Legal and Ethical Issues of
Live Streaming

Legal and Ethical Issues of Live Streaming

Edited by
Shing-Ling S. Chen,
Zhuojun Joyce Chen, and Nicole Allaire

LEXINGTON BOOKS
Lanham • Boulder • New York • London

Published by Lexington Books
An imprint of The Rowman & Littlefield Publishing Group, Inc.
4501 Forbes Boulevard, Suite 200, Lanham, Maryland 20706
www.rowman.com

6 Tinworth Street, London SE11 5AL, United Kingdom

British Library Cataloguing in Publication Information Available

Library of Congress Control Number: 2020943919

ISBN: 978-1-7936-1541-1 (cloth)
ISBN: 978-1-7936-1543-5 (pbk)
ISBN: 978-1-7936-1542-8 (electronic)

Dedicated to

Clifford G. Christians

A Father of Modern Media Ethics

Contents

Chapter One

Introduction

The Sacredness of Life as Protonorm

Clifford G. Christians

Studies of media technology that include live streaming are typically instrumentalist and functional. This technical framework is a basis for creating live stream platforms and programs, but it presumes media technologies are neutral and therefore is silent on moral and legal issues. Live streaming is a technological phenomenon, and it can only be understood within the larger context of the digital era in which it is possible. As this book documents, the liveness motif is a journalism tool in electronic communication; television news uses this strategy following the journalism value of immediacy. But, live streaming driven by social media is a transformation of this communicative style. Chapter-by-chapter, a distinctive approach is developed in this book, one that is sophisticated on digital technology and substantive on the issues of ethics and law. It is a profound book of research, history, and case studies that establishes the basis for informed public discussion of this communication genre in its urgent forms today.

A decisive shift in media technology has taken place and today's online media that make live streaming iconic cannot be understood in reductionist, mechanical terms as electronic artifacts. Since technologies are value-laden, fundamental work on the nature of social media technology is necessary for the long term. The scholarly challenge is to identify the internal properties of live stream technology in order to know it distinctively as its own. By doing so, it is the unique and strategic character of this book to give this powerful form of contemporary communication the critical assessment its importance warrants. However, the technological context as a whole is the framework within which legal and ethical considerations of live streaming are intellectually credible and relevant to professional practices and public policy.

1

HISTORY OF MEDIA TECHNOLOGIES

This book's understanding of live streaming as a technological phenomenon needs elaboration. An exploratory history of media technologies will clarify how and why live streaming is a formidable issue in the digital era. This intellectual journey will explain that research and scholarship by communication scholars is imperative, though the complications of live stream technology invite academics from multiple fields to analyze it.

Language is the public agent through which human existence is possible and realized. In a symbolic approach to communications, human beings are considered able to integrate specific acts and messages within the larger project of cultural formation. Beyond the need to survive is the need for meaningfulness in human interaction; we comprehend ourselves by interpreting the symbolic meanings that our lifeworld represents (Cassirer, 1953–1957, 1966). Communication is the creative process of building and reaffirming the social order through symbols, with cultures the human habitat that results. In a symbolic approach to communication, concepts are not isolated from their representations. The social and individual dimensions of language are a unified whole. In James Carey's terms, "The media of communication are vast social metaphors that not only transmit information but determine what is knowledge, that not only orient us to the world but tell us what kind of world exists" (1967, p. 8). Obviously, symbols are not identical to that which they symbolize, but symbols do participate in their meaning. In literature and cinema, or YouTube Live, Stream2Watch, Hulu and Hotstar, the indispensable features of their inner dialectics—the point of departure, setting, overall tone, their digital coding, and resolution of conflict—all reflect their cultures' value system and only on that deep-seated level can these mediations be understood. Symbols share the significance of that which they represent, and thereby the symbolic theory of communication avoids the subject-object dualism.

The contemporary communication enterprise is technological in character, requiring our analysis of cyberspace to pay explicit attention to the mediated form in which the content is structured. From the perspective of technology as a distinct cultural enterprise, live stream communication as with all media technologies is not a tool per se but a cultural practice of making meaning. Terrorists with weapons need the visual and audio to make their actions intelligible, and to them, worthwhile. Suicidal voyeurs want their dying to live so it won't be meaningless. Media technology symbolizes human events without which the human species cannot exist; therefore, the assertion is credible that communications specialists are best equipped to analyze the live stream phenomenon.

Martin Heidegger (1962) calls human being *Dasein* (literally "there being") to indicate that human beingness is not an unchanging essence, but an existential being located in history (Heidegger, 1966).[1] In modernity, our humanness is understood most clearly through the technological phenomenon; for example, we laud humans as "the genius inventors." The human life-world has a technological texture that stipulates what existence means. In *The Question Concerning Technology* (Heidegger, 1977b), the modern era is technological in character, and Being *(Dasein)* is technicized as a result. In Heidegger's summary, technology is the primary mode of human existence in societies of advanced technology, and therefore the foremost avenue for coming to grips conceptually with the sociopolitical world. As the French thinker, Jacques Ellul, puts it, technology is not only decisive for understanding economics and politics, but it dominates the symbolic formation of contemporary culture (Ellul, 1954, 1978). Though exhibiting the structural elements of all technical artifacts, communications media are the arena where the meaning of the technological era is most clearly exposed (Ellul, 1965). The challenge technological societies face is not that from machines and products per se, but from a technological pervasiveness that erodes our language about Being. This includes not only live streamers themselves, but social media users of live streaming, educator ethicists focusing on it, and politicians who administer the legal system in dealing with it.

Language is the *sine qua non* of humanness and the organizing motif for the social order; therefore, when the human communication capacity is structured in fundamentally different mediations than before, the impact is substantial and extensive. From a media ecology perspective, when symbolic systems are transformed technologically, the changes in human life and culture must be calibrated historically and evaluated for beneficence and deficit. In the communication-as-symbolic theory, today's massive digital intrusion into human culture and institutions means that our definitions of reality must be recreated (Ong, 2002). Given symbolic theory's presumption that the history of communications is central to the history of civilization, it follows that social change results from media transformations and that structural changes in symbolic formations profoundly impact human consciousness.

The Canadian communications scholar Harold Innis (1951), for instance, studied the introduction of papyrus, the printing press, radio, and the telegraph—and documented in each a bias regarding space and time. Oral communication systems, he argued, are biased toward time; they give history continuity while making space outside the oral-aural range discontinuous. Print systems, by contrast, have a propensity toward space, giving the geography of empires continuity and breaking time into distinct units such as ancient and medieval. Thus, from the introduction of cuneiform writing to contemporary communication satellites, fiber optics, and cyberspace, media technologies have attracted historical and sociology attention—scholars in the symbolic tradition examining all important shifts in technological form, associating with them differentiations in culture and in perception. Within this theory of bias in communication systems, the conceptual demand is to identify the distinctive features of particular media technologies such as books, radio, cinema, television, live stream, Twitter, YouNow, and WeChat.

For today's computer-based era in which live streaming flourishes, we need for digital technology a composite of concepts geared to the electromagnetic spectrum. With digital platforms and wireless networks, we confront particular vibrations of sound and images of light that fade away and subsist unevenly. Print and broadcast modes become secondary when our basis of knowing is digital platforms and wireless networks. The new media congeries of wireless optics, cloud data storage, crowdsourcing, algorithmic models, personal websites, and smartphones are the world of everyday communications in societies North, South, East, and West. With the social media, the heart and soul of the Web 2.0 phenomenon, humans participate in cyberspace as the facilitators and weavers of networks. Theorizing live stream communication and seeking a pathway forward requires a competent understanding of the larger technological framework that live streaming represents.[2]

In Grant Kien's *Global Technography: Ethnography in the Age of Mobility* (2009), there is a "seismic shift" to fluidity in the social media era. Similarly, in Zygmunt Bauman's (2005) terms, cultural systems, and social structures in modernity have become liquid. The new social media have "reinvented" electronic space as "mobile territory" and "transit itself is the new normal" (Kien, 2009, p. 2). As Harold Innis explained with his idea of media bias, time, and space are fundamental features of human cognition; therefore, changes in the technology of symbol systems alter perceptions of time and space. Kien (2009) sees the time and space mediations operating intensely in cyberspace. Different from print and broadcast, space becomes "teledistanced" (Heidegger, 1977b) while time becomes "telepresent" (Virillio, 2000); through "digital mediation, network users experience omnipresence in time and space" (Kien, 2009, p. 65). Instead of satellites and wireless networks bringing distant things near to set them apart conceptually, "uniform distancelessness obliterates the distance required for meaningful interpretation" (Heidegger, 1971, p. 164). With live streaming, the idea of time is reoriented. History is resymbolized so that, for example, the centuries of Islamic achievement become "Muslims are the enemies of civilization." Presenting cultures chronologically in terms of past, present and future is recast by live streaming into present time; the history of cultures is rejected and their future is precarious.

Following Heidegger, Kien observes that we need the structure of time and a sense of distance to avoid solipsism and to understand ourselves as belonging in the world, but "distancelessness" preempts such authenticity. With the compression of history into the momentary and the demise of spatial limits, our basis of knowing changes to an anytime, anywhere experience with humans "the signifiers of selfhood . . . equally described as existing everywhere always and nowhere never" (Kien 2009, pp. 125–41). This is the dilemma of instantaneous technologies, particularly pertinent to the educational, political, and everyday world in which live streaming is used and critiqued. How can we give live stream technology a moral and legal assessment, when in the digital era history is compressed into the momentary, and the spatial limits needed for adequate understanding are eviscerated?

Ellul understands the history of media technology in these time-and-space terms. His *The Technological Society* was one of the earliest to define the shift to electronic media. And he gives today's media revolution a deeper assessment that is especially pertinent to the legal and moral emphases of the chapters that follow. Ellul works within the Martin Heidegger tradition, where technology is intertwined with the structure of human beings. As Patrick Troude-Chastenet puts it, "Fourteen years before Heidegger's first lectures on the subject, Ellul already thought technique and not politics was now at the heart of things" (2006, p. 5).

In Ellul's radical framework, modern pervasive means of communication are not instruments of information through which citizens guide their public life. The Web 2.0 is not a communication network of understanding, but through it the human symbolic system is absorbed into an efficiency-dominated culture. In *Propaganda, Humiliation of the Word,* and *The Technological Bluff,* Ellul constructs the various forms of electronic media in terms of *la technique. La technique* is for him the world of machineness behind machines, an internal efficient bureaucratizing that saturates human values, culture, and institutions. We are enveloped in data, absorbed into a one-dimensional world of shibboleths and memes. People's own views and identity are replaced by a generalized machinic mind-set (Ellul, 1965, p. 163).

Of particular importance for this book, Ellul describes modern technological systems in terms of means and ends. The dualism of means and ends is a crucial trajectory in both the law and ethics chapters of this book, but Ellul sees today's computer-based media systems as revolutionizing this dualism. In his view, technological societies have committed their creative, educational, and financial resources overwhelmingly to products, the invention of tools, engineering, and science, the world of means; together, they suffocate society's concern for ends. "We have forgotten our collective ends. . . . In this terrible dance of means which has been unleashed, no one knows where we are going; the aim of life has been forgotten" (Ellul, 1951, pp. 63, 69). Obviously politicians still invoke ends such as progress and entertainment programs to promote happiness. However, Ellul contends, these goals no longer inspire; certainly "no one would die for them" (1951, p. 67). As technological societies advance, the concept of ends becomes marginal to the demands of perfecting strategies. For Ellul, the existential problem in technological societies is the disappearance of tangible ends. He concludes in *The Technological Bluff* that when machinic efficiency replaces normative goods, peoples' inner life is impoverished and automatism replaces their creativity (Ellul, 1990).

The crisis in electronic societies is not only solipsism as described above but the demise of the moral point of view. The predicament in this era of the technological revolution is not just the violation of norms first of all, but the vacuum of normlessness. Moral commitments are displaced by advanced techniques, making it difficult for this book's emphasis on ethics to be understood in such an era.

In other words, the prevailing worldview in industrial societies is instrumentalism—the idea that technology is neutral and expands in terms of its own technical character without conditioning our humanness.[3] This is a mechanical model that promotes technological imperatives where the capabilities of media technologies set the agenda and define the issues. Beginning in the late nineteenth century in industrial societies, technological developments have multiplied so rapidly that little viable space remains for setting limits and proper direction. In the face of technology's complexity and pervasiveness, and given the sophistication of twenty-first-century technology when social impact can rarely be calculated anymore, "we are abandoned to a haphazard scattering of goods and evils, of productive and destructive tendencies," rather than guided by an agreed-upon concept of the common good (Hood, 1972, p. 352).

Instead of following human ends, the instrumental philosophy of technology promotes muscular values. With its diffusion-of-tools mentality, instrumentalism begins and ends with the technological reality itself and offers strategies for accomplishing technical goals through it. In instrumentalism, our scientific prowess and financial resources are channeled into high technology, into improving the power and speed of technological instruments. Therefore, instead of looking for technical improvements to the instrumentalist framework, we need to reconceive technology itself. Transmission theories of neutral media are grounded in an instrumentalist worldview, and that value system needs to be revolutionized. Rather than be content with critique only, and live unproductively with the traditional dualism of means and ends, the instrumentalist worldview needs to be confronted head-on. The epistemology of the instrumental view is wrong. Ellul's warnings about technicism as a whole apply to live stream mediations. Ellul denies technical solutions and predicts the ineffectiveness of legal and administrative options. A credible ethics and law for the live stream niche of twenty-first-century communications require a different approach to technology as neutral instruments.

SACREDNESS OF LIFE

This intellectual history of media technology raises fundamental issues that surround live streaming as a technological phenomenon. This introductory chapter works on the foundational level so that the chapters that follow can credibly deal with important legal and ethical problems in live streaming. Taken as a whole, instead of shrill outrage over trauma caused by live stream bullies and voyeurists, this book opens an educational pathway forward.

The question in this history of technology is ontological, that is, the nature of being, specifically the character of human beings. Following Heidegger and Ellul, and as argued in Innis's theory of communication, technology and humanness are intertwined. Our understanding of human existence in the modern era typically has a technological inflection. Within that framework, what is profoundly at stake in live stream technology is the sacredness of human life.[4] Live streaming of suicides, of murdering terrorists, of live stream news where privacy is invaded, and reputations are compromised, denigrate human life. The opposite of what live streaming communicates is the declaration: "all life is sacred." The horrendous Christchurch, New Zealand live stream discussed throughout this book is the most brutal assault possible on the sacredness of life, a revengeful, raw, primal scream that human life is zero (cf. Aslam, 2019).

The sacredness of life is not a pleasantry, but a bedrock concept for the survival of the human species. This proposition is self-evident, regardless of cultures and competing ideologies. It is a natural reality, that is, an intrinsic moral claim on us for its own sake and in its own right. In order that this norm—human life is sacred—not be trivialized or affirmed perfunctorily, the centrality and deeper meaning of this idea needs to be developed and clarified.

For the German philosopher Hans Jonas, nature is not a spiritless matter. In Jonas's perspective, the purpose is embedded in the animate world, and its purposiveness is evident in bringing forth life. Animation is so prevailing that it can be meaningfully said that "nature evinces at least one determinate goal—life itself" (Jonas, 1984, p. 74). To be ethical means to show the same reverence for every animate being's will-to-live as one does for one's own livelihood. Peukert's summary is helpful: "Human beings have certain inescapable claims on one another which we cannot renounce except at the cost of our humanity" (1981, p. 11). Reverence for life on earth is the rationale for human action.

In his book-length etymological study, David Gushee (2013) concludes that "the sacredness of life," "sanctity of life," and "social worth" are used interchangeably. In the history of ideas, these terms refer to both human existence and to moral duty regarding it (p. 13).[5] The rationale for valuing human beings as worthy varies from humans as image-bearers of God to the evolutionary chain of life. However, across that range of rationales, the concept is not limited to analytical definition, but given moral status. The "sanctity of life" (referring to all forms of life) and the "sacredness of human life," nearly without exception, occur in sentences and phrases requiring a human commitment. Respect is considered a necessary response to all forms of life and to human life, and for both, destroying it is indefensible (Gushee, 2013, pp. 17–20).

Among human beings, the sacredness of life is a common understanding of their primal existence as lingual beings. The communications context is especially appropriate for understanding the scope and character of reverence for life. For the *Legal and Ethical Issues of Live Streaming*, the murder of human life is not only criminally illegal, but the desecration of life by rhetoric is morally unacceptable. The symbolic theory of communication clarifies the complex relationship between specific human interactions and the web of life that words and actions ought to honor. As we generate and maintain symbolic systems, we acknowledge boundaries between moral norms and actual behavior, even as we situate them both in the natural order understood as purposive (Wuthnow, 1987).

Albert Schweitzer (1875–1965) made the sacredness of life famous in the twentieth century (cf. Mayer, 2002). With Ph.D. credentials, he was an influential Kantian scholar, and he also specialized in theology at the University of Strasbourg. An accomplished musician, his book *Johann Sebastian Bach*, still influences the way Bach's music is taught and critiqued. Trained as a physician, he considered his greatest achievement as founding of the Lambaréné Hospital in Gabon, Africa (Schweitzer, 2009). In 1952 he received the Nobel Peace Prize, and his address on that occasion, "The Problem of Peace," is considered the most intellectually profound statement on the reverence for life ever made.

In his *Philosophy of Civilization*, Schweitzer argues that "true philosophy must start from the most immediate and comprehensive fact of consciousness" (1987, ch. 26). Respect for life, resulting from the contemplation of one's own conscious will to live, motivates people to live meaningfully by serving their species and all living organisms (cf. Goodin, 2013). Schweitzer sharpens Jonas's purposiveness of life in his well-known summary line: "I am life that wants to live, in the midst of life that wants to live" (1987, ch. 26). In reviewing Schweitzer's *The Philosophy of Civilization*, Greg Smith (2003) calls it a monumental book, a "classic of global civilization."[6]

Reflecting the same mind as Schweitzer's, for Václev Havel, Czechoslovakia's playwright and president appeal to human rights and freedom are meaningless if they do not derive from esteem for "the miracle of Being, the miracle of our existence" (1994, p. 615). Through human solidarity, rooted in a reverence for life, we respect ourselves and genuinely value others in an increasingly technological age where "everything appears possible but almost nothing is certain" (Havel, 1994, p. 614; cf. Vladislav, 1990).

Protonorms

The sacredness of life is a protonorm, that is, an underlying norm about which there can be cross-cultural agreement. One meaning of *proto* is before or initial or first, as in prototype where a model is fabricated and engineers then reproduce copies in a manufacturing process. That is not the definition here. *Proto* in Greek also means underlying or lying beneath, as in the proto-Germanic, proto Sino-Tibetan, and proto Indo-European languages. Such "proto" families are lingual predecessors underlying the actual languages that exist in recorded history. These earliest lingual forms can be reconstructed from the languages we know. The veneration of human life is a protonorm in this sense, an underlying presupposition that is indispensable for systematic ethical reasoning. A protonorm is a belief about human existence shared by those who belong to that category.[7] The preservation of life is a presumption, and adherence to presuppositions,

> is a matter of commitment, not of epistemic certainty. We initiate any inquiry or action with presuppositions, because we must do so, not because they have been demonstrated. One's commitments are always open to question and thus are liable to be modified or replaced. But one cannot proceed in any enterprise without taking something as given. (Johnstone, 1994, p. 301)

Similarly, it is argued here that presuppositions are the primordial first step in theorizing about or analyzing the live stream process. The sacredness of life is a pretheoretical belief fundamental to the legal and moral reasoning on live stream technology in this book.

In epistemological terms, thinking is impossible without taking something as a starting point. Aristotle's "unmoved mover" is a truism; human knowledge is incoherent if there is infinite regression. Theories are not mathematically neutral but are interpretive schemes for elaborating on our basic values. The theoretical world is grounded in first beliefs. Systematic work in ethics and law is conditioned by our beliefs about the world.[8] Research on and debate about live streaming that is rooted in the protonorm "sacredness of life" enables public discussion and inspires us to act strategically. Pretheoretical givens represent the researcher's presumptions about reality. A dualism that regards the natural world as objective cannot account for the purposiveness of life. This introductory chapter contends that reverence for life on earth is a pretheoretical taken-for-granted that gives substance and direction to this book's moral and legal reflections on live stream technologies.

Sacredness of Life as Coherence

The sacredness of life, as presented here, is a coherence concept. This norm applies to all actions. It enables each person to choose wisely and each institution to act justly among the alternatives. When this protonorm actually serves as a coherence principle, there is the possibility, in principle at least, that debate over the role of live streaming in society, and struggles over the tragic uses of live stream technologies, can be worked on constructively. As an underlying presupposition, coherence across a spectrum of circumstances is what the sacredness entails, or at least promises.

Following the coherence mode, the live streaming of murders in the act of promoting death or enabling others to experience it voyeuristically, is to be understood as immoral violations of the protonorm. The sacredness of life is primal to human existence, not simply an intuition but the declaration given when new life appears and acted on in the interaction of humans' ordinary deference to the others' existence. The legal apparatus may determine in specific instances that its violation was a mental disorder and not a first-degree criminal act, but live streamers of mass shootings pleading ignorance of the sacredness of life is indefensible. Its core reality is symbolized in human language from the very beginning of human interaction.

For those encountering live stream tragedy, whether personally or in mediations (such as the Live.me social media app), the sacredness of life is the catalyst for outrage, horror, pain, cries of anguish and tears. Whoever may revel in the horrifics of live streamed suicide ideation and attempts in real-time, or pander when live stream news degrades and mocks the sacredness of a living being's existence, must be corrected by this declaration and as a protonorm, the correction will be understood as legitimate. A disconcerting phenomenon is the transfer of anti-life streaming to electronic networks and platforms. Individuals and institutions caught up in the machinic mind of instrumentalism, and who thereby serve as a module without conscience in the social media cyberspace, may not be legally culpable but are morally blameworthy.[9]

For politicians and government officials in jurisprudence, the sacredness of life serves as a protonorm also. In basic terms, for legal experts and politicians, victims have priority and not the speech rights of the live stream-ing terrorist. The Prime Minister of New Zealand honors the norm by never saying the live streamer's name, privileging the victims by making their names live and denying a hearing to anti-life voices in all their mediated forms. The government of New Zealand legitimately impounds both the killing spree's live stream and Brenton Turrant's 16,000-word statement on behalf of "Europeans who wish to live in their own lands and practice their own traditions" and now "take revenge" so that "the invaders will never conquer our homelands or replace our people" (Önnerfors, 2019). The socio-political order cannot exist without the sacredness of life as its foundation; there is no rights-of-free-expression law ever devised that can rule otherwise. Its violation warrants no weak-minded excuses. Norway does not extermi-nate Anders Breivik or it would violate the ideal. But for the protection of

Norway's livelihood as a country, his electronic manifesto of 1,500 pages will never be heard and his outrageous brutality of murdering 77 and wounding 242 will be mourned but not retold in the courts or the media. In public policy and making courtroom judgments, the philosophy underneath is the sacredness of life. As the chapters on law in this book make explicit, the sacredness of life as a norm works across the heterogeneity of a nation-state, and across national boundaries, regardless of political theory (Hanitzsch et al., 2011). With live streaming across borders an actuality in both acts and networking, an international protonorm enables the world community to work cooperatively in addressing it.

For social science research as developed in a chapter following, live streamed video footage requires ethical guidelines that are explicit and comprehensive. The sacredness of life provides an overall framework for live streamed data in the study of mass violence. For scholars and teachers of ethics, the sacredness of life as a pre-theoretical given, leads them away from utilitarianism, because this tradition presumes the neutrality of autonomous actors. In utilitarian ethics, harm to society occurs by default in the analysis and is addressed in utilitarian terms that are weakly constructed and on the whole irrelevant. By the coherence motif, utilitarian ethical theory is dismissed as incoherent (Christians, 2007b). Neo-Kantian theories, such as Habermas's discourse ethics, are defensible because humans as ends in themselves in Kant, reflects the sacredness-of-human-life presupposition (cf. Benhabib, 1986). All systematic ethical analysis of specific issues such as live streaming requires four distinct steps: (a) precise account of the facts of the problem or case; (b) review of the professional, social and legal values involved in the decision-making process; (c) determination of the most appropriate ethical principle; and (d) identifying who or what institutions have priority (Christians, Fackler, Richardson, & Kreshel, 2020, pp. 4–31). The pre-theoretical sacredness of life gives coherence to the multiple levels in each stage and to coordinating the four steps into a unified whole.

Journalists who report on live stream dehumanization, as accounted for throughout this book, are challenged by the sacredness of life in their values and practices.[10] For professional journalists honoring the protonorm, truth by itself is not sufficient in live streaming since the live stream is actual data (Christians, 2007a). Journalists who recognize that they cannot be neutral, and are committed to reverence for life on earth, will enable those audiences, readers, and users—who likewise believe that human life is sacred—to act and think productively. But as the chapters following document, the complications for journalists are deep and wide-ranging. Breivik and Tarrant are homegrown, killing their fellow citizens; some live streamers are outsiders. The sources of live streaming inside and outside, the many reasons are given for the violence, and live streaming's surprise and unpredictability indicate that news coverage of terrorism is complicated; for journalists to think morally about attacks on human life cannot be superficial. The sacredness of life as a protonorm enables journalists to identify the relevant considerations and give them their appropriate weight.

Since New Zealand's Prime Minister refuses to say the attacker's name, should the news media do likewise? New Zealand's and the world's television had to decide how to cover the dead bodies. Immediately after the ordeal, internet users sent some shocking footage but not others. What safeguards must Facebook, Twitter, and YouTube use to prevent Tarrant's bloody live streaming? Tarrant cited Anders Breivik approvingly in his manifesto; should that detail be repeated in the news media, or does it give Breivik notoriety? Is it more important to tell the truth, journalists ask themselves, or to preserve privacy? Liveness is valued in a public safety crisis, but as a following chapter elaborates, speculation and misinformation ordinarily increase for live reporting of mass shootings. Any single decision involves a host of values that must be sorted out.

Newspeople hold several values regarding professional reporting: for example, they prize immediacy, skepticism, and their own independence. The public has a right to know, but the responsible media do not provide personal information about victims unless it has officially been verified. Overall, professionals value distributing information without hesitation, but ought to recognize the protonorm of the sacredness of life when there are both psychological and physical injuries to others. In sizing up the circumstances and asking what values are relevant, the sacredness of life as protonorm helps journalists discuss conflicts of opinion constructively and indicates in the decision-making process where additional analysis is needed. When journalism values are grounded in the sacredness of life, there is a frame of reference for interpreting episodes of live streaming terror and their aftermath. The crucial question is whether the professional media in reporting and editorials affirm the sacredness of life. Mechanistic and bureaucratic criteria for judging the live stream phenomenon are made secondary to the sacredness of life as a normative ideal.[11]

CIVIL SOCIETY AS THE PATHWAY FORWARD

The writers of this book who know ethics and law, and understand live streaming as a technological phenomenon, make explicit in their chapters how the sacredness of life is the coherence norm. And in order that these authors may be understood as *Legal and Ethical Issues of Live Streaming* works its way into schools and government offices and public arenas, foundational work is essential so that in the digital age this book's vocabulary, distinctions, conclusions, recommendations, and analyses can be understood and discussed productively. This deeper and long-term task with its larger agenda calls for enriching civil society.[12] When the civil society prospers, discussions of live streaming in sacredness-of-life terms will replace live streaming in technical and functional terms. Humans are lingual beings. We need to have our symbolic world of meaning synchronized around the sacredness of life for effective communication about live stream technology to be possible.

Civil society is the composite term for the sociocultural domain beyond the political and commercial. While government and business tend to dominate the social order, the civil society of home, schools, religion, medicine, neighborhoods, charities, and non-governmental organizations is essential for promoting language and action based on the sacredness of life. Our everyday practices, values, and life's meaning are typically learned and negotiated in civil society communities, where human worth typically receives its fullest understanding and most effective application. As described above, the sacredness of life belongs to all human beings as human beings, but it needs to be activated and become embedded in people's consciousness. Homes, schools, religious centers—and the other arenas of civil society—are the major habitats for this enculturation.

Throughout this book, the digital revolution is seen as transformative for civil society's culture as it is for politics and business. For Harold Innis (1951, 1952) and the media ecology tradition, communications media never exist innocently and equally alongside one another. New forms of communication tend to monopolize human knowledge and render other forms residual. In today's instrumentalism, digital knowledge is primary, and other forms of communication are secondary. In the broadcast era, visual technology dominated our way of thinking and social structures, leaving print and oral modes no longer the standard of truth or the centerpiece of education and politics (Ong, 2002). Given the explosive growth of digital technology and our lionizing it, cyberspace tends to monopolize our political-economic-educational institutions now. Twitter, Facebook, WhatsApp, Wiebo, and Renren monopolize human communication, and oral and print forms become marginal.

The digital revolution that has given epic proportions to live streaming is decisive, but in the civil society framework, decisive does not mean veneration for the new media technologies. With the sacredness of life as pretheoretical, the social media frame is not rejected but seen to operate in a different paradigm as supplemental. The issue in the approach advocated in this book is to research and analyze live streaming in terms of the rapid development of the new technologies, but at the same time ensure that other communication forms such as oral, print and broadcast are not eclipsed.[13] In other words, the imperative for communication studies in the digital era is multimedia abundance instead of the Web 2.0's monopoly of knowledge. One aspect of the necessary foundational work long-term is developing civil society into a pluralism of multimedia communities. For example, as one application of the language-as-a-symbolic-system for understanding digital networks, the requirement for communication studies in the internet era is multimedia abundance instead of allowing computer-based information to monopolize educational curricula and research.

Paulo Freire's *Education for Critical Consciousness* clarifies the long-term agenda. This Brazilian linguist is concerned that in culture, its language, ideas, forms of communication engender critical thinking (Freire, 1973).[14] In his perspective, instead of being modules in an information network, humans to be healthy in mind and spirit ought to energize their consciousness. Monopolies of knowledge drive humans into cultures of silence. Speaking the true word is our ontological vocation. The aim is not first of all engineering data speed but deepening the dialogue. The goal is not a torrent of statistical data and staccato outrage in the same lingual form as live streaming itself, but educational symbolic forms that inspire human subjectivity.[15]

Reflecting the sacredness-of-human-life protonorm, for Freire, the central problem in his literacy campaigns with and for agricultural laborers is dehumanization.[16] When *Campesinos* become critically conscious, the status quo is seen as repressive, and the status quo's power begins to break down. The struggle against dehumanization involves the double process of "overcoming social alienation and the affirmation of people as persons" (Freire, 1970, p. 28). For Freire (1970), "the great humanistic and historical task of the oppressed" is to "liberate both themselves and their oppressors" (p. 28) by speaking the true word that every human being without exception has intrinsic worth. When people groups gain a critical consciousness, they are able to live outside the status quo, in our case here, outside the digital monopoly of knowledge.

Alternative Communities

Giving priority to civil society as the pathway forward can be given focus through the strategy of alternative communities. Alternative communities are an active variation on the civil society legacy. While working out the ethical and legal perspectives on live streaming, this chapter advocates developing alternative communities where the ethical and legal issues can be discussed and applied. In a digital age under instrumentalism, the legal and moral aspects have little bearing.

Following the sacredness of life principle, our task is to nurture and evoke a worldview alternative to the nowhere never consciousness of the dominant culture of instrumentalism. The civil society imagination does not mean primarily addressing specific public crises, but addressing the dominant and resilient crisis of having the education, social science, religious centers, neighborhoods and voluntary associations co-opted and domesticated to the means of technicism rather than the ends of the common good.

Alternative communities represent a radical break with the social reality of computer-based communication that monopolizes knowledge. To be a genuine alternative, they are rooted not in righteous indignation but in an alternative philosophy (that is, the sacredness of life as protonorm) and in a different sociology than the instrumentalism of efficiency and amorality. "The evocation of an alternative reality consists at least in part as the battle for language and the legitimatization of a new rhetoric" (Brueggemann, 2018, p.18).

Nancy Fraser's "Rethinking the Public Sphere" (1992) and her *Justus Interruptus* (1997) argue for times and places of withdrawal and reconnection, "sub-altern counter publics" that have an emancipatory purpose. In these alternative communities—she calls them "discursive arenas"—members of social groups create counter discourses as oppositional interpretations of their circumstances and interests. Focusing on the discursive character of social identities, they create a vocabulary on issues that are overlooked or ignored or suppressed by the existing authorities. Likewise, Clemencia Rodriguez (2001, 2011) researches local movements that create and control their own systems of meaning. These different discourses resist the dominant narrative—in this chapter's case, the digital, machinic commitment in which other forms of media atrophy. Ideally, outside the uniformity of the majority public sphere, in these interpretive communities (Benson, 2009), discussion of and belief in the sacredness of life flourishes as live streaming is experienced personally or discussed as news or programmed into marketing campaigns.[17] Within these alternative communities, the ethics and law of live streaming in the information age is done. This is an academic version of Saul Alinsky's (1946) community movements[18] and Harry Boyte's everyday politics (2004).

In addition to sociological and cultural perspectives on alternative communities, philosophical reflection on them deepens our civil society agenda. Dwelling is a key concept in Heidegger, that is, living in community, feeling at home, settled. "To dwell, to be set at peace, means to remain at peace within the preserve, the free space that safeguards each thing in its preserve. The fundamental character of dwelling is sparing" (Heidegger, 1977a, p. 327). Living with ubiquitous social media replaces our natural human habitat in time and space. Frenetic doing becomes the substitute for meditative dwelling. The worldview of efficiency that drives modernity's instrumentalism buries the emotional experience of memory, safety, peace, and rootedness. In the original Greek, ethics is *ethos,* abode, dwelling place, the human domain for moral discernment. Homelessness, no fixed abode, means the absence of the sacredness of life as a moral anchor, that is, moral indifference. As Heidegger puts it, "only if we are capable of dwelling, only then can we build" (1977a, p. 338). In his *Poetry, Language and Thought* (Heidegger, 1971), the arts illuminate the mystery of being. The artistic genre "opens new ways of saying Being." Based on his work on language, symbol, art, and poetry, Heidegger expects of artists a dwelling place that enriches human existence.

In Hannah Arendt's *The Human Condition*, the lifeworld of human association is pre-political; human relationships are non-hierarchical. What she calls the *vita activa* is the biological life that must be nurtured for the survival of the species. Belonging to all, the *vita activa* is the world that we enter when we are born, live in primarily through oral-aural communication, and what we leave behind when we die (Arendt, 1998 [1958], p. 55). The *vita activa* is the existential condition of the entire human species. In this domain, where the sacredness of life operates, association with one another is by respect, approval, and agreement. The *vita activa* is the aspect of our being where the sacredness of life can actually become our worldview (cf. Benhabib, 2003).

For the educational domain of civil society, the sacredness of life requires the humanities in order to flourish. The arts, music, history, philosophy, literature, and humanistic social science can best develop a non-instrumental understanding of the human condition. Scholarship, the classroom, and academic administration can be alternative life worlds where the sacredness-of-life worldview can be illustrated, taught, and learned.

The solution—civil society institutions with a critical consciousness—is long term, and the authors of *Legal and Ethical Issues of Live Streaming* plead with our readers to be involved in the struggle. Through education, our commitment to the social media's monopoly of knowledge can change, and when our values are transformed, a different use of technological mediations will follow. Social media voyeurism ought to be replaced with values rooted in the sacredness of human life. Rather than emphasizing live stream drama for its own sake in mechanized terms, the language of the humanities ought to be promoted instead. In civil society, the arts, music, philosophy, and literature should prosper, not just engineering and electronic gadgetry. Then an educational culture can be developed in which the sacredness of life is the preeminent social value, and the ethical and legal questions regarding live stream phenomena are productively addressed.

NOTES

1. Heidegger is widely considered one of the three greatest Western philosophers of the twentieth century. However, his reputation continues to be controversial regarding his relationship to German national socialism prior to and during World War II, to which he offered no apology before his death in 1967 (cf. Lyotard, 1990; Wolin, 1993). Rockmore (1995, pp. 128–144) offers one account that is plausible intellectually: Heidegger's transpersonal concep-

tion of Being differs essentially from the democratic subject and therefore tolerates within itself an anti-democratic politics.

2. M. Rex Miller (2004) researches changes in society by focusing on the major transformations in communication technology throughout history. He studies the revolutions that occurred in the dominant media of communications, that is, the shift from oral communication to print media in the fifteenth century, and the shift to broadcasting in the twentieth. His *Millennium Matrix* sees these alterations as fundamental changes in a society's worldview, enabling him to describe the basic features of the digital world that technological societies are living in now, and experiencing live stream phenomena in particularly powerful form. Whereas in oral cultures, the human brain orientation was intimate and relational; in print culture rational and abstract; and in broadcast visceral and emotional; the brain's orientation in digital societies is characterized by the disembodied intimacy of electronic linkage. Miller calls each of these historic changes, "a cultural revolution."

3. Regarding worldview epistemology, the empirical is embodied in human experience rather than becoming statistical and abstract empiricism. It does not commit the fallacy of naturalistic theorizing, where rationality determines both the genesis and the conclusion.

4. The interdependence of people, animals, and plant life is in contrast to the prevailing concept in history that the human species is dominant over other forms of life. Since this book's focus is on the human experience of live streaming, this chapter privileges human life while committed to the unified web of organic existence.

5. The term "sacredness" is standard in religious vocabulary, with the word referring to deity. But it is also an anthropological concept with its etymology from the Latin *sanctum*, meaning "set apart." The protonorm of sacred life is presuppositional, primordial. On that deep level, sacredness as a term grants extraordinariness to human life but does not invoke the specialized domain of organized religion, its doctrines, and institutions.

6. Greg Smith (2003) concludes about Schweitzer: "Einstein was not *the* person of the 20th century. Not by a long shot. Albert Schweitzer wins that distinction hands down. He weaved a legacy of the most accomplished Renaissance Man in the last 200 years. Combining intellectual brilliance with an amazing thirst for humanitarian service . . . he accomplished more in a lifetime than anyone I can think of. He should be the standard by which all global thought is measured" (August 9, 2003).

7. Ruth Kempson's *Presupposition and the Delimitation of Semantics* (1975) is the classical work on presuppositions in communication theory, analyzing both philosophical and linguistic approaches. Her book includes detailed application to such issues as circular reasoning, inference from presuppositions, and presupposing what is untrue.

8. Thomas Kuhn's *The Structure of Scientific Revolutions* (1996) is an influential contradiction of value-free theory formation. For Kuhn, theorizing is a paradigm construction, rather than the usual science of verifying that propositions are externally and internally valid. Theories as paradigms are an intricate mixture of politics, creativity, intuition and beliefs. The chapters of this book represent theory in these terms. They are schooled in the humanities where theories are postulates about reality. For them, theories elucidate our fundamental beliefs about the world. From this perspective, questions of method are secondary to the basic belief system that guides theoreticians in epistemologically fundamental ways. Communication theory, in its semantic derivations, requires the mutually known and therefore is value-conditioned.

9. Given the character of social media technology as described above, maintaining the sacredness of human life during this communication phase is nearly impossible. As Lawrence Bennett puts it in his classic *News: The Politics of Illusion*, "The rise of blogs, discussion forums, instant polls, YouTube channels, social networking sites," and citizens reporting news stories "on cell phones and digital cameras" are a dramatic technological transformation, but of uncertain benefit (2016, p. 153). People often "stream news chaotically, checking for shallow updates" without taking time "for reflection or critical processing" (240). Communication of this sort faces the dangers of extreme splintering and individual isolation. The "babel of information" in these new media technologies "may produce individuals who before informed only about issues and perspectives that suit their personal lifestyle and beliefs" (p. 24).

10. The distinction between journalists and non-journalists is currently in tension and crisis. With eyewitness footage shot and sent by social media, the legal and ethical predicaments for

trained journalists working for news organizations are serious and require the full-chapter treatment in this book. This introductory chapter focuses on the established news media, expecting of professional journalists' serious attention in their careers to the sacredness-of-life protonorm.

11. For a similar argument about journalism responsibility in the live streaming of tragedy, but oriented toward peace journalism, see Rukhsana Aslam (2019), "Christchurch Mosques Shooting: Reflections and Confessions."

12. The concept of civil society originated with the philosopher G. W. F. Hegel (1770–1831). In the early nineteenth century, in his *Philosophy of Right* (Hegel, 1896), he identified self-supporting citizens with their own centers of gravity as entities distinct from the political state (Reidel, 1984). Charles Taylor (1992) helpfully situates Hegel's notion of civil society in the context of other political theories such as those of Locke and Montesquieu. For *Civil Society: History and Possibilities* (Kaviraj & Khilnani, 2001), Hegel is the basis of contemporary understandings of civil society. Research on civil society in India includes Gandhi's people movements as a strategy for implementing this idea (Kaviraj & Khilnani, 2001).

13. The communication theory of media ecology provides the argument for media variety in the civil society. Personal relations that characterize primary groups in civil society are best fostered by oral communication, whereas digital technology is most efficient at the machine-to-machine transmission. Walter Ong's *Orality and Literacy* (2002), for example, uses a historical perspective to specify the fundamental difference between print literacy and oral-aural communication, and in the process contends that orality is basic for all humans universally (as far as has been researched) and therefore is the standard by which all mediations should be compared.

14. Freire's *Education for Critical Consciousness* is an operationalized version for cultural discourse of Jürgen Habermas's (1984) communicative rationality in the public sphere. As with Freire, Habermas shifts the emphasis on the idea of rationality from the conceptual to the social. Relevant to this chapter's commitment to the sacredness of life as a protonorm, Habermas argues that for shared understanding to be possible among speakers and listeners, they must agree on universal validity claims (cf. Habermas, 1990).

15. Freire adopts his philosophy of communication from Karl Jaspers's *Origin and Goal of History* (1953), as interpreted by the Spanish philosopher Eduardo Nicol's *Los Principos de la Ciencia* (1965).

16. Freire was exiled after the 1964 military *coup d'etat* in Brazil. In Chile, he continued to apply his method to *campesinos,* working for the Chilean agricultural reform program and in rural extension, that is, in literacy education empowering them as Freire called it.

17. While subaltern communities require active aural-oral symbolization to maintain the sacredness of life, social media communities are not categorically excluded. Bennett and Segerberg (2013) in *The Logic of Connective Action* identify digital networks that use "broadly inclusive, easily personalized action frames as a basis for technology-assisted" human collective action. Typically, virtual communities are one-interest groups and demographic tribes, but there are examples of cyberspace promoting the sacredness of life instead of a machinic instrumentalism.

18. Alinsky's thinking and action were based on Robert E. Park (his professor at the University of Chicago) who saw in communities "reflections of the larger processes of an urban society" (Park, 1952). Park's understanding of communities as hubs of society-as-a-whole is reflected in this chapter as the pathway to socio-cultural change through alternative communities (cf. Christians, 2004).

REFERENCES

Alinsky, S. D. (1946). *Reveille for radicals.* New York: Vintage Random House.

Arendt, H. (1998). *The human condition* (2nd ed). Chicago: University of Chicago Press. (Original work published 1958).

Aslam, R. (2019). Christchurch Mosques shooting: Reflections and confessions. *Ethical Space: The International Journal of Communication Ethics, 16*(4), 48–56. (Paperback: https://www.amazon.com/Ethical-Space-Vol-16-Issue-4/dp/1845497546)

Bauman, Z. (2005). *Liquid life*. Cambridge, UK: Polity Press.

Benhabib, S. (1986). *Critique, norm and utopia: A study of normative foundations of critical theory*. New York: Columbia University Press.

Benhabib, S. (2003). *The reluctant Modernism of Hannah Arendt*. Lanham, MD: Rowman & Littlefield.

Bennett, W. L. (2016). *News: The politics of illusion* (10th ed). Chicago: University of Chicago Press.

Bennett, W. L., & Segerberg, A. (2013). *The logic of connective action: Digital media and the personalization of contentious politics*. New York: Cambridge University Press.

Benson, R. (2009). Shaping the public sphere: Habermas and beyond. *The American Sociologist, 40*(3), 175–97. https://doi.org/10.1007/s12108-009-9071-4

Boyte, H. C. (2004). *Everyday politics: Reconnecting citizens and public life*. Philadelphia: University of Pennsylvania Press.

Brueggemann, W. (2018). *The prophetic imagination*. Minneapolis: Fortress Press.

Carey, J. W. (1967). Harold Adams Innis and Marshall McLuhan. *Antioch Review, 27*(1), 5–39. doi:10.2307/4610816

Cassirer, E. (1953–1957, 1966). *The philosophy of symbolic forms* (4 vols.) (R. Manheim & J. M. Krois, Trans.). New Haven, CT: Yale University Press. (Original work published 1923–1929).

Christians, C. (2004). *Ubuntu* and communitarianism in media ethics. *Ecquid Novi: South African Journal for Journalism Research, 25*(2), 235–56. Retrieved from https://www.researchgate.net/publication/237466200_Ubuntu_and_communitarianism_in_media_ethics

Christians, C. (2007a). Neutral science and the ethics of resistance. In M. Gardina, & N. Denzin (Eds.), *Ethical futures in qualitative research: Decolonizing the politics of knowledge* (pp. 47–66). Walnut Creek, CA: Left Coast Press.

Christians, C. (2007b). Utilitarianism in media ethics and its discontents. *Journal of Mass Media Ethics, 22*(2–3), 113–31. https://doi.org/10.1080/08900520701315640

Christians, C. G., Fackler, P. M., Richardson, K. B., & Kreshel, P. J. (2020). *Media ethics: Cases and moral reasoning* (11th ed.). New York: Routledge.

Ellul , J. (1951). *The presence of the kingdom* (O. Wyon, Trans.). Philadelphia, PA: Westminster.

Ellul, J. (1954). *The technological society* (J. Wilkinson, Trans.). New York: Random Vintage.

Ellul, J. (1965). *Propaganda: The formation of men's attitudes* (K. Kellen & J. Lerner, Trans.). New York: Alfred A. Knopf.

Ellul, J. (1978). Symbolic function, technology and society. *Journal of Social and Biological Structure, 1*(3), 207–18. https://doi.org/10.1016/0140-1750(78)90023-4

Ellul, J. (1990). *The technological bluff* (G. W. Bromiley, Trans.). Grand Rapids, MI: William B. Eerdmans.

Fraser, N. (1992). Rethinking the public sphere: A contribution to the critique of actually existing democracy. In C. Calhoun (Ed.), *Habermas and the public sphere* (pp. 109–42). Cambridge, MA: MIT Press.

Fraser, N. (1997). *Justus interruptus*. New York: Routledge.

Freire, P. (1970). *Pedagogy of the oppressed*. New York: Seabury Press.

Freire, P. (1973). *Education for critical consciousness*. New York: Seabury Press.

Goodin, D. (2013). *The new rationalism: Albert Schweitzer's philosophy of reverence for life*. Montreal: McGill Queen's University Press.

Gushee, D. P. (2013). *The sacredness of human life*. Grand Rapids, MI: William B. Eerdmans Publishing Company.

Habermas, J. (1984). *The theory of communicative action* (Vol. 1): *Reason and the rationalization of society* (T. McCarthy, Trans.). Boston, MA: Beacon Press.

Habermas, J. (1990). *Moral consciousness and communicative action* (C. Lenhardt & S. W. Nicholsen, Trans.). Cambridge, MA: MIT Press.

Hanitzsch, T., Hanusch, F., Mellado, C., Anikina, M., Berganza, R., Cangoz, I., Coman, M., Hamada, B., Hernández, M. E., Karadjov, C. D., Moreira, S. V., Mwesige, P. G., Plaisance, P. L., Reich, Z., Seethaler, J., Skewes, E. A., Noor, D. V., & Yuen, E. K. W. (2011).

Mapping journalism cultures across nations: A comparative study of 18 countries. Journalism Studies , 12 (3), 273–93. https://doi.org/10.1080/1461670X.2010.512502

Havel, V. (1994). Post-modernism: The search for universal laws. *Vital Speeches of the Day, 60*(20), 613–15. Retrieved from https://www.vsotd.com/issue/1994-20/post-modernism

Hegel, G. F. W. (1896). *Philosophy of right* (S. W. Dyde, Trans.). London: George Bell and Sons.

Heidegger, M. (1962). *Being and time [Sein und Zeit]* (J. Macquarrie & E. Robinson, Trans.). New York: Harper & Row. (Original work published 1927)

Heidegger, M. (1966). *Discourse on thinking.* New York: Harper & Row.

Heidegger, M. (1971). *Poetry, language, thought* (A. Hofstadter, Trans.). New York: Harper & Row.

Heidegger, M. (1977a). Building dwelling thinking. In D. F. Krell (Ed.). (2008), *Martin Heidegger: Basic writings from Being and Time to The Task of Thinking* (D. F. Krell, Trans.) (pp. 319–39). New York: Harper & Row.

Heidegger, M. (1977b). *The question concerning technology and other essays* (W. Lovitt, Trans.). New York: Harper & Row.

Hood, W. F. (1972). The Aristotelian versus the Heideggerian approach to the problem of technology. In C. Mitcham & R. Mackey (Eds.), *Philosophy and technology: Readings in the philosophical problems of technology* (pp. 347–63). New York: Free Press.

Innis, H. (1951). *The bias of communication.* Toronto: University of Toronto Press.

Innis, H. (1952). *Empire and communication.* Toronto: University of Toronto Press.

Jaspers, K. (1953). *The origin and goal of history.* London: Routledge and Kegan Paul.

Johnstone, C. L. (1994). Ontological vision as ground for communication ethics: A response to the challenge of Postmodernism. *Proceedings of the Third National Communication Ethics Conference, 299–302.* Annandale, VA: Speech Communication Association.

Jonas, H. (1984). *The imperative of responsibility: In search of an ethics for the technological age. [Macht oder Ohnmacht der Subjektivität? Das Lieb-Seele problem im Vorfeld des Prinzips Verantwortung]* Chicago: University of Chicago Press.

Kaviraj, S., & Khilnani, S. (Eds.). (2001). *Civil society: History and possibilities.* Cambridge, UK: Cambridge University Press.

Kempson, R. M. (1975). *Presupposition and the delimitation of semantics.* Cambridge, UK: Cambridge University Press.

Kien, G. (2009). *Global technography: Ethnography in the age of mobility.* New York: Peter Lang.

Kuhn, T. S. (1996). *The structure of scientific revolutions* (3rd ed). Chicago: University of Chicago Press.

Lyotard, J. F. (1990). *Heidegger and the Jews* (A. Michel & M. S. Roberts, Trans.). Minneapolis: University of Minnesota Press.

Mayer, M. (Ed.). (2002). *Reverence for life: The ethics of Albert Schweitzer for the twenty-first century.* Syracuse, NY: Syracuse University Press.

Miller, M. R. (2004). *The millenium matrix: Reclaiming the past, reframing the future of the church.* San Francisco: Jossey-Bass.

Nicol, E. (1965). *Los principios de la ciencia [The principle of knowing].* Mexico: Fundo de Cultura Economica.

Ong, W. J. (2002). *Orality and literacy: The technologizing of the word* (2nd ed.). New York: Routledge. (Original work published 1982)

Önnerfors, A. (2019, March 18). "The great replacement"—Decoding the Christchurch terrorist manifesto. CARR (Center for Analysis of the Radical Right). Retrieved from https://www.radicalrightanalysis.com/2019/03/18/the-great-replacement-decoding-the-christchurch-terrorist-manifesto/

Park, R. E. (1952). *Human communities: The city and human ecology.* New York: The Free Press.

Peukert, H. (1981). Universal solidarity as the goal of communication. *Media Development, 28*(4), 10–12.

Reidel, M. (1984). *Between tradition and revolution: The Hegelian transformation of political philosophy.* Cambridge, UK: Cambridge University Press.

Rockmore, T. (1995). *Heidegger and French philosophy: Humanism, Antihumanism and Being.* New York: Routledge.

Rodriguez, C. (2001). *Fissures in the mediascape: An international study of citizens' media.* Cresskill, NJ: Hampton.

Rodriguez, C. (2011). *Citizens' media against armed conflict: Disrupting violence in Colombia.* Minneapolis: University of Minnesota Press.

Schweitzer, A. (1987). *The philosophy of civilization.* New York: Prometheus Books.

Schweitzer, A. (2009). *Out of my life and thought: An autobiography.* Baltimore, MD: Johns Hopkins University Press.

Smith, G. T. (2003, August 9). Customer review: *Philosophy of civilization* by Albert Schweitzer. Retrieved from https://www.amazon.ca/gp/customer-reviews/R135D6MAG8LO3L/ref=cm_cr_srp_d_rvw_ttl?ie=UTF8&ASIN=0879754036

Taylor, C. (1992). Civil society in the western tradition. In E. Groffier & M. Paradis (Eds.), *The notion of tolerance in human rights* (pp. 117–36). Ottawa: Carleton University Press.

Troude-Chastenet, P. (2006). The political thought of Jacques Ellul: A 20th Century man (E. A. Tumanova, Trans.). *The Ellul Forum, 38,* 3–12. Retrieved from https://journals.wheaton.edu/index.php/ellul/issue/view/63/63

Virillio, P. (2000). The information bomb (C. Turner, Trans.). New York: Verso.

Vladislav, J. (Ed.). (1990). *Vaclav Havel: Or living in truth by Havel, Vaclav.* London: Farber and Farber.

Wolin, R. (Ed.) (1993). *The Heidegger controversy: A critical reader.* Cambridge, MA: MIT Press.

Wuthnow, R. (1987). *Meaning and moral order: Explorations in cultural analysis.* Berkeley: University of California Press.

Chapter Two

The Dark Side of Watching

*Theoretical and Ethical Challenges of
Live Streamed Suicides*

Matt Corr and Tim Michaels

*Authors' Note: The contents of this chapter engage with theories and examples
of suicide and other forms of self-harm. While we have done our best to
present this content with care and empathy, readers may find much of it to be
emotionally challenging and potentially triggering due to the very nature of
the subject.*

INTRODUCTION

On December 30, 2016, a 12-year-old girl began a live stream on the Live.me
social media app, just as so many of her peers do across the variety of social
media platforms available (Phillips, 2017). This stream, however, was tragi-
cally different; rather than a jovial banter with friends or a review of a
favorite movie, the subject turned to the darkest of human thoughts. Once she
had an online audience, she utilized the medium to disclose her ongoing
struggle with depression, which had been triggered after a member of her
own family had sexually abused her. After 40 minutes, the stream ended
abruptly when, horrifyingly, the youth committed suicide on camera for all
viewers to see. The video spread quickly across multiple social media platforms, yet major websites like YouTube struggled to keep it from reappear-
ing no matter how many times it had been deleted (Phillips, 2017). It became
a live streamed suicide that haunted the Internet.

This tragic incident is just one example of the growing phenomenon of
live streaming suicides to online audiences. Suicide rates have been steadily

increasing in recent years, and, according to the American Foundation for Suicide Prevention, suicide is now the tenth leading cause of death in the United States, claiming the lives of more than 47,000 U.S. citizens in 2017. Presently, the exact number of these deaths that are live streamed is unknown, but the examples continue to accumulate.

As early as 2008, online streaming platforms became targets for making suicides public, when a 19-year-old used Justin.tv to stream an intentional overdose (Stelter, 2008). A year after the suicide described in the opening, a similar incident played out as a 14-year-old used Facebook Live to broadcast her own hanging (Bever, 2017). That same year, Facebook's live streaming capabilities were also used by a 33-year-old actor who shot himself in the head after being charged with domestic violence (Wilcox, 2017). While these first three examples are only in the United States, the problem is undoubtedly global, with incidents occurring in France (Williamson, 2016), Sweden (Westerlund, Hadlaczky, & Wasserman, 2015), and China (Ma, Zhang, Harris, Chen, & Xu, 2016) to name a few. The situation has become prevalent enough to prompt an editorial on Facebook from Mark Zuckerberg (2017). Morbid as it may be, the issue certainly warrants consideration in academic research.

It is an unfortunate fact that suicide rates are steadily on the rise in the United States. While the proliferation of legal and ethical challenges of live streaming has generated a lot of conversation, the unique challenges of live streamed suicides has, hitherto, remained on the periphery. The intent of this chapter is, in part, to more directly assess the relationship between live streaming and suicide. In order to address this unique phenomenon, this chapter will apply insights from both communication and sociological theory to instances of suicide ideation, attempts, and imagery appearing in real time on various social media platforms. In particular, we seek to understand the potential causes and, especially, the consequences of live streamed suicides.

While the majority of mainstream research on suicide emerges from the fields of psychology and sociology, this chapter approaches the subject from a framework of communication theory and ethics. From this perspective, the inherent socio-interactional factors of suicidal motives, as well as the media-ecological nature of live streaming as a communication medium, become co-influential with unique ethical implications. This approach is not intended to supplant extant theoretical approaches to suicide research but rather to supplement them with an additional point-of-view. In short, this chapter offers an additional voice to an important, ongoing conversation.

This chapter consists of four primary sections. In the first section, we introduce the field of suicidology to offer an overview of literature from psychology, sociology, and philosophy to explain potential motives for suicide in the general sense. We follow this section by then questioning why an individual might also wish to live stream his or her own suicide to a digital audience. The third section addresses the potential societal impact of live streamed suicides by using already established media effects as theoretical proxies. Lastly, this chapter considers the ethical implications of live streaming suicides in terms of the duty of the actor, the audience, and the stage. As a whole, this chapter presents a case for the dark side of live streaming and the unique challenges it initiates.

SUICIDAL MOTIVES: A PRIMER ON SUICIDOLOGY

To best understand live streamed suicides, one must first understand what might drive an individual to take their own life in the first place. After all, these deaths represent a significant dereliction of the animalistic instinct of self-preservation. Of course, there is no singular theory to explain an act driven by the unique experiences and emotions of an individual; however, it is fruitful to review the literature of suicidologists in order to acquire a broad understanding of the explanations at hand. Rather than being exhaustive or even representative, we instead focus here on theories and perspectives of suicidal behavior that best explain why an individual might live stream their own suicide.

Current research in the social sciences that seeks to understand suicide better is becoming increasingly visible in mainstream literature. For instance, the *Diagnostic and Statistical Manual of Mental Disorders* (*DSM*-5), the premier resource for mental health professionals published by the American Psychiatric Association (APA), has included suicide risk as a corresponding concern for patients diagnosed with numerous disorders. Some wide-ranging examples include bulimia nervosa, opioid use disorder, major depressive disorder, posttraumatic stress disorder, and schizophrenia, among many others. The most current edition of the *DSM-5*, however, includes Suicidal Behavior Disorder as one of its "Conditions for Further Study," which are conditions that the APA deems important enough to encourage future research but do not yet have "criteria sets" sufficient enough for clinical use (2017, p. 783). The proposed criteria for Suicidal Behavior Disorder include previous suicide attempts within the past two years "with at least some intent to die" which is separate from the similarly proposed condition of nonsuicidal self-injury (2017, p. 801). While it remains to be seen how suicide will be featured in the next *DSM*, it is important that researchers continue to track this growing and dynamic health risk. That said, many experts across multiple fields have already explored suicidal motivation with significant depth.

The famous philosopher Albert Camus opens *The Myth of Sisyphus* with the assertion, "There is but one truly serious philosophical problem, and that is suicide. Judging whether life is or is not worth living amounts to answering the fundamental question of philosophy" (1983, p. 3). Camus believes that when an individual asks themselves this fundamental question, they are responding to the absurd nature of existence itself; namely, that we continue to seek clarity and meaning from an irrational and unreasonable world. It is noteworthy that Camus believes that philosophy guides action; therefore, if we deem life meaningless, then our beliefs direct our responses (1983). Camus suggests that people commit suicide "because they judge life is not worth living" (1983, p. 4). Camus's treatise does not submit to suicide as deterministic, but begs the question: In a world devoid of meaning, how do we continue to live our lives despite the experience of absurdity?

Camus was not the only thinker to reflect on the phenomena of suicide. French sociologist Émile Durkheim's *Le Suicide* (1951/1897) identifies social forces that may contribute to suicidal behavior, specifically social integration and moral regulation. Durkheim categorizes four types of suicide that manifest as a result of these social forces. The first kind of suicide is *egoistic suicide*, characterized by a sense of isolation from social groups and a lack of connection to others. The second kind, *altruistic suicide*, describes those in which individuals are deeply tied to society or a particular social group, but see their individual contributions to that group as being inferior to or even threatening the strength of the group. The suicide is for the good of the group. The third type of suicide is *anomic suicide*. These suicides are the result of extreme disappointment with their lives compared to expectations. Individuals in this category are often morally confused; or have surrendered any possibility of a guiding social ethic to a system of continual disappointment by unmet expectations. Durkheim's fourth, and final, type of suicide is *fatalistic suicide*. This kind of suicide occurs when some individuals feel so trapped by oppression that they would rather die than keep living.

Durkheim's sociological theory was revolutionary because "he was the first to attempt a systematic, comprehensive, coherent, and testable theory of suicide" (Joiner, 2005, p. 35). Durkheim's work shifted thinking about suicidal causes from an individual disposition to social forces. Thomas Joiner, inspired by Durkheim and confronting staggering increases in domestic suicide rates, was frustrated by the lack of research on the topic. He argued that "science about suicide is not especially well developed and has certainly not permeated the public consciousness" (Joiner, 2005, p. 25). To help fill this void, Joiner (2005) proposed a model of suicidal behavior, which he published in his book *Why People Die by Suicide*. Driven, in part, by his father's suicide, Joiner sought to understand suicidal motives better. In order to improve prevention, "people need a clearer understanding of how and why people die by suicide" (Joiner, 2005, p. 25).

Searching for answers, Joiner references the work of Edwin Shneidman,[1] a psychologist and suicidologist who focused on thwarted psychological needs leading to psychological pain. This *psychache* results from "the introspective experience of negative emotions such as dread, despair, fear, grief, shame, guilt, frustrated love, loneliness, and loss" (Shneidman, 1998). The introspective pain "is the core of suicide. Suicide is an exclusively human response to extreme psychological pain" (Shneidman, 1998, p. 181). The pain associated with one's consciousness likened to Camus's concept of absurdity, the experience of meaninglessness and disconnection from the world and others. This existential crisis, this feeling of homelessness within our own being, has been approached ontologically and phenomenologically by philosopher Martin Heidegger. What Camus calls absurdity, Heidegger (2000) calls *Geworfenheit*, or thrownness, a feeling of being thrown into existence with arbitrary social conventions and an acute awareness of the arbitrary nature of being. Being in the world, itself, causes a sense of alienation which we must cope with throughout our lives.

Many people cope with the aforementioned alienation through escapism. Consequently, a colleague of Joiner, Roy Baumeister, has proposed the escape theory of suicide. The theory posits a series of steps escalating to suicidal behavior. The first step is similar to Durkheim's *anomic suicides*, catalyzed by extreme discrepancies between expectations and reality. These shortcomings result in self-blame and feelings of worthlessness; thus, "awareness of the self's inadequacies generate negative affect, and the individual, therefore, desires to escape from self-awareness" (Baumeister, 1990, p. 90) and the associated negative feelings. The individual escalates into "cognitive deconstruction (constricted temporal focus, concrete thinking, immediate or proximal goals, cognitive rigidity, and rejection of meaning), which helps prevent meaningful self-awareness and emotion" (Baumeister, 1990, p. 90). This clouded thinking may result in irrational behavior, the most extreme of which is attempted suicide.

Blending Durkheim's insights on "social disconnection" (Joiner, 2005, p. 35), Baumeister's theory of escapism, and Shneidman's concept of *psychache*, Joiner formulates his interpersonal-psychological theory of suicidal behavior. This theory proposes that in order for an individual to commit suicide, they must have suicidal desires as well as the ability to overcome instincts of self-preservation. Joiner begins by trying to understand the social and psychological elements that constitute psychache and suicidal motivation. It is here that Joiner finds utility in the insights from Durkheim and Shneidman. In Joiner's words, "perceived burdensomeness combined with failed belongingness constitutes psychache" (2005, p. 37). Joiner finds additional insight from psychologist and suicide theorist Aaron Beck.[2]

Aaron Beck et al. (1990) approached suicide from cognition and finds a strong correlation between successful suicides and hopelessness (Beck et al., 1990). Beck believed that "depressed people are convinced in their hearts of three related beliefs, known as *Beck's cognitive triad of depression*. These are: 'I'm no good.' 'My world is bleak,' and 'My future is hopeless'" (Haidt, 2006, p. 38). A 1990 study finds that those with suicidal ideation are eleven times more likely to die by suicide if they register high scores of hopeless-ness (Beck et al., 1990). Joiner considers the idea of hopelessness is incom-plete, "what in particular are suicidal people hopeless about?" (2005, p. 39). Joiner believes these individuals are hopeless about their "burdensomeness and failed belongingness" (2005, p. 39).

Low Belongingness/Social Alienation

Émile Durkheim's groundbreaking study in 1897 showed that the greatest factor determining suicide risk was social constraints. People that are less obligated to others were more likely to commit suicide. "People living alone were most likely to kill themselves; married people, less; married people with children, still less." Durkheim concluded that "people need obligations and constraints to provide structure and meaning to their lives" (Haidt, 2006, p. 133). Having a low sense of belongingness is a feeling of alienation from others. These individuals are not dependent on others and instead rely only on themselves and "recognize no other rules of conduct than what are founded on his private interests" (Durkheim, 1951, p. 209). Recent longitudi-nal studies show the importance of social relationships to happiness and longevity. The benefits extend even to those who prefer little social interac-tion (Haidt, 2006, p. 133). We seem to have an innate need to interact with one another; that is, we simply need to belong (Baumeister & Leary, 1995).

Perceived Burdensomeness

This suicide risk factor is characterized by perceived low self-worth to family, social groups, or society as a whole. Individuals experiencing feelings of burden-someness have the misperception that the world would be better off without them. They feel ineffective in their contributions to their family, friends, and other social groups. Intrigued by a study that suggested a correlation between suicidal ideation and perceived burdensomeness (De Catanzaro, 1995), Join-er tested this connection by analyzing suicide notes. Joiner et al. (2002) found that when the letters expressed feelings of burdensomeness, individu-als were more likely to have succeeded in their suicide attempts and were more likely to use "violent means" of suicide. However, in addition to low belongingness and perceived burdensomeness, an individual has to acquire the ability to carry out the means of death.

Ability to Overcome Self-Preservation

While researching suicide, Shneidman realized that "only a small minority of cases of excessive psychological pain result in suicide, but every case of suicide stems from excessive psychache" (Shneidman, 1996, p. 58). Joiner understood that psychological pain is not sufficient for suicidal behavior;

there must be another factor at play. Thus, Joiner's theory of suicide has three necessary components, including perceived burdensomeness, social alienation, and an ability to overcome the fear of dying. Joiner looks to Durkheim, Shneidman, Baumeister, and Beck for insight into the first two, but Joiner's theory is unique in that it includes an achieved ability to overcome the natural fear of dying.

Joiner (2005) writes, "When self-injury and other dangerous experiences become unthreatening and mundane—when people work up to the act of death by suicide by getting used to its threat and danger—that is when we might lose them" (p. 48). This ability to enact self-harm remains constant, unlike *psych-ache*, which ebbs and flows from hour-to-hour or day-to-day. Therefore, just because an individual has built up an ability for lethality, does not necessarily mean that they want to die. Suicidal individuals may, in fact, be ambivalent. The suppressed instincts for self-preservation often reincarnate as a desire to be rescued. Could this "desire for someone to save them" be a hidden motive for live streaming suicides? To better understand the motives for live streaming suicides, we look first to motives for live streaming.

MOTIVES FOR LIVE STREAMING

According to the Center for Disease Control and Prevention (CDC), suicide is the second leading cause of death among those ages 15 to 34 (Hedegaard et al., 2018). Consequently, according to the streaming demographics research company, Leichtman Research Group, individuals 18 to 34 years of age are currently driving the live streaming trend via "Internet-delivered pay-TV service" (Leichtman Research Group, 2018). These two statistics overlap almost perfectly. Understanding this particularly vulnerable demographic may be key in understanding suicides carried out in this online public space.

Live streaming has rapidly evolved over the last ten years. This rapid evolution is part of the reason for the lack of research. Live streaming has exploded in popularity since Justin.tv emerged in 2007. YouNow launched in 2011, and Snapchat began to offer live elements to its app in 2014. As live streaming gravitated more toward video game live streaming, services such as Twitch became popular in 2014. The following year saw the launch of two rival live streaming services, Meerkat and Periscope. Meerkat made its debut in February and gained popularity in March at the South by Southwest Festival in Austin, Texas. Around the same time, Twitter purchased Periscope and began aggressively competing with Meerkat for new customer accounts. Four months after its release, Periscope surpassed ten million accounts. Within the following year live streaming was integrated into the Twitter app. In 2016, Facebook expanded live streaming services for all users, enhanced by the ability for real-time comments and floating emojis over video. Today,

Periscope (including Twitter) and Facebook Live (including Instagram) represent the most popular general live streaming options.

What makes live streaming such a popular means of communication? Although at present, relatively little empirical research exists to explore this question as it relates to suicide, we may be able to learn from the research on the interface between new technologies and human interaction.

Technological Mediation

For more than 30 years, Sherry Turkle[3] has been researching interactions between humans and technology. Her first book on the subject, *The Second Self* (1984) suggests that computers are not merely a tool, but alter our psychology and influence the way we interact with one another. This idea expanded in *Alone Together* (2011). Turkle (2011) argues that "Technology is seductive when what it offers meets our human vulnerabilities. As it turns out, we are very vulnerable, indeed. We are lonely but fearful of intimacy" (p. 1). In response to our fear, we substitute unpredictable relationships with ones we can control. Computers applications and social networks "offer the illusion of companionship without the demands of friendship [and] the illusion of friendship without the demands of intimacy" (Turkle, 2015, p. 7). Turkle (2015) suggests that it is real conversation that builds empathy and builds "intimacy, community, and communion" (p. 7). Furthermore, conversations allow us to "build narratives" or stories that connect ourselves to history, culture, places, and each other. Narratives, in short, give us meaning.

However, the online relationships we gravitate to are ones we can control. "Online communication makes us feel more in charge of our time and self-presentation" (Turkle, 2015, p. 21). These are relationships built around image management and efficiency. "But human relationships are rich, messy, and demanding. When we clean them up with technology, we move from conversation to the efficiencies of mere connection. I fear we forget the difference" (Turkle, 2015, p. 21). Individuals dealing with what Shneidman calls *psychache* often see the world as meaningless. If we gain meaning through narratives built during face-to-face conversation, we may be looking online for something that does not exist there. "We slip into thinking that always being connected is going to make us less lonely. But we are at risk because it is actually the reverse" (Turkle, 2015, p. 23).

When depressed and suicidal individuals turn to the internet for the connection they lack in the real world, they may end up feeling more emotionally disconnected, and may not realize it. A recent study paired up college friends and had them communicate in one of "four different ways: face-to-face conversation, video chat, audio chat, and online instant messaging" (Turkle, 2015, p. 23). The researchers then tested "the degree of emotional bonding" that occurred during their interactions. "The results were clear: In-person conversation led to the most emotional connection, and online messaging led to the least" (Turkle, 2015, p. 23). If low belongingness is a risk factor for suicidal behavior, then this study offers a remedy in the form of face-to-face conversation.

Turkle's insights gained support by a 2017 study in the *American Journal of Epidemiology,* which found that while in-person conversations improve health, regular communication via Facebook decreased an individual's well-being. "Exposure to the carefully curated images from others' lives leads to negative self-comparison, and the sheer quantity of social media interactions may detract from more meaningful real-life experiences" (Shakya & Christakis, 2017). Remember that Durkheim's *anomic suicides* are caused by large discrepancies between expectations and reality, which lead to feelings of ineffectiveness and/or worthlessness.

Turkle's research can be useful in suicide prevention research. When people use technology to replace face-to-face communication, they lose the ability to empathize, they are more depressed, and they miss out on the narratives of life that imbue it with meaning. Many of the side effects that occur as humans communicate through *and to* technology are very similar to the elements of Shneidman's *psychache.*

We have explored Sherry Turkle's insights into motivations for choosing online communities over those in real life. We have also seen some undesirable side effects of those mediated interactions. Turkle's psychological and social analyses are insightful in terms of how and why we turn to online communities, but there has been some research that takes a more empirical approach.

Uses and Gratifications

Uses and gratifications literature attempts to explain the way people use certain communication channels, among other resources, to satisfy their needs and achieve their goals (Katz, Blumler, & Gurevitch, 1974). Uses and gratifications is a psychological perspective, with three main objectives. The first tries to explain how people use media to satisfy particular needs. The second is to understand media behavior motives better. The third main objective of uses and gratifications research is to identify consequences that result from needs, motives, and behavior (Rubin, 2002). Due to the recent development of live streaming technology and the rapidity of its inception, little is actually known about user motivations in this medium. Thus, we begin by trying to answer the three uses and gratifications questions: How are people using live streaming? Why live stream? And what are the consequences of live streaming?

A 2018 study published in *Computers in Human Behavior* examined users' motivations for live streaming on Twitch. The researchers collected

2,227 surveys and placed responses into six different motivation categories. According to their study, people engaged Twitch for "social interaction, sense of community, meeting new people, entertainment, information seeking, and a lack of external support in real life" (Hilvert-Bruce et al., 2018, p. 58). Three additional findings from the study were that social interaction was a motivator for all types of engagement, "viewers who lacked external support spent more time watching live streams" (Hilvert-Bruce et al., 2018, p. 58), and those that "preferred smaller channels were more motivated by social engagement" (Hilvert-Bruce et al., 2018, p. 58).

Analyzing this study from the perspective of Joiner's interpersonal theory of suicidal behavior, we can see individuals live streaming to fulfill the desire to belong (people live stream for social interaction, a sense of community, and because they lack a healthy support network in the life). While many seek an online sense of community as a supplement to healthy real-life social groups, there are undoubtedly others that seek these communities because they lack them in real life.

Motivations for Live Streaming Suicides

While the CDC does not have data on the number of social media suicides, it is clear that "social media is becoming a new platform for public suicide" (Bever, 2017). The uses and gratifications literature and insight from Sherry Turkle may help understand why some people turn to live streaming as a replacement for healthy, real world social interaction; however, motives for live streaming one's death are speculative at best. Why would someone want to die in front of a live, online audience? Clinical psychologists, Nadine Kaslow[4] and Sarah Dunn[5] hypothesize that "teens and young adults may choose to end their lives online for a number of reasons." For instance, "those who have been victims of cyberbullying may do it as a form of revenge or to retaliate against the bullies" (Bever, 2017). Some may do it "as a way to memorialize themselves" (Bever, 2017). While others may broadcast their suicide attempts "hoping that viewers will step in to stop them" (Bever, 2017). Dunn adds that "There seems to be a link between what goes on on social media and suicides on social media" (Bever, 2017). Dunn implies a blurring between the boundaries of real and online worlds. Online interactions most certainly have real-world consequences.

MEDIA EFFECTS OF LIVE STREAMED SUICIDES

Any type of media with a significant audience, including live streams, is bound to influence that audience substantively. These measurable impacts of mass communication are referred to as media effects. One of the first media effects that is of concern for live streamed suicides is known simply as the "copycat effect." This broad term refers to the phenomenon of members of audiences to imitate something witnessed in the media. Loren Coleman (2004) further defines the copycat effect as "the power of the mass communication and culture to create an epidemic of similar behaviors" (p. 1). Importantly, as Coleman (2004) argues, such contagions are not limited to just news reporting, but rather are the result of all widely consumed communication media, including books, movies, television, and music. According to Coleman (2004), one of the results of the copycat effect is an epidemic of imitated suicides.

While Coleman does not make mention of live streaming as a medium for stimulating the copycat effect; indeed, the publication of his work largely predates the widespread use of that technology, it certainly should not be excluded. The plethora of examples of behaviors and trends emerging from social media of all kinds are nearly endless, as so-called influencers have utilized Facebook Live and YouTube to extend their reach across audiences. Internet-based communication media are arguably the most impactful today in terms of replicating actions and behaviors. This, of course, begs the question: do live streamed suicides result in the copycat effect? To better answer this question, we now turn to two corresponding media effects more specific to the subject: the Werther Effect and the Papageno Effect.

The Werther Effect

While the specific effects of live streamed suicides have received little research, we believe that the well-established co-related phenomena of the Werther Effect and the Papageno Effect offer important theoretical proxies. The former was first conceived in 1974 by sociologist David P. Phillips, who, after studying highly publicized suicides in the United States and the United Kingdom, concluded that there was a correlation between suicide portrayals in media and subsequent surges in suicide rates. Phillips (1974) dubbed this phenomenon the Werther Effect in acknowledgment of one of the first recorded cases of its existence: a contagion of copycat suicides in Europe following the publication of Johann Wolfgang von Goethe's novel *The Sorrows of Young Werther* in 1774. In Goethe's work, the titular character ultimately decides that the only resolution of the love triangle he is entangled in is to remove himself entirely through suicide. According to Phillips (1974), the immediate popularity of the work apparently instigated a slew of copycat suicides, many of which even reportedly mimicked Werther's method for doing so. Despite being merely a fictional character, Werther demonstrated the power that a representation of suicide can have on an audience.

The focus of Phillips's (1974) original work on the Werther Effect, as well as the bulk of subsequent scholarship, focused on how media coverage of suicides could prompt imitations. For Phillips, the media's inherent power of suggestion is the driving force behind copycat suicides. Quantitative analyses of suicide rates following highly reported suicide events have largely corroborated Phillips's (1974) theory (see: Wasserman, 1984; Yip et al., 2006; Fu & Yip, 2007). The results demonstrate that nearly any medium with a large audience can result in what Gould, Wallenstein, and Davidson (1989) call a "suicide cluster" (p. 17). Suicide clusters represent a measurable result of the Werther Effect, a sizable surge in suicide victims linked by a key commonality, usually within just a few weeks of the inciting incident.

Changes in communication technology and consumption have more recently pushed the types of media that induce the Werther Effect beyond journalism coverage and literature. Michaels and Corr (2018) have noted the contemporary infatuation with celebrities, for example, result in suicide clusters when famous actors, musicians, and artists take their own life. The same can be true of fictional portrayals of suicide. In 2017, suicide clusters were tied to the broadcast of the television series *13 Reasons Why*, the plot of which is based on the suicide of a teenage character (Devitt, 2017), further demonstrating the reach of the Werther Effect.

As of writing, the necessary data is unavailable to either confirm or deny the potential of live streamed suicides to invoke the Werther Effect and create suicide clusters. However, the literature on the subject has demonstrated that mediums of communicating or representing suicide do not seem to limit or deter the effects; indeed, it is consistent through journalism, literature, celebrity status, television, and social media. We may conclude, then, that it is unlikely that live streamed suicides are somehow exempt from the Werther Effect. Given the unfiltered presentation and immediacy of these platforms, live streams have the potential to exacerbate the already climbing suicide rates. To be clear, there is no direct evidence to prove this argument; however, the examples of teenage girls hanging themselves during live streams just weeks apart mentioned earlier in this chapter bear many of the characteristics of the Werther Effect. If indeed live streamed suicides inspire copycats that go as far as mimicking the live streaming component of the event, a contagion of clusters could result. Which means, then, that live streaming platforms hold the power to multiply suicides.

The Papageno Effect

We have been warned of the Werther Effect and the potential influence in inspiring suicidal individuals to carry out their final acts; however, there is an optimistic counter. While the Werther Effect inspires tragic acts, the Papageno Effect inspires alternatives. *The Magic Flute*, an eighteenth-century opera by Mozart, tells the tale of Papageno and his struggles with suicidal thinking. During the opera, other characters give Papageno alternatives to killing himself, which ultimately convinces him that suicide would be a mistake (Niederkrotenthaler et al., 2010). The lesson of Papageno is that carefully conceived messages can deter suicides.

The Papageno Effect was first postulated by Niederkrotenthaler et al. (2010) as an effort to assess the difference that specific media content and framing may have as an effect when portraying or reporting suicides. Niederkrotenthaler et al. (2010) determined that, when media coverage of a high-profile suicide minimizes glorification while emphasizing avenues for assistance, the Werther Effect can be nullified or even reversed. The media, whether a major broadcaster or a social media platform, can effectively take an active role in decreasing copycat suicides by offering alternatives (Sisask & Värnik, 2017). This effect has prompted news agencies, particularly in Europe, to adopt stringent standards for covering stories involving suicides or suicide attempts (Sisask & Värnik, 2017). The World Health Organization has even offered a universal guide for journalists covering suicides, which codifies these standards, requiring that the story emphasize education over sensationalism.

The Papageno Effect can also be initiated outside of the traditional news media. According to Michaels and Corr (2018), a notable example of this success has been in the way celebrity suicides are framed. Michaels and Corr (2018) have also noted that celebrities have been able to leverage their social media presence to raise additional awareness, even managing to spike suicide help hotlines after doing so. In short, although suicide representations in media can lead to imitation as a media effect, it can also stimulate education depending on the thoughtfulness of the broadcast.

Live streaming can be a powerful tool for offering these alternatives; however, it is ultimately up to the streamer, the audience, and the platform to enact responsible countermeasures to suicidal ideation. Herein lies perhaps the largest dilemma for the media effects of live streamed suicides. Traditional news media is capable of producing the Papageno Effect because of the high level of preparation that is required of the journalistic process. These professionals are able to carefully craft their messages to favor Papageno over Werther. Even most social media platforms like Facebook and Twitter can, at least to some extent, claim this same advantage, as ordinary postings can be framed in the same manner.

Live streams, however, have an inherent immediacy and a rawness that differentiates them from the former two communication media. As such, leveraging live streamed suicides to invoke the Papageno Effect seems immensely challenging if not outright impossible. For one, the suicidal individual is certainly unlikely to be suggesting to the audience that potential alternatives to suicide are available and directing them to sources of help. Furthermore, the audience is unlikely to intervene in the way Papageno's friends did. Not only are they far removed from the situation, actual examples of live streamed suicides have shown that audience members often doubt the individual's motives, but many have actually *encouraged* the individual to go through with it, such as in the case of Abraham Biggs (Madkour, 2008). Lastly, live streaming platforms are relatively passive; that is to say that live streams are not actively monitored, edited, or restricted. This essentially prohibits the meticulous planning that journalists and mainstream broadcasters have successfully employed in invoking the Papageno Effect. As a result, the direct and raw nature of a live stream is largely unable to receive the careful framing of suicides that have been used elsewhere. We conclude with the concern that live streamed suicides are much more likely to invoke the Werther Effect than the Papageno Effect, making them even more dangerous than one might initially expect. In the next section, however, we will consider some possibilities for mitigation as we investigate the ethical implications of live streamed suicides.

ETHICAL IMPLICATIONS: THE ACTOR, THE AUDIENCE, AND THE STAGE

The media effects established as relevant to live streamed suicides call into question the duties of those involved. At this juncture, this chapter will consider the ethical implications brought about by suicides that have been live streamed. Because we have largely established this phenomenon as a sort of digital interaction, we now turn to communication ethics specifically in order to consider the ethical implications for three components of these performances: the actor, the audience, and the stage.

The Actor

Is killing yourself unethical? It is a common debate in the context of terminally ill patients experiencing daily pain and anguish from their condition. Those debating this topic often take one of two ethical positions. The deontological position relies on absolute principles such as "Thou shall not kill." Regardless of the situation, this principle is to be upheld; however, deontological positions often come into conflict with each other and require breaking the principle. For example, ectopic pregnancies usually require an abortion to save the life of the expecting mother. The absolute positions almost always have exceptions and become arbitrary in application. Another common ethical approach to suicide is the principle of autonomy. A person can act in any way that they choose as long as it is lawful and does not violate the autonomy of another. An interesting caveat of applying this principle in a medical context is that patient autonomy is often not granted to mentally unstable individuals, such as severely depressed people wanting to die.

While debates for the right-to-die are relevant to live streaming suicide, there is another ethical consideration that is unique to live stream one's suicide for public consumption. Joiner's interpersonal theory of suicidal behavior includes the ability to overcome the instincts for self-preservation over time. Clinical psychologists Kaslow is concerned that when viewers watch a suicide online, sometimes over and over again, it "could give others who are struggling a greater sense of 'acquired capability'—the idea that, 'If you can do it, I can do it'" (Bever, 2017). Those publicly broadcasting their suicide could inspire a member of their live audience or someone who watches at a later date to harm themselves.

Those with suicidal intentions have often untethered themselves from living under a guiding social ethic (remember Durkheim's *anomic suicides*); however, if their act can potentially harm others, this is contradictory to the ideas of *altruistic suicide* or perceived burdensomeness and may elicit cognitive dissonance. This new ethical dilemma may force the self-harmer to confront the idea that publicly harming themselves may harm another individual that they were trying to "help" by their suicide. This brings up another ethical approach to suicide: consequentialism. A consequentialist approach, such as utilitarianism, aims to minimize any harm and maximize the good. This approach considers more of the situation; however, it relies on subjective definitions of good and bad.

The Audience

Abraham Biggs hated himself and wanted to die. He announced his intentions to carry out his suicide on a bodybuilding website by live streaming over Justin.tv. Biggs overdosed on a combination of benzodiazepines and opiates prescribed for his bipolar disorder. Over the next 12 hours, people watched him die. Biggs was one of the people first to live stream their suicide. While Biggs slowly died, some members of his audience "cracked jokes" and "encouraged him to do it" while others "tried to talk him out of it" (Madkour, 2008).

If we care about our humanity, we must respond to the other when they are in trouble. This was the view of the twentieth-century Jewish philosopher, author, and ethicist, Emmanuel Levinas. For Levinas, communication begins by listening, not speaking. Whether listening to a friend, or a stranger, listening connects us to an "ethical echo" (Arnett, 2009, p. 200). This echo links us to the very foundation of human existence and "turns us towards the face of the Other that moves us toward an accompanying attentive response" (Arnett, 2009, p. 200). Levinas believes we all have a fundamental responsibility to respond and attend to one another. His justification is that because we are social creatures by nature, we need one another. Without the other, there is no I; thus, if we neglect the other, "we cease to be human" (Arnett, 2009, p. 203). Our responsibilities begin with what is in front of us. The visual phenomenon of encountering the actual face of the Other reminds us of our ethical obligation. If this is true in the real world, then this must be true online as well.

The Stage

Companies such as Facebook and Twitter have given a global stage to anyone that wants to broadcast live content. At the same time, they have almost complete autonomy in determining how to monitor their content. While these companies and others have content guidelines, it is mainly up to channel audiences to flag videos. With thousands of videos being streamed simultaneously, there are "tens of millions of reports a week about potentially objectionable content" (Terdiman, 2018). The sheer volume of reports makes managing content nearly impossible. Thus, many violent videos are available for days before they are removed.

Both Facebook, Twitter (Periscope), and China's Live.me have implemented artificial intelligence (AI) to help recognize potentially objectionable content. Facebook, for instance, is focusing on seven areas, including "nudity, graphic violence, terrorism, hate speech, spam, fake accounts, and suicide prevention" (Terdiman, 2018). Facebook's AI software "will scan all posts for patterns of suicidal thoughts, and when necessary send mental health resources to the user at risk or their friends, or contact local first-responders" (Constine, 2017). Early results are promising. AI is becoming very accurate at predicting suicidal behavior. A 2017 Florida State University study analyzed health records and "used machine learning to predict with 80 to 90 percent accuracy whether or not someone will attempt suicide, as far off as two years in the future" (Molteni, 2017). This is a similar technique being used by Facebook to mine data and flag posts as "suicide or self-injury," which could prompt immediate intervention during a live video stream. One of the challenges is that the AI mines posted content and not orally delivered content. Thus, the current software is reliant on viewer comments. Additionally, while innovations in suicide prevention software continue, another ethical dilemma comes to the forefront, specifically user privacy. How much of our privacy are we willing to sacrifice for AI to be effective?

While each stakeholder (the potential victim, the audience, and the platform) has its own ethical considerations, they are not independent of one another. Those that provide the stage, such as Facebook and Twitter, have acknowledged their responsibility to provide the audience with reporting tools. The audience, then, is charged with recognizing the difference between entertainment and genuine calls for help by using the available tools in an act of attending to the Other.

Sherry Turkle (2015) warns us that online communication does not replace face-to-face conversation. The very human need to belong is not nurtured online. The social and personal relationships that give meaning to our lives are cultivated in real life. If we rely on artificial intelligent machines to "fix" the growing trend of live streaming suicides, then we miss the point. When someone is struggling with *psychache* and reaches out for help, do we heed Emmanuel Levinas and attend to the face of the Other, or do we let AI answer the call? And what does this mean for our humanity?

CONCLUSION AND FUTURE RESEARCH

Throughout this chapter, we have aimed to answer many questions with regards to live streamed suicides. This chapter first reviewed the extant literature in psychology, sociology, and philosophy to provide a background on the general motivations for suicidal behavior. We then turned to media ecology to explain why those experiencing such motivations might ultimately execute them during a live stream; that is, primarily, they desire an audience with which to communicate. With that in mind, this chapter shifted attention to the ways in which an audience may be influenced by a live streamed suicide, arguing that, due to the lack of framing on these platforms, this phenomenon risks encouraging copycat suicides vis-à-vis the Papageno Effect. Lastly, this chapter considered the ethics of live streamed suicides, in which we suggested that there is more that can be done by the platforms themselves to mitigate these events and preventing subsequent suicide clusters.

While we have endeavored to provide a comprehensive assessment of live streamed suicides given what information is available, we hope that this chapter is a catalyst for an extended conversation on this subject. While there are many avenues for future research on this subject, we wish to particularly encourage the following three. First, we recognize the speculative nature of much of this chapter, and, although we are confident in our assertions, especially regarding media effects, we concede that they carry limited authority without data to support them. We hope that the data will become available for empirical research to examine the Werther Effect and Papageno Effect following live streamed suicides. Second, as new technologies such as artificial intelligence develop, social media platforms must find ways to incorporate it into live streams of attempted suicides promptly and effectively. While the potential is there, the approach and application has yet to determined. Lastly, while we considered the ethical implications of the actor, audience, and stage, the legal ramifications are unclear. Recent case law has sought to establish the liability of various social media platforms for the content that they carry, and if live streamed suicides continue to happen, it seems inevitable that at some point litigation will follow. Investigating these answers will offer an even fuller picture of this emergent trend.

In closing, the authors wish to reiterate that suicides are a real-world problem with the gravest of consequences. Extended scholarly discussion of the subject can sometimes make it abstract, but, as we have learned in this chapter, face-to-face social networks with real-world others can prevent someone from taking their own life. If you, or anyone you know, are showing signs of suicidal ideation or behavior, take the situation seriously and encourage them, like Papageno, to consider the alternatives. Thoughtfully direct them to seek the help of a professional counselor or call the national suicide hotline at 1-800-273-8255. Live streamed or not; all suicides are preventable.

NOTES

1. In addition to his work in clinical psychology, Edwin Shneidman founded the American Association of Suicidology, a leading advocate for suicide prevention. He also started *Suicide and Life Threatening Behavior*, a prominent journal in the field of suicide scholarship.
2. Aaron Beck is professor emeritus at the University of Pennsylvania and is known as the founder of cognitive therapy.
3. Sherry Turkle is a *New York Times* bestselling author and professor at M.I.T.
4. Nadine Kaslow is professor of psychology at the Emory School of Medicine and the former president of the American Psychological Association.
5. Sarah Dunn directs the suicide prevention project at Grady Memorial Hospital called Grady Nia Project.

REFERENCES

American Foundation for Suicide Prevention. (2019, April 16). Suicide statistics. Retrieved from https://afsp.org/about-suicide/suicide-statistics/
American Psychiatric Association. (2017). *Diagnostic and statistical manual of mental disorders: DSM-5*. Arlington, VA.
Arnett, R. C. (2009). Emmanuel Levinas: Priority of the Other. In C. G. Christians & J. C. Merrill (Eds.), *Ethical communication: Moral stances in human dialogue* (pp. 200–206). Columbia, MO: University of Missouri Press.
Baumeister, R. F. (1990). Suicide as escape from self. *Psychological Review, 97*(1), 90–113. https://doi.org/10.1037/0033-295x.97.1.90
Baumeister, R. F., & Leary, M. R. (1995). The need to belong: Desire for interpersonal attachments as a fundamental human motivation. *Psychological Bulletin, 117*(3), 497–529. https://doi.org/10.1037//0033-2909.117.3.497
Beck, A. T., Brown, G., Berchick, R. J., Stewart B. L., & Steer, R. A. (1990). Relationship between hopelessness and ultimate suicide: A replication with psychiatric outpatients. *American Journal of Psychiatry, 147*(2), 190–95. https://doi.org/10.1176/ajp.147.2.190
Bever, L. (2017, February 8). The disturbing trend of live-streamed suicides. Retrieved from https://www.chicagotribune.com/lifestyles/health/ct-the-disturbing-trend-of-live-streamed-suicides-20170208-story.html
Camus, A. (1983). *Myth of Sisyphus*. New York: Vintage.
Coleman, L. (2004). *The copycat effect: How the media and popular culture trigger the mayhem in tomorrow's headlines*. New York: Paraview Pocket Books.
Constine, J. (2017, November 27). Facebook rolls out AI to detect suicidal posts before they're reported. Retrieved from https://techcrunch.com/2017/11/27/facebook-ai-suicide-prevention/
De Catanzaro, D. D. (1995). Reproductive status, family interactions, and suicidal ideation: Surveys of the general public and high-risk groups. *Ethology and Sociobiology, 16*(5), 385–94. https://doi.org/10.1016/0162-3095(95)00055-0
Devitt, P. (2017, May 8). *13 Reasons why and suicide contagion*. Retrieved from https://www.scientificamerican.com/article/13-reasons-why-and-suicide-contagion1

Durkheim, É. (1951/1897). *Suicide.* (J.A. Spalding & G. Simpson, Trans.). New York: Free Press.

Fu, K. W., & Yip, P. S. F. (2007). Long-term impact of celebrity suicide on suicidal ideation: Results from a population-based study. *Journal of Epidemiology & Community Health, 61*(6), 540–46. https://doi.org/10.1136/jech.2005.045005

Gould, M. S., Wallenstein, S., & Davidson, L. (1989). Suicide clusters: A critical review. *Suicide and Life-Threatening Behavior, 19*(1), 17–29. https://doi.org/10.1111/j.1943-278x.1989.tb00363.x

Haidt, J. (2006). *Happiness hypothesis: Finding modern truth in ancient wisdom.* New York: Basic Books.

Hedegaard, H., Curtin, S. C., & Warner M. (2018, November). Suicide mortality in the United States, 1999–2017 (NCHS Data Brief No. 330). Retrieved from https://www.cdc.gov/nchs/products/databriefs/db330.htm

Heidegger, M. (2000). *Being and time.* (Macquarrie J & Robinson E, Trans.). London: Blackwell Publishing.

Hilvert-Bruce, Z., Neill, J. T., Sjöblom, M., & Hamari, J. (2018). Social motivations of live-streaming viewer engagement on Twitch. *Computers in Human Behavior, 84*, 58–67. https://doi.org/10.1016/j.chb.2018.02.013

Joiner, T. E., Pettit, J. W., Walker, R. L., Voelz, Z. R., Cruz, J., Rudd, M. D., & Lester, D. (2002). Perceived burdensomeness and suicidality: Two studies on the suicide notes of those attempting and those completing suicide. *Journal of Social and Clinical Psychology, 21*(5), 531–45. https://doi.org/10.1521/jscp.21.5.531.22624

Joiner, T. (2005). *Why people die by suicide.* Cambridge, MA: Harvard University Press.

Katz, E., Blumler, J., & Gurevitch, M. (1974). Utilization of mass communication by the individual. In J. G. Blumler & E. Katz (Eds.), *The uses of mass communications: Current perspectives on gratifications research* (pp. 19–32). Beverly Hills, CA: Sage.

Leichtman Research Group. (2018, April). Streaming pay-tv services augmenting video consumption in the household. Retrieved from https://www.leichtmanresearch.com/2018/04/

Ma, J., Zhang, W., Harris, K., Chen, Q., & Xu, X. (2016). Dying online: Live broadcasts of Chinese emerging adult suicides and crisis response behaviors. *BMC Public Health (Open Access), 16*:774. https://doi.org/10.1186/s12889-016-3415-0

Madkour, R. (2008, November 24). Family outraged over teen's online suicide. Retrieved from https://www.cbsnews.com/news/family-outraged-over-teens-online-suicide/

Michaels, T., & Corr, M. (2018). Life, death, and the stars: Public reaction to celebrity suicides. In C.M. Madere (Ed.), *How celebrity lives affect our own: Understanding the impact on Americans' public and private lives* (pp. 1–14). Lanham, MD: Lexington Books.

Molteni, M. (2017, June 3). Facebook's AI is learning to predict and prevent suicide. Retrieved from https://www.wired.com/2017/03/artificial-intelligence-learning-predict-prevent-suicide/

Niederkrotenthaler, T., Voracek, M., Herberth, A., Till, B., Strauss, M., Etzersdorfer, E., Eisenwort, B., & Sonneck, G. (2010). Role of media reports in completed and prevented suicide: Werther v. Papageno effects. *British Journal of Psychiatry, 197*(3), 234–43. https://doi.org/10.1192/bjp.bp.109.074633

Phillips, D. P. (1974). The influence of suggestion on suicide: Substantive and theoretical implications of the Werther Effect. *American Sociological Review, 39*(3), 340–54. https://doi.org/10.2307/2094294

Phillips, K. (2017, January 15). A 12-year-old girl live-streamed her suicide. it took two weeks for Facebook to take the video down. *The Washington Post.* Retrieved from https://www.washingtonpost.com/news/the-intersect/wp/2017/01/15/a-12-year-old-girl-live-streamed-her-suicide-it-took-two-weeks-for-facebook-to-take-the-video-down/

Rubin, A. (2002). The uses and gratifications perspective on media effects. In J. Bryant & D. Zillman (Eds.), *Media effects: Advances in theory and research* (2nd ed., pp. 525–48). Mahwah, NJ: Lawrence Erlbaum Associates.

Shakya, H.B., & Christakis, N.A. (February, 2017). Association of Facebook use with compromised well-being: A longitudinal study. *American Journal of Epidemiology, 185* (3): 203–11. https://doi.org/10.1093/aje/kww189

Shneidman, E. S. (1993). Suicide as psychache. *Journal of Nervous and Mental Disease, 181*, 145–47. https://doi.org/10.1097/00005053-199303000-00001

Shneidman, E. S. (1996). *The suicidal mind*. Oxford: Oxford Univ. Press.

Shneidman, E. S. (1998). Perspectives on suicidology. Further reflections on suicide and psychache. *Suicide and Life Threatening Behavior, 28*(3), 245–50. https://doi.org/10.1111/j.1943-278X.1998.tb00854.x

Sisask, M., & Värnik, A. (2012). Media roles in suicide prevention: A systematic review. *International Journal of Environmental Research and Public Health, 9*(1): 123–38. https://doi.org/10.3390/ijerph9010123

Stelter, B. (2008, November 25). Web suicide viewed live and reaction spur a debate. *New York Times*.

Terdiman, D. (2018, May 2). Here's how Facebook uses AI to detect many kinds of bad content. Retrieved from https://www.fastcompany.com/40566786/heres-how-facebook-uses-ai-to-detect-many-kinds-of-bad-content.

Turkle, S. (1984). *The second self: Computers and the human spirit*. London: Granada.

Turkle, S. (2011). *Alone together: Why we expect more from technology and less from each other*. New York: Basic Books.

Turkle, S. (2015). *Reclaiming conversation: The power of talk in a digital age*. New York: Penguin Press.

Wasserman, I. M. (1984). Imitation and suicide: A reexamination of the Werther Effect. *American Sociological Review, 49*(3), 427. https://doi.org/10.2307/2095285

Westerlund, M., Hadlaczky, G., & Wasserman, D. (2015). Case study of posts before and after a suicide on a Swedish Internet forum. *British Journal of Psychiatry, 207*(6), 476–82. https://doi.org/10.1192/bjp.bp.114.154484

Wilcox, G. J. (2017, January 25). Actor kills himself on Facebook Live. Retrieved from https://www.mercurynews.com/2017/01/25/actor-kills-himself-on-facebook-live/.

Williamson, L. (2016, May 13). French Periscope death stirs social media safety fears. Retrieved from https://www.bbc.com/news/world-europe-36274051.

World Health Organization (2000). *Preventing suicide: A resource for media professionals*. Geneva, Switzerland: WHO.

Yip, P. S., Fu, K., Yang, K. C., Ip, B. Y., Chan, C. L., Chen, E. Y., & Hawton, K. (2006). The effects of a celebrity suicide on suicide rates in Hong Kong. *Journal of Affective Disorders, 93*(1–3), 245–52. https://doi.org/10.1016/j.jad.2006.03.015

Zuckerberg, M. (2017, February 18). Building global community. Retrieved from https://www.facebook.com/notes/mark-zuckerberg/building-global-community/10154544292806634.

Chapter Three

Are We All Journalists Now?

Professional Ideology and the Legal and Ethical Implications of Live Streaming

Wendy M. Weinhold

These are remarkable times for the First Amendment. Many people shoot and share live streams via smartphones, tablets, and social media, and they bring with them a host of opportunities and challenges to test the strength of laws protecting freedom of expression in the United States. Live streaming applications, such as Facebook Live, Instagram Live, YouTube Live, and Periscope (via Twitter), leave journalists rushing to contend with new competitors and struggling to assert their roles as the world tunes in online (Bock, Suran, & González, 2018). Live streams are among the most commonly viewed eyewitness videos shot by journalists and non-journalists alike and serve as increasingly popular resources for journalists. As a result, scholars suggest it is likely the First Amendment protects live streaming activities when people engage in journalistic activities despite serious shortcomings in law and policy (Stewart & Littau, 2016; Studer, 2017). News companies and audiences have embraced live streaming, and they are reshaping journalists' work and the laws that define them.

Live streaming has also redefined journalists' audiences, who now play active roles in the production and dissemination of news. The abundance of live streaming options has opened the doors to many more voices and transformed social media users into unwitting journalists who contribute to the digital public sphere (Artwick, 2018; Bock, Suran, & González, 2018; Jackson, 2017). As Bock (2016) notes, "The ubiquity of the smartphone has changed life in mundane and profound ways, often with the same technological application" (p. 13). Consequently, people with no journalism training or experience now have unparalleled access to the basic digital tools used by journalists. Unlike journalists, whose professional ideology emphasizes objectivity in their reporting and values public service as a measure guiding what they should (and should not) report, live streaming users are not inherently compelled by the same ethical imperatives (Carlson & Lewis, 2015; Ferrucci & Vos, 2017). Live streaming has furthered and quickened the transformation of the "people formerly known as the audience" from consumers into producers (Rosen, 2012, p.13).

The changes have reshaped journalism's principles and practices, as journalists face new pressures to protect private individuals and provide content that profits their employers. Deuze and Witschge (2018) contend that the advent of digital journalism fundamentally changed the nature of journalism's professional ideology and practices. The traditional values guiding journalists' labor—among them objectivity, public service, and autonomy—do not always fit in the digital landscape (Lewis, 2012). The rush to the "real" demands consideration of the basic tenets of responsible journalism in order to ensure protections for the rights and privacy of those being filmed, as well as for those filming.

Often in times of definitional crisis, journalists have looked to the law for the protection of their labor and products. This chapter uses legal research methodology to consider the ways the current and ever-changing media landscape presents legal and ethical predicaments for live streaming users and journalists, their work, and their definitions. Efforts to define journalists in the United States illustrate how defining who is a "real" journalist and what is "real" journalism is a gradual and communal project (Deuze, 2005). The purpose of this analysis is to answer the question posed in this chapter's title: Are we all journalists now? In the following pages, an answer to the question is crafted by unpacking law and ideology that inform definitions of journalists in the United States. This analysis has two goals: first, to examine the two most influential sources defining journalists, the law and journalists' professional ideology, and second, to draw conclusions about the future of these definitions and the people they protect.

SOURCES DEFINING JOURNALISTS

While clear codes and definitions are available for careers in highly specialized occupations—medicine, law, and cosmetology, for example—definitions of journalists are beset by the amorphous nature of journalists' work. Carlson (2015) suggests, "Struggles over journalism are often struggles over boundaries" (p. 2). Without clear boundaries to define journalists, legal sources are key to understanding who can and should be recognized as a journalist. Legal sources, including constitutional law, statutory sources, and special privileges, represent some of the clearest efforts to define journalists (Artwick, 2018; Black, 2010; Peters & Tandoc, 2013; Ugland & Henderson, 2007). This section begins by reviewing literature dedicated to the legal definition of journalists, and then considers the ways journalists' occupational ideology that has been contested and challenged by digital innovators working at the boundaries of journalism.

Legal Definitions of Journalists

Journalists' work in a variety of mediums and forms is recognized through protections granted at all levels of law in the United States. Fargo (2019) describes these laws as "a crazy quilt of protection for journalists" (p. 152). Technological and economic shifts have occurred rapidly in recent decades and brought with them a host of new challenges for defining journalists in the law. Ugland and Henderson (2007) describe the legal definition of journalists as "expansive," noting that legal definitions are shaped by the assumption that "society is best served by removing all but the most essential barriers to free expression" (p. 243). Repeated efforts to enact a federal shield law have failed, so state shield laws provide the clearest definitions of journalists. Constitutional law, statutory law, special privileges, and shield laws all contribute to legal definitions of journalists.

Constitutional Law: First Amendment and Branzburg v. Hayes

The First Amendment's freedom of the press and freedom of speech clauses serve as the foundations for federal law defining journalists. The U.S. Supreme Court has long held that the freedom of the press "lies at the foundation of free government by free men" (*Schneider v. State*, 1939, Page 308 U.S. 161, para. 2). Traditional definitions of journalists and the Supreme Court's interpretation of the First Amendment have and will certainly continue to face challenges from digital technologies. Lewis, Sanders, and Carmody (2019) explain that the Court has extended First Amendment protections to a variety of content produced via new and emerging technologies, but the Court leans toward inclusion only after the technologies have been widely adopted by the public. It is important to note that because the First Amendment applies only to government action, social media platforms, which operate as private businesses, are free to censor users, and many have.

Branzburg v. Hayes represents the first and only time the Supreme Court has considered the question of whether a reporter's privilege exists. The Court ruled in *Branzburg* that a journalist could not claim First Amendment protection as grounds to refuse to testify when questioned by a grand jury (*Branzburg v. Hayes,* 1972). Justice Byron R. White, writing for a 5–4 majority, declined to create a reporter's privilege on the grounds that the effective functioning of a grand jury and trial proceedings were of greater concern than the real but speculative danger of diminished news-gathering should reporters be required to testify (Calvert, 1999). White's words reveal the difficulty of defining a journalist:

> The administration of a constitutional newsman's privilege would present practical and conceptual difficulties of a high order. Sooner or later, it would be necessary to define those categories of newsmen who qualified for the privilege, a questionable procedure in light of the traditional doctrine that liberty of the press is the right of the lonely pamphleteer who uses carbon paper or a mimeograph just as much as of the large metropolitan publisher who utilizes the latest photocomposition methods. The informative function asserted by representatives of the organized press in the present cases is also performed by lecturers, political pollsters, novelists, academic researchers, and dramatists. Almost any author may quite accurately assert that he is contributing to the flow of information to the public, that he relies on confidential sources of information, and that these sources will be silenced if he is forced to make disclosures before a grand jury. (*Branzburg v. Hayes,* 1972, pp. 703–5)

The Court expressly left the decision to grant journalists evidentiary privilege up to the states and asserted that "[t]here is also merit in leaving state legislators free within First Amendment limits, to fashion their own standards" (p. 706). In the end, the Court stopped short of offering a comprehensive definition of journalists.

Reporter's Privilege Takes Shape after Branzburg

Federal law defining journalists has been murky since the 1972 Supreme Court decision in *Branzburg v. Hayes* that journalists have no First Amendment privilege to withhold confidential sources from a grand jury investigation (Peters & Tandoc, 2013). Lower court rulings have helped to further shape the legal definition of a journalist. Decisions from the circuit courts have upheld the ideal that efforts of the press to investigate and report the news advance key First Amendment values (Benkler, 2011). These rulings are distinct in which they do not proffer employment, training, or other advantages as a qualification for protection under the reporter's privilege. Hayes, Singer, and Ceppos (2007) summarize the results: "legal rulings also support the argument that journalism is a 'verb' (Jarvis, 2005); that is, one 'does' journalism" (p. 267). Ugland and Henderson (2007) explain that these "more wide-ranging decisions . . . have effectively solved the 'special rights' dilemma by making the privilege available to any citizen industrious enough to seek and report the news" (p. 247). In short, the federal appeals courts have embraced a wide-ranging scope of contemporary newsgathering practices. The following paragraphs review a sample of these rulings.

The Second Circuit's decision in *Von Bulow v. Von Bulow* (1987) provided a key test for determining who qualifies for the reporter's privilege.

The opinion reasons that from the moment a person begins to gather news, her intent must go beyond private use, and she must display the intent to distribute information to the public. This decision produced the *Von Bulow* test of intent as a foundation for claiming the reporter's privilege. The Third Circuit grappled with the issue for the first time *In re: Madden* (1998). In *Madden*, a man asked the courts for protection under the journalist's privilege after he was found writing and then taping 900-number promotional telephone messages for his employer, the World Championship Wrestling, Inc. In its ruling, the appellate court observed, "Although we have determined that a journalist's privilege exists, we have never decided who qualifies as a 'journalist' for purposes of asserting it" (*In re: Madden*, 1998, III. 12). The court found the man was not eligible for protection because his work was neither investigative in nature, part of the traditional press, nor news intended for publication. The case of *Madden* is particularly relevant to live streaming because it was the first case to explicitly mention the World Wide Web when considering who is a journalist.

In one of the most well-documented cases of a nontraditional journalist attempting to claim the journalist's privilege, the Ninth Circuit utilized the *Von Bulow* test to expand the privilege based upon intent and substance of the reporter rather than employment or publication venue (Eliason, 2006). The court found an investigative book author eligible for the journalist's privilege because "what makes journalism is not its format but its content" (*Shoen v. Shoen*, 1993, 5 F.3d 1293, IV A, para. 4). This case and its focus on content is also highly relevant to live streaming and emphasizes how the subject of the streamed video, rather than the technology or application used for streaming, will likely influence a court's decision over who is protected by the legal definition of journalists.

Cases such as these suggest that the door for qualification under the reporter's privilege is likely to open further to include more people working outside the traditional media (Gant, 2007; Peters & Tandoc, 2013). In summary, decisions in lower courts have prioritized functional benchmarks over employment or expertise, thus expanding the potential for more people to fall under the definition of "journalist." In other words, there is wiggle room in the law to suggest live streaming could qualify as journalism.

Statutory Law: State Shield Laws

Statutory law contains a number of unique protections, particularly in the form of state reporters' shield laws. The clearest and most narrow legal definitions of journalists reside in statutory law (Ugland & Henderson, 2007). Because this analysis seeks to understand the legal definitions of journalists, it is important to note the scope of analysis will be limited to the definitions provided in these statutory laws and will not delve deeply into the protections the laws provide.

Reporters' shield laws in most states represent the bulk of statutory law. A majority of states, beginning with Maryland in 1896, have enacted shield laws that recognize journalists as a special class worthy of unique protections (Fargo, 2019). Court interpretations of statutes enacted before access to the Internet was widely available usually shared two general conditions: first, protection was dependent upon employment by the traditional media; and second, traditional media activities were favored (Docter, 2010). By prioritizing employment status and traditional forms of publication, the state statutes emphasized an insider's approach to newsgathering and definitional status. Ugland and Henderson (2007) describe this as an "expert conception of the press" (p. 248).

Journalists' autonomy is another key to the expert model of the press espoused in many legal decisions (Ugland & Henderson, 2007). Ugland and Henderson (2007) explain that in law, the expert model views journalists as a distinctly skilled, professional class of people who serve the public interest by creating and publishing news. Furthermore, the concept of journalistic autonomy reassures journalists that it is possible for them to work free of market influences and be protected from censors. This approach is unrealistic in today's media landscape, however. Singer (2007) explains:

> The Internet is a network—an environment in which no single message is discrete and in which message producers and consumers are not only interchangeable but also inextricably linked. All communicators and all communication in this environment are connected. The notion of autonomy, therefore, becomes unavoidably contested. Professional communicators lose control over their messages as those messages become freely copied, exchanged, extended, and challenged by anyone with a mind (and a modem) to do so. (p. 90)

As Hayes, Singer, and Ceppos (2007) note, "Oversight of professional behavior has become a team sport, and journalists no longer control who gets to play" (p. 274). The interactive nature of online content enables anyone to perform as reporter and editor, publishing material instantaneously, and setting the news agenda. Legal definitions have been slow to recognize this change. Their tautological reasoning works this way: Journalists cannot function without editors, so only people with editors are journalists. Clearly, legal definitions of journalists can no longer stand apart from the communities and the people journalists cover.

More recent interpretation of statutory law has expanded to include people working exclusively online as part of the protected class of journalists (Robinson, 2012). For example, since 2010, statutes in Wisconsin, Arkansas, West Virginia, New York, Massachusetts, and Kansas have extended protection to journalists who publish entirely online (Robinson, 2012). Robinson (2012) suggests:

> The reach and influence of blogs and other forms of new media as sources of news and information continues to increase. And there is little reason why blogs and bloggers that operate in role(s) of information providers to their readership should not be covered by shield laws. (p. 43)

At the time of this writing, shield laws protecting journalists from certain subpoenas are enacted in 40 states and the District of Columbia.[1]

Nine other states have protection in case law.[2] Wyoming is the only state without some kind of statutory protection for or definition of journalists. West Virginia, Wisconsin, and Kansas are the most recent states to pass shield laws in 2011, 2009, and 2010 respectively. West Virginia's law, which went into effect June 10, 2011, does not provide people working online without pay with protection from subpoena to reveal confidential sources (W. Va. Code 57-3-10). Many of the states with shield laws do grant employed online and traditional journalists legal protections, including retraction and long-arm statutes (Dougherty, 2012). Fee waivers in many states' Freedom of Information Act (FOIA) laws also recognize journalists as experts whose abilities merit special access to scrutinize and distribute information (Anderson, 2002). In general, state protections for people working online vary and generally depend upon employment for consideration under their definition of journalists.

Definitions of journalists in the state statutes vary and have varying results. The lack of consensus in shield laws has sometimes resulted in jurisdictional clashes (Johnston & Wallace, 2017). Zelnick (2005) explains that most state shield laws "seek to strike a balance between the importance of the information, its relevance to the case at bar, and the possibility of developing it from other sources" (p. 549). In California, the protection is encoded for a "publisher, editor, reporter, or other person connected with or employed upon a newspaper, magazine or other periodical publication, or by a press association or wire service, or any person who has been so connected or employed" (California Reporters' Shield Law, 2013–2014, para. 1). Pennsylvania's law defines journalists as those "engaged in, connected with, or employed by any newspaper . . . or magazine of general circulation" (42 Pa. Cons. Stat. § 5942 (a)). One of the broadest laws, *Free Flow of Information Act*, Nebraska's statute provides protection to those who "gather, write, edit, or disseminate news or other information to the public" (Neb. Rev. Stat. 20-144 to 20-147, 1973, 20-144 (1)). Many states specify frequent or regular employment as a journalist to qualify for an exemption. For example, statutes in Alaska, Oklahoma, and Louisiana require journalists to be "regularly engaged" in journalistic work in order to qualify, whereas Illinois allows reporters to qualify for protection if they work for news media organizations on even a part-time basis (AS 09.25. 230; Okla. Stat. tit. 12 § 2506; La. RS 45:1451-1459; 735 ILCS 5/). For examples of other state shield statutes, see Cohen (2007). Many of the states recognize people working online as covered under reporters' shield laws, but employment remains key in many states.

Courts have looked to state and federal court rulings and state reporters' shield laws and found robust support to protect the identities of anonymous posters to Internet sites of newspapers and media organizations, such as Yahoo! (Burnham & Freivogel, 2010; Jones, 2012). According to Burnham and Freivogel (2010), anonymous posters on the Internet represent "a new issue of anonymity that is a hybrid of the anonymous source and anonymous pamphleteer" (p. 5). *Doty v. Molnar* (2008) is an example of a case where a newspaper utilized state shield law to protect the identities of anonymous online posters. In this 2008 Montana civil defamation claim, *The Billings Gazette* successfully argued that Montana's Media Confidentiality Act (Montana Code Annotated, 2019, 26-1-901 to 26-1-903) protected the newspaper from having to reveal the IP and e-mail addresses of commenters to its website (Burnham & Freivogel, 2010). According to Burnham and Freivogel, the judge in this case "gave broad protection to anonymous posters not because of their value but because of their lack of value" (p. 7). The issue of anonymous posters highlights the complexities of legal definitions of journalists.

Courts have varied in their willingness to apply shield law protections cases from anonymous sources to anonymous online posters, but cases such as *Doty* worry Burnham and Freivogel (2010). They contend rulings that protect "speech that contributes little if anything, of value to public debate" risk diminishing the privileges state shield laws grant anonymous sources (p. 18). Burnham & Freivogel (2010) argue,

> Anonymous sources are the basis of some of the most important news of the day, while anonymous posters are not. . . . News organizations should continue to protect anonymous posters against flimsy legal attempts to unmask them. But they should do so while cognizant of the potential risk to other legal protections that have far more value to their mission of reporting the news. (p. 19)

Jones (2012) and Reader (2010) disagree, countering that protecting the freedom to speak anonymously is part of the responsibility of the law and of the press, which defend the First Amendment. Reader (2010) writes, "anonymity is the one true cultural equalizer, and that it is what the First Amendment was meant to protect all along" (p. 17). Rulings that have granted legal recognition to anonymous posters have the capacity to expand the law's view of who contributes to journalism, if not adding to a more expansive view of who is a journalist.

Special Privileges: Passes, Access, and Public Relations

The next area of law worthy of note comes in the form of privileges government officials grant exclusively to journalists. Time, space, and cost force a host of governmental bodies to limit the nets they cast to recognize and even attract media interest. Journalists are afforded special privileges in the form of press passes, press rooms, special seating and cameras in courtrooms, press secretaries, waived Freedom of Information Act fees, as well as being protected against discriminatory taxation (Dilts, 2002; Gant, 2007; West, 2011). People working in online media are granted access to a host of major news events, such as seats on the floor of the Democratic and Republican National Conventions, permission to live blog and Tweet inside courtrooms, and access to the Super Bowl Press Box. The abundance and demand for live streaming of major events provides an incentive for controlling public relations; by granting exclusive access and streaming rights to journalists, events get to control their message.

Access to special privileges has historically depended upon a journalist's access to a mass audience and employment by a recognized news medium in order for the person seeking access to qualify. Bock, Suran, and González (2018) explain how special privileges, such as press passes to police news conferences, function to insulate and reify boundaries: "Whatever their form, credentials can be seen as a mark of professionalism, as a link between journalists and their sources, and, from the perspective of police departments, a means of managing public relations" (p. 350). The White House first granted press credentials to a blogger in 2005, but access to privileged government spaces continues to be limited largely to journalists employed by the traditional, commercial news media (Russo, 2006; Cohen, 2011). Hall, Critcher, and Jefferson (1978) described the ways of the relationship between police and media "reproduce the definitions of the powerful" (pp. 59–60). When seeking access to the White House Press Room or a high-profile trial, nontraditional journalists often find themselves left out because they do not have a history of access to those in power, their medium is unlike traditional forms, and their work is perceived as unlikely to reach the mass audience for which those press-centered activities were staged.

Federal Shield Law Efforts

This section concludes the chapter's legal analysis by reviewing attempts to establish a reporters' shield law at the federal level. There have been frequent failed attempts to institute a federal reporters' shield that would protect journalists from having to reveal confidential sources and unpublished information. More than 100 bills, including three in the 2010s, proposing the creation of a federal shield law have been introduced in Congress since U.S. Supreme Court made the decision on *Branzburg v. Hayes*, June 29, 1972 (Tucker &

Wermiel, 2008). Lee (2012) explains the challenges of defining the journalist via a federal shield law:

> Justice Scalia facetiously asked if the term press meant people wearing fedoras with a ticket saying "Press" in the hatband—in short, the classic old school image of a journalist. The fedora definition of journalist, however, is no more outdated and limiting than the definitions contained in many state shield laws. Defining who is entitled to coverage under a shield law is a most vexing problem; if coverage is too broadly defined, the law may protect terrorists or other criminal organizations. (p. 35)

The abundance of attempts to issue a federal shield reflects the recognition, by journalists and legislators, that the definition of journalists changes fast (Fargo, 2019). Dougherty (2012) explains recent attempts to pass federal shield laws were understood to be "favorable to digital journalists generally" but still depended upon fulltime employment for protection (p. 310). Previous versions of the bill, including 2009, 2011, 2013, and 2017 versions, utilizing broad, functional definitions of journalists, took and included people engaged in online news production under the definition of "journalist." Fargo (2019) claims "the complexity of amending multiple whistleblower protection laws and changing the government's document classification system" (p. 145 [Abstract]).

Much like the previous versions, the most recent iteration of the federal shield, H.R. 4382, died in committee. Commonly known as the "*Free Flow of Information Act of 2017*" bill introduced in House (11/14/2017) by Mr. Raskin (for himself and Mr. Jordan), was referred to the Committee on the Judiciary. In Section 4 Definitions, journalism is defined as follows:

> (5) JOURNALISM.—The term "journalism" means the gathering, preparing, collecting, photographing, recording, writing, editing, reporting, or publishing of news or information that concerns local, national, or international events or other matters of public interest for dissemination to the public. (*Free Flow of Information Act of 2017*, 2017, p.10)

Unlike previous iterations, a companion bill was never introduced in the Senate.

A discussion of the federal shield law would be incomplete without mentioning a few recent cases—most notably that of former *New York Times* reporter Judith Miller. In one of the most significant media stories from the dawn of the twenty-first century, Miller was jailed for 85 days in 2005 when she initially refused to identify vice presidential aide I. Lewis "Scooter" Libby as her source for unpublished information that Valerie Plame was a covert CIA agent (Freivogel, 2009a). Miller's case helped fuel renewed calls for a federal shield law. Miller's case highlights the federal courts' changing interpretations of *Branzburg v. Hayes* (Freivogel, 2009b). After three decades of rulings that found support for "creative math" to interpret the Supreme Court's decision in *Branzburg* to be supportive of constitutional grounds for a reporter-source privilege, the court in the Miller case switched course (Freivogel, 2009a). The court failed to recognize a constitutional protection for a journalist to withhold confidential information. Another relevant case that highlights the complexities of static legal definitions of journalists in the contemporary media climate came in 2007. Kurtz (2007) describes how Josh Wolf, a then-24-year-old blogger and videographer, spent more than 200 days in jail (a record for contempt of court cases). Wolf refused to turn over a video he shot of a San Francisco protest that turned violent during a G-8 meeting. According to Kurtz (2007), federal prosecutors emphasized how Wolf was an ordinary person when he recorded events in public with his video camera while the Reporters' Committee for Freedom of the Press joined groups filing briefs supporting Wolf. Wolf was not working for a media outlet when he recorded his footage, but he had previously sold the video to news outlets (Kurtz, 2007). Wolf's case is highly relevant to issues surrounding live streaming, especially given the propensity for commercial news media to rebroadcast videos originally published as live streams on social media sites.

The setting for this project is a time when journalists struggle to assert their role as the world was online. As Studer (2017) contends, "what constitutes speech becomes increasingly more complex since online communication includes an assortment of print, audio, photography, video, and now interactive real-time communication" (p. 636). Technological change is a constant in journalism, and legal definitions of journalists have been hesitant to rely on definitions that forward a technologically determinist view of journalism. Changes in media, especially the growth of social media and online news, and the resulting growth in the volume of news production and competition for audiences complicate conversations about legal protections governing freedom of speech and freedom of the press. Based on the legal analysis, it can be concluded that legal definitions reflect the many public and private sources that inform descriptions of who is a journalist.

Beginning with the First Amendment, the legal sources that define journalists are as varied as the definitions they offer, and their implications are significant in this climate of digital innovation. Ultimately, when it comes to legal definitions of journalists, Ugland (2019) contends, "Americans are going to have to re-engage the debate about the meaning and scope of the First Amendment" (p. 289). It should also be clear that the First Amendment does not provide journalists with any rights beyond those granted to all Americans (Rulffes, 2018). In other words, journalists stand in citizens' shoes. Many of those citizens are live streaming.

Ideological Definitions of Journalists

Ideology is an essential tool for understanding who chooses to define as a journalist and who does not. Deuze (2005) defines ideology as "a system of beliefs characteristic of a particular group, including—but not limited to—the general process of the production of meanings and ideas" (p. 445). Legal definitions of journalists, scholarly definitions of journalists, and journalists' conversations about their work inform journalists' ideological definitions. Just as legal definitions of journalists have evolved to emphasize intent over content, ideological definitions focus on *why* and *how* journalists do journalism and not *what* journalists do. The ideological forces that inform definitions of journalists reflect the growing professionalism of journalism during journalism's heyday in the twentieth century (Schiller, 1981). In many ways, ideology reflects and is shaped by journalists' work experiences. Ample scholarship has written about journalists' ideology, yet there is little agreement between journalism scholars and journalism practitioners about ideology's role in journalism. Deuze (2005, 2007b) tracks scholarship to outline the five traits or values that journalists generally agree upon and adopt. Deuze (2007b) summarizes the values as follows:

1. Public service: journalists provide a public service (as watchdogs or "newshounds," active collectors and disseminators of information);
2. Objectivity: journalists are impartial, neutral, objective, fair, and (thus) credible;
3. Autonomy: journalists must be autonomous, free, and independent in their work;
4. Immediacy: journalists have a sense of immediacy, actuality, and speed (inherent in the concept of "news");
5. Ethics: journalists have a clear sense of ethics, validity, and legitimacy. (p. 163)

These values form crucial components of journalists' identities and "give legitimacy and credibility to what they do" (Deuze, 2005, p. 446). Even in an evolving news ecosystem, journalists rely on the values to give meaning to their work.

Decades of journalism studies have produced many references to professional journalism as an ideology. For journalists, like all professional identities, ideologies develop over time and function to reify some views and invalidate others (Bettig & Hall, 2012; Deuze, 2007b). Scholarly references to ideology in journalism abound (e.g. Deuze, 2005; Golding & Elliott, 1979; Reese, 1997; Soloski, 1990; Zelizer, 1993). According to Gans (1979), "Journalists are neither much interested in ideology nor aware that they, too, promulgate ideology" (p. 68). Schudson (2001) describes the occupational ideology of journalists as cultural knowledge stemming from a deeply embedded consciousness that forms their news judgment. Lewis (2011) defines journalists' ideology as a mechanism of control. He explains ideology leads journalists to "take for granted the idea that society needs them as journalists—and journalists alone—to fulfill the functions of watchdog publishing, truth-telling, independence, timeliness, and ethical adherence in the context of news and public affairs information" (Lewis, 2011, p. 16). Live streaming introduced new watchdogs, and they have the potential to push the boundaries of journalism's ideology.

Despite rapid changes in media, scholars contend journalism's ideology remained relatively unchanged until the digital milieu (Deuze & Witschge, 2018). The notion that journalists' ideology has been slow to change reflects the ways ideological values "sustain operational closure, keeping outside forces at bay" (Deuze, 2005, p. 447). The ideology of journalism functions to normalize journalism and justify its social utility. Live reporting is not new to journalism. What is new is that anyone with a smartphone can report live from anywhere. It is no wonder that live streaming has joined the list of threats challenging traditional journalism. Journalists' ideology relies on routines and 'strategic rituals' that have long-shaped and reinforced the definition of journalism (Tuchman, 1972). Efforts to define journalists have particularly come under question since the rise of online news publications and the emergence of a generation of new watchdogs (Eldridge, 2013; Lewis, 2012; Shirky, 2008). As Hindman and Thomas (2014) suggest, "Journalists—once the dominant institutional actors in the mass communication of information—must now share the media jungle with new (and excitable) beasts" (p. 544). Journalists' ideology helps reinforce the boundaries of who can claim membership in the community of journalists, and those boundaries are much more porous today.

Deuze (2007b) notes how the values are regular conversation topics for journalists, who "talk about them every time they articulate, defend or critique the decisions they or their peers make" (p. 163). Deuze (2007a) explains,

> As self-proclaimed gatekeepers, journalists have only their occupational ideology and news culture to rely on as a defense against either commercial intrusion or special interests. In doing so, journalism's representation of society tends to stay the same while at the same time reporting on a rapidly changing world. . . . journalism makes sense of a modernity that seems unsettling at best, and out of touch with the everyday lives of most of its inhabitants at worst. (p. 671)

While these values may seem less relevant in the context of digital journalism, Ferrucci and Vos (2017) found the values still have a significant role in the ways fulltime digital journalists construct their identity and determine "who's in, who's out" (p. 868). Similarly, in a study of BuzzFeed's entry into journalism, Tandoc (2017) found that news produced at BuzzFeed sought recognition and legitimation through adherence to the traditional rules of journalism. What is old is often important in shaping what is new.

Live Streaming Ferguson: A Test for Redefining Journalists

Live streaming of civil unrest in Ferguson, Missouri, is largely credited with propelling #BlackLivesMatter, racial violence, and police misconduct to the forefront of national conversations in 2014. When protests erupted in Ferguson after Darren Wilson, a white police officer, fatally shot Michael Brown, a black teenager, people who live streamed from the streets were the first to publicize "the stunningly hostile, often violent demeanor of police officers toward protesters" (Dewey & Ohlheiser, 2016, para. 10). Barnard (2018) describes the ways activists and journalists used Twitter to network and disseminate information quickly. Twitter emerged as a place where the events in Ferguson unfolded play by play. Less than a year later, Twitter's acquisition of Periscope was complete, and live streaming about Ferguson became commonplace on Twitter.

Ferguson represents a model of the hybridity of journalism and activism that offers a useful lens through which to consider journalists' changing identities. Live streaming in Ferguson has offered extended, locally focused coverage and helped mobilize and expand democratic opportunities to communities in need of a voice (Tewksbury, 2018). On the one hand, the events in Ferguson that began August 9, 2014, after Michael Brown was shot and killed, have unfolded over days, weeks, and years. Unlike the shootings in Christchurch, New Zealand, or other major news events that have been the focus of live streaming, Ferguson cannot be reduced to a single incident that mobilized people to live stream. Instead, the unfolding nature of the events in Ferguson is noteworthy, particularly because of the challenges it presents to standard journalism. Newcomers to journalism, such as people who live stream, helped to answer some of those challenges in part because they were doing grassroots work, meaning that many people participated in and contributed to live stream coverage of Ferguson. Ferguson demonstrates the ways live streaming can serve as a journalistic tool to expand democratic opportunities for new voices and perspectives.

The work of people who live stream in Ferguson offers a case to test and expand on the definitions of journalism discussed in the preceding pages. Using Deuze's (2005, 2007b) five-tiered model of the occupational ideology of journalists, live streaming and its effect on journalism about Ferguson demonstrates similarities and differences in the ideological imperatives driving journalists and people who live stream. The five values—public service, objectivity, autonomy, immediacy, and ethics—are explored in the following pages.

First, public service, which Deuze (2005, 2007b) describes as journalism's watchdog function, emphasizes the importance of keeping those in power in check. Journalists' watchdog roles are often ones that involve wary embraces of public officials, but they are embracers, nonetheless. In contrast, many people who live stream events in Ferguson are interested, most importantly, in social justice, which in their case means rejection of and revolt against institutions such as the police. People using Twitter in Ferguson in 2014 helped propel #BlackLivesMatter, Michael Brown's death, and police violence into the national news. Live streaming helped Twitter become synonymous with social justice and revolution, and other live streaming applications followed to embrace this mantra (Blevins, Lee, McCabe, & Edgerton, 2019). In essence, live streamers redefine public service as social justice, which is often interested in transformation rather than fortification of government power.

The second value is objectivity, which Deuze (2005, 2007b) describes as journalists' focus on credibility and unbiased reporting. This value emphasizes fairness. Social justice warriors, such as activists in Ferguson, argue fairness is a farce. Objectivity has been critiqued, muddled, and reassembled throughout much of journalism's history (Eliasoph, 1997; Schiller, 1981; Schudson, 1978, 2001; Tuchman, 1972). Live streaming is one of many digital tools that may be used to put the final nail in objectivity's coffin. Live streaming makes proximity to news events essential. For journalists, this erodes the pretense of physical, intellectual, and emotional distance that objectivity advocates. Live streamers have to be where the action happens, and they have pushed journalists to be closer to the news and the people they cover.

Third, autonomy, which Deuze (2005, 2007b) describes as independence and editorial oversight, is most importantly, a function of the commercial context in which professional journalism functions. Autonomy reassures journalists that it is possible for them to work free of market influences and protected from censors. Yet the news is a "contested commodity" where Capitalist and journalistic imperatives are often at odds (Jackson, 2009, p. 146). Live streaming also emphasizes independence, but those who use live streaming to shed light on experiences of people living in Ferguson are interested in live streaming as a tool that allows them to get their message out while maintaining their independence from mainstream news media (LeFebvre & Armstrong, 2018). However, while live streaming accommodates voices that are often marginalized in mainstream news, the most commonly used live streaming applications, including streaming on sites such as Twitter, Facebook, Instagram, and YouTube, tether users to major players in the media industrial complex. Live streaming is no more autonomous from mainstream media or advertising than professional journalism.

The fourth value, immediacy, is the place where live streaming and journalism's ideology most clearly align. Deuze (2005, 2007b) explains the emphasis on immediacy reflects the 24/7 news cycle where everything is breaking news, and none of it matters. Just as journalism values eyewitness accounts and perspectives, live streams are inherently eyewitness products. Immediacy has a new meaning—delivering important news quickly and with an intimate knowledge of the story.

Finally, ethics informs every part of journalists' identity, explains Deuze (2005, 2007b). Terms such as "watchdog" and "gatekeeper" reference the urgency of journalists' ethical value. These kinds of roles assume a top-down form of message control reliant upon journalists working in traditional news. People who live stream do not depend upon employment in news media to get their message out, but employment and training have long been necessary components in definitions of journalism and in creating quality journalism. As Carpenter and Kanver (2017) suggest, "While journalists may no longer hold a monopoly over certain technical and nontechnical skills due to the low costs of technologies, they may still be able to employ these skills in a more complex way than the general public" (p. 205). Legal questions of journalists' intent are hard to separate from ethics, which are hard to separate from journalism training and education. The ethics of eye-witnessing point to tensions about who has the right to video and publish someone's suffering in an area where professional journalism has long held a monopoly. Martini (2018) explains the ways live streaming poses challenges to journalistic notions of ethics and witnessing: "This rising tension between top-down and bottom-up forms of truth-making is indicative of a radical change in the relationship between video-makers and networked publics" (p. 4039). Ethical guidelines are an essential issue for live streaming to contend with as more people use and view live streams of the human experience in all its complexity.

Live Streaming and the Future of Journalism

Despite its morphing face, journalism has been a key part of democracy in the United States since the Founding Fathers granted freedom of the press among citizens' essential liberties. Technological advancements, particularly the Internet, have ushered in a new era of concerns over who is guaranteed protection under the First Amendment. Consequently, defining journalists is a difficult task. It seems clear that the more media that are included in legal definitions, the more those working in traditional journalistic endeavors lose control over the definitional boundaries of their professional identities. As Deuze and Witschge (2018) suggest, "going beyond boundaries is what is productive in this time of flux" (p. 177). Live streaming challenges journalists to keep pushing beyond boundaries to improve and bring journalism closer to something everyone does and wants to do.

This chapter argues that good journalists are at their core engaged citizens. Journalists do the work of citizens, and that work is possible because it is labor worthy of compensation. Important criticisms have been made by many, including the author of this chapter, about the dangers of commercial imperatives that override and erode the democratic function of journalism (Deuze & Witschge, 2018; McChesney, 2016; Weinhold, 2008, 2010). It follows that profit and privacy are among the many significant challenges live streaming presents, as the lines distinguishing journalists from other people have blurred in the digital age. Live streaming services make information collection and dissemination instantaneous, which makes privacy violations almost certain and creates new competitors for journalists' already dwindling audiences and revenues (Jackson, 2017; Stewart & Littau, 2016). However, while laws addressing issues such as privacy and copyright often relate to and influence journalists' work, these laws do not contain specific language defining journalists and thus are outside the scope of this project. Future studies are needed to address these issues.

Changing media, innovations in practice, and challenging markets color journalism's complex history. Journalists who have survived these changes favor innovation, not tradition. The endless growth of media with uncertain terms and uses serves to further blur the definitional boundaries of journalists (Singer, 2007). It matters less and less if journalists work for traditional news corporations or if they publish in 140-character blasts. As Deuze (2007b) explains, "Technology is not an independent factor influencing the work of journalists from the 'outside,' but rather it must be seen in terms of its implementation, and therefore how it extends and amplifies previous ways of doing things" (p. 153). References to "traditional journalists" wrongly represent journalists as monoliths when it is the journalists' ideology—not journalists—that is anchored in convention. Furthermore, as journalism moves forward, media law and policy need to do so as well. The review of legal sources offered in this chapter recounts how the law has slowly shifted to accommodate more expansive definitions of journalists. The literature reviewed here shows how law and ideological definitions of journalists are connected. Law and ideology are often reinforced by one another and the social contexts in which they operate. Thus, the ambiguity of the law opens possibilities for changes in the ideological definitions of journalists.

People who live stream are challenging the canons of journalism. The definitions of journalists considered in this chapter recognize journalists and journalism as a process. This process has changed and will continue to change as people embrace new technologies to tell stories that need to be told. From this perspective, journalists do not materialize in specific acts per se, but instead, form through routines that may encompass a number of activities. Routinized adherence to the rules of journalism defines and confines the definitions of journalists, but people who live stream are pushing the boundaries of these definitions. The institution of law defines journalism—its mores, canons, and actors—and demands that journalists engage in repetition in order to maintain their membership as journalists. Through ideological repetition, a journalist is constantly becoming the individual and collective Journalist—exemplified in legal definitions, employment, press passes, press conferences, and bylines. As journalism's ideology changes, more people, including people who live stream, have access to the institutional power of and opportunity to demand more of journalism. Are we all journalists now? If we want to be, the answer is yes.

NOTES

1. The 40 states with shield laws are as follows: Alabama, Alaska, Arizona, Arkansas, California, Colorado, Connecticut, Delaware, Florida, Georgia, Hawaii, Illinois, Indiana, Kansas, Kentucky, Louisiana, Maine, Maryland, Michigan, Minnesota, Montana, Nebraska, Nevada, New Jersey, New Mexico, New York, North Carolina, North Dakota, Ohio, Oklahoma, Oregon, Pennsylvania, Rhode Island, South Carolina, Tennessee, Texas, Utah, Washington, West Virginia, and Wisconsin.

2. The nine states where courts have granted reporters some form of shield are as follows: Idaho, Iowa, Massachusetts, Mississippi, Missouri, New Hampshire, South Dakota, Vermont, and Virginia.

REFERENCES

[Alaska Reporters' Shield Law] AS 09.25. 230 (300–390) [Renumbered as AS 09.25.400.]. (2019). Article 2. Privilege of public officials and reporters. Retrieved from http://www.akleg.gov/basis/statutes.asp#09.25.230

Anderson, D. A. (2002). Freedom of the press. *Texas Law Review, 80*(3), 429–530. [article excerpt] retrieved from https://www.questia.com/library/journal/1P3-110217487/freedom-of-the-press)

Artwick, C. G. (2018). *Social media livestreaming: Design for disruption?* London: Routledge.

Barnard, S. R. (2018). Tweeting# Ferguson: Mediatized fields and the new activist journalist. *New Media & Society, 20*(7), 2252–71. https://doi.org/10.1177/1461444817712723

Benkler, Y. (2011). A free irresponsible press: Wikileaks and the battle over the soul of the networked Fourth Estate. *Harvard Civil Rights-Civil Liberties Law Review, 46*, 311–97. Retrieved from http://benkler.org/Benkler_Wikileaks_current.pdf

Bettig, R. V., & Hall, J. L. (2012). *Big media, big money: Cultural texts and political economics*. Lanham, MD: Rowman & Littlefield.

Black, J. (2010). Who is a journalist. In C. Meyers (Ed.), *Journalism ethics: A philosophical approach* (pp. 103–16). New York: Oxford University Press.

Blevins, J. L., Lee, J. J., McCabe, E. E., & Edgerton, E. (2019). Tweeting for social justice in# Ferguson: Affective discourse in Twitter hashtags. *New Media & Society, 21*(7), 1636–53. https://doi.org/10.1177/1461444819827030

Bock, M. A. (2016). Film the police! Cop-watching and its embodied narratives. *Journal of Communication, 66*(1), 13–34. https://doi.org/10.1111/jcom.12204

Bock, M. A., Suran, M., & González, L. M. B. (2018). Badges? Who needs them? Police press credential policies, professionalism, and the new media environment. *Journalism, 19*(3), 349–65. https://doi.org/10.1177/1464884916667655

Branzburg v. Hayes, 408 U.S. 665. (1972). *US Supreme Court*. Retrieved from https://supreme.justia.com/cases/federal/us/408/665/

Burnham, L., & Freivogel, W. (2010, August). *The anonymous poster: Today's hybrid of the anonymous pamphleteer and anonymous source?* Paper presented at the annual meeting of the Association for Education in Journalism and Mass Communication, Denver, CO.

California Reporters' Shield Law. (2013–2014). Senate Bill No. 558, Chapter 519. (2013). *California Legislative Information.* Retrieved from https://leginfo.legislature.ca.gov/faces/billTextClient.xhtml?bill_id=201320140SB558

Calvert, C. (1999). And you call yourself a "journalist?" Wrestling with a definition of "journalist" in the law. *Dickinson Law Review of the Pennsylvania State University, 103,* 411–51. https://heinonline.org/HOL/LandingPage?collection=journals&handle=hein.journals/dlr103&div=20&id=&page=

Carlson, M. (2015). Introduction: The many boundaries of journalism. In M. Carlson & S. C. Lewis (Eds.), *Boundaries of journalism: Professionalism, practices and participation* (pp. 1–18). Routledge.

Carlson, M., & Lewis, S. C. (2015). *Boundaries of journalism: Professionalism, practices and participation.* London: Routledge.

Carpenter, S., & Kanver, D. (2017). Journalistic expertise: A communicative approach. *Communication and the Public, 2*(3), 197–209. https://doi.org/10.1177/2057047317720218

Cohen, A. (2011, November). The media that need citizens: The First Amendment and the fifth estate. *Southern California Law Review, 85,* 1–84. https://southerncalifornialawreview.com/2011/11/05/the-media-that-need-citizens-the-first-amendment-and-the-fifth-estate-article-by-adam-cohen/

Cohen, H. (2007). *Journalists' privilege to withhold information in judicial and other proceedings: State shield statutes* (Report No. RL32806). Library of Congress Washington, DC: Congressional Research Service. https://fas.org/sgp/crs/secrecy/RL32806.pdf

Dewey, C., & Ohlheiser, A. (2016, July 8). How live-streaming has forever changed the way we view violence. *The Washington Post.* Retrieved from https://www.washingtonpost.com/news/the-intersect/wp/2016/07/08/how-live-streaming-has-forever-changed-the-way-we-view-violence/

Deuze, M. (2005). What is journalism? *Journalism, 6*(4), 442–64. https://doi.org/10.1177/1464884905056815

Deuze, M. (2007a). Journalism in liquid modern times. *Journalism Studies, 8*(4), 671–79. https://doi.org/10.1080/14616700701412233

Deuze, M. (2007b). *Media work.* Cambridge: Polity Press.

Deuze, M., & Witschge, T. (2018). Beyond journalism: Theorizing the transformation of journalism. *Journalism, 19*(2), 165–81. https://doi.org/10.1177/1464884916688550

Dilts, J. P. (2002). The press clause and press behavior: Revisiting the implications of citizenship. *Communication Law & Policy, 7,* 25–49. https://doi.org/10.1207/S15326926CLP0701_02

Docter, S. (2010). Blogging and journalism: Extending shield law protection to new media forms. *Journal of Broadcasting & Electronic Media, 54*(4), 588–602. https://doi.org/10.1080/08838151.2010.519809

Doty v. Molnar, No. DV 07-022 (Mont. Dist. Ct.). (2008). [Referring to *Digital Media Law Project* (dmjp.org)]. Retrieved from http://www.dmlp.org/sites/citmedialaw/files/2008-09-03-Hearing%20and%20Oral%20Ruling%20on%20Billings%20Gazette%20Motion%20to%20Quash.pdf

Dougherty, J. (2012). Obsidian Financial Group, LLC v. Cox and reformulating shield laws to protect digital journalism in an evolving media world. *North Carolina Journal of Law & Technology, 13,* 287–322. http://cite.ncjolt.org/13NCJOLTOnlineEd287

Eldridge, I. I. (2013). Perceiving professional threats: Journalism's discursive reaction to the rise of new media entities. *Journal of Applied Journalism & Media Studies, 2*(2), 281–99. https://doi.org/10.1386/ajms.2.2.281_1

Eliason, R. D. (2006). Leakers, bloggers, and fourth estate inmates: The misguided pursuit of a reporter's privilege. *Cardozo Arts & Entertainment Law Journal, 24,* 385–446. http://cardozoaelj.com/wp-content/uploads/Journal%20Issues/Volume%2024/Issue%202/Eliason.pdf

Eliasoph, N. (1997). Routines and the making of oppositional news. In D. Berkowitz (Ed.), *Social meanings of news* (pp. 230–53). Thousand Oaks, CA: Sage.

Fargo, A. L. (2019). Protecting journalists' sources without a shield: Four proposals. *Communication Law and Policy, 24*(2), 145–89. https://doi.org/10.1080/10811680.2019.1586405

Ferrucci, P., & Vos, T. (2017). Who's in, who's out? Constructing the identity of digital journalists. *Digital Journalism, 5*(7), 868–83. https://doi.org/10.1080/21670811.2016.1208054

Free Flow of Information Act of 2017. (2017). H.R. 4382, 115th Congress, First Session. Retrieved from https://www.congress.gov/115/bills/hr4382/BILLS-115hr4382ih.pdf

Freivogel, W. H. (2009a, November 16). Despite weaknesses, media lawyers tend to support Senate bill on federal shield law. *St. Louis Beacon.* Retrieved from http://stlbeacon.org

Freivogel, W. H. (2009b). Publishing national security secrets: The case for "benign indeterminacy." *Journal of National Security Law & Policy, 3*(1), 95–119. Retrieved from https://jnslp.com/wp-content/uploads/2010/08/03-Freivogel_ver_16_9-21-09.pdf

Gans, H. (1979). *Deciding what's news: A study of CBS Evening News, NBC Nightly News, Newsweek and Time.* New York: Vintage Books.

Gant, S. (2007). *We're all journalists now: The transformation of the press and reshaping of the law in the Internet Age.* New York: Free Press.

Golding, P., & Elliott, P. (1979). *Making the news.* London: Longman.

Hall, S., Critcher, C., & Jefferson, T. (1978). *Policing the crisis: Mugging, the state, and law and order.* London: Macmillan.

Hayes, A. C., Singer, J. B., & Ceppos, J. (2007). Shifting roles, enduring values: The credible journalist in a digital age. *Journal of Mass Media Ethics, 22*(4), 262–79. https://doi.org/10.1080/08900520701583545

Hindman, E. B., & Thomas, R. J. (2014). When old and new media collide: The case of WikiLeaks. *New Media & Society, 16*(4), 541–58. https://doi.org/10.1177/1461444813489504

[Illinois Reporters' Shield Law] 735 ILCS 5/(Code of Civil Procedure) Art. VIII Chapter 9. Reporter's Privilege. *Illinois General Assembly.* Retrieved from http://www.ilga.gov/legislation/ilcs/ilcs4.asp?DocName=073500050HArt%2E+VIII+Pt%2E+9&ActID=2017&ChapterID=56&SeqStart=57600000&SeqEnd=58600000

In re: Mark Madden, 151 F.3d 125, 128 (3d Cir. 1998). (1998). Titan Sports, Inc., A Delaware Corporation v. Turner Broadcasting Systems. *Court Listener.* Retrieved from https://www.courtlistener.com/opinion/756667/in-re-mark-madden-titan-sports-inc-a-delaware-corporation-v-turner/

Jackson, K. (2017). I spy: Addressing the privacy implications of live streaming technology and the current inadequacies of the law. The *Columbia Journal of Law & the Arts, 41,* 125. Retrieved from https://academiccommons.columbia.edu/doi/10.7916/D8DV31X1

Jackson, P. T. (2009). News as a contested commodity: A clash of capitalist and journalistic imperatives. *Journal of Mass Media Ethics, 24*(2–3), 146–63. https://doi.org/10.1080/08900520902905349

Jarvis, J. (2005, March 30). Journalism is a verb, not a noun. *BuzzMachine.* Retrieved from http://www.buzzmachine.com/archives/2005_03_30.html

Johnston, J., & Wallace, A. (2017). Who is a journalist? Changing legal definitions in a deterritorialised media space. *Digital Journalism, 5*(7), 850–67. https://doi.org/10.1080/21670811.2016.1196592

Jones, R. A. (2012). Rethinking reporter's privilege. *Michigan Law Review, 111*(7), 1221–82. Retrieved from https://repository.law.umich.edu/mlr/vol111/iss7/1

Kurtz, H. (2007, March 8). Jailed man is a videographer and a blogger but is he a journalist? *The Washington Post.* Retrieved from https://www.washingtonpost.com/wp-dyn/content/article/2007/03/07/AR2007030702454.html

Lee, W. E. (2012). The demise of the federal shield law. *Cardozo Arts & Entertainment Law Journal, 30,* 27–38. Retrieved from http://www.cardozoaelj.com/wp-content/uploads/Journal%20Issues/Volume%2030/Issue%201/Lee.pdf

LeFebvre, R. K., & Armstrong, C. (2018). Grievance-based social movement mobilization in the# Ferguson Twitter storm. *New Media & Society, 20*(1), 8–28. https://doi.org/10.1177/1461444816644697

Lewis, S. (2011). The sociology of professions, boundary work, and participation in journalism: A review of the literature. Top faculty paper presented to the Journalism Studies Division of the International Communication Association, May, 2011, Boston, MA. Retrieved from https:// www.academia.edu/667807/The_Sociology_of_Professions_Boundary_Work_and_Participatio n_in_Journalism_A_Review_of_the_Literature

Lewis, S. C. (2012). The tension between professional control and open participation: Journalism and its boundaries. *Information, Communication & Society, 15*(6), 836–66. https:// doi.org/10.1080/1369118X.2012.674150

Lewis, S. C., Sanders, A. K., & Carmody, C. (2019). Libel by algorithm? Automated journalism and the threat of legal liability. *Journalism & Mass Communication Quarterly, 96*(1), 60–81. https://doi.org/10.1177/1077699018755983

[Louisiana's Reporters' Shield Law] La. RS 45:1451-1459. (1964). Chapter 11. News Media. Part I. Reporters. *Louisiana State Legislature.* Retrieved from https://www.legis.la.gov/Legis/ Law.aspx?d=99896

Martini, M. (2018). Online distant witnessing and live-streaming activism: Emerging differences in the activation of networked publics. *New Media & Society, 20*(11), 4035–55. https://doi.org/ 10.1177/1461444818766703

McChesney, R. W. (2016). *Rich media, poor democracy: Communication politics in dubious times.* New York: The New Press.

[Montana Reporters' Shield Law] Montana Coded Annotated 2019, Title 26, Chapter 1, Part 9: 26-1-901 to 26-1-903. (2019). Media Confidentiality Act. *Laws.* Retrieved from https:// leg.mt.gov/bills/mca/title_0260/chapter_0010/part_0090/sections_index.html

[Nebraska Reporters' Shield Law] Neb. Rev. Stat. 20-144 to 20-147. (1973). Free Flow of Information Act. *Nebraska Legislature.* Retrieved from https://nebraskalegislature.gov/ laws/statutes.php?statute=20-144

[Oklahoma Reporters' Shield Law] Okla. Stat. tit. 12 § 2506. (1978). Journalist's privilege. [Added by Laws 1978, c. 285, § 506, eff. Oct. 1, 1978. Amended by Laws 2002, c. 468, § 36, eff. Nov. 1, 2002]. *Casetext.* Retrieved from https://casetext.com/statute/oklahoma-statutes/title-12-civil-procedure/12-2506-journalists-privilege

[Pennsylvania Reporters' Shield Law] 42 Pa. Cons. Stat. § 5942. (2016). Confidential communications to news reporters. *Pennsylvania General Assembly.* Retrieved from https:// www.legis.state.pa.us/cfdocs/legis/LI/consCheck.cfm?txtType=HTM&ttl=42&div=0& chpt=59&sctn=42&subsctn=0

Peters, J., & Tandoc, E. (2013). People who aren't really reporters at all, who have no professional qualifications: Defining a journalist and deciding who may claim the privileges. *NYU Journal of Legislation and Public Policy Quorum, 34*, 34–63. Retrieved from https:// nyujlpp.org/wp-content/uploads/2013/03/Peters-Tandoc-Quorum-2013.pdf

Reader, B. (2010, Fall). We the (anonymous) people. *American Journalism Review, 32*(3), 17. Retrieved from https://ajrarchive.org/Article.asp?id=4916.&id=4916.

Reese, S. D. (1997). The news paradigm and the ideology of objectivity. In D. Berkowitz (Ed.), *Social meanings of news* (pp. 420–40). London: Sage.

Robinson, E. P. (2012, Fall). With judges' decision, Illinois joins states with shield law protection for bloggers. *Gateway Journalism Review, 42*(328), 42–43. Retrieved from http:// www.dmlp.org/blog/2012/reconsideration-illinois-judge-holds-blog-protected-shield-law

Rosen, J. (2012). The people formerly known as the audience. In M. Mandiberg (Ed.), *The social media reader* (pp. 13–16). New York: NYU Press.

Rulffes, A. (2018). The First Amendment in times of crisis: An analysis of free press issues in Ferguson, Missouri. *Syracuse Law Review, 68*, 607–34. Retrieved from https://lawrev iew.syr.edu/wp-content/uploads/2018/10/M-Rulffes-FINAL-v4.pdf

Russo, M. (2006). Are bloggers representatives of the news media under the Freedom of Information Act? *Columbia Journal of Law and Social Problems, 40*, 225–66. Retrieved from https://heinonline.org/HOL/LandingPage?handle=hein.journals/collsp40&div=14& id=&page=

Schiller, D. (1981). *Objectivity and the news.* Philadelphia: University of Pennsylvania Press.

Schneider v. State, 308 U.S. 147, (N.J. 1939). (1939). Opinions: Case. *JUSTIA.* Retrieved from https://supreme.justia.com/cases/federal/us/308/147/

Schudson, M. (1978). *Discovering the news.* New York: Basic Books.
Schudson, M. (2001). The objectivity norm in American journalism. *Journalism, 2*(2), 149–70. https://doi.org/10.1177/146488490100200201
Shirky, C. (2008). *Here comes everybody: The power of organizing without organizations.* London: Penguin.
Shoen v. Shoen, 5 F.3d 1289, 1292 (9th Cir. 1993). [Regarding investigative journalist]. Retrieved from https://casetext.com/case/shoen-v-shoen-3
Singer, J. B. (2007). Contested autonomy. *Journalism Studies, 8*(1), 79–95. https://doi.org/10.1080/14616700601056866
Soloski, J. (1990). News reporting and professionalism: Some constraints on the reporter of the news. *Media, Culture & Society, 11*(4), 207–28. https://doi.org/10.1177/016344389011002005
Stewart, D. R. C., & Littau, J. (2016). Up, periscope: Mobile streaming video technologies, privacy in public, and the right to record. *Journalism & Mass Communication Quarterly, 93*(2), 312–31. https://doi.org/10.1177/1077699016637106
Studer, G. (2017). Live streaming violence over social media: An ethical dilemma. *Charleston Law Review, 11*, 621. Retrieved from https://heinonline.org/HOL/LandingPage?handle=hein.journals/charlwrev11&div=26&id=&page=
Tandoc, E. C. (2017). Five ways BuzzFeed is preserving (or transforming) the journalistic field. *Journalism, 19*(2), 200–216. https://doi.org/10.1177/1464884917691785
Tewksbury, D. (2018). Networking #Ferguson: An ethnographic study of Ferguson protesters' online-offline community mobilization. *Democratic Communiqué, 27*(2), 53–68. Retrieved from https://journals.flvc.org/demcom/article/view/106334
Tuchman, G. (1972). Objectivity as strategic ritual: An examination of newsmen's notions of objectivity. *The American Journal of Sociology, 77*(4), 660–79. Retrieved from https://www.jstor.org/stable/2776752
Tucker, J., & Wermiel, S. (2008). Enacting a reasonable federal shield law: A reply to professors Clymer and Eliason. *American University Law Review, 57*, 1291–1339. Retrieved from http://digitalcommons.wcl.american.edu/aulr/vol57/iss5/4
Ugland, E. (2019). Expanding media law and policy education: Confronting power, defining freedom, awakening participation. *Communication Law and Policy, 24*(2), 271–306. https://doi.org/10.1080/10811680.2019.1586407
Ugland, E., & Henderson, J. (2007). Who is a journalist and why does it matter: Disentangling the legal and ethical arguments. *Journal of Mass Media Ethics, 2*(4), 241–61. https://doi.org/10.1080/08900520701583511
Von Bulow by Auersperg v. Von Bulow, 811 F.2d 136, 142 (2d Cir. 1987). *Leagle.* Retrieved from https://www.leagle.com/decision/1987947811f2d1361929
Weinhold, W. M. (2008). Newspaper negotiations: the crossroads of community newspaper journalists' values and labor. *Journalism Practice, 2*(3), 476–86. https://doi.org/10.1080/17512780802281222
Weinhold, W. (2010). Letters from the editors: American journalists, multimedia, and the future of journalism. *Journalism Practice, 4*(3), 394–404. https://doi.org/10.1080/17512781003643228
West Virginia Legislature (2017). West Virginia Code 57-3-10: Reporters' privilege. Retrieved from http://www.wvlegislature.gov/wvcode/ChapterEntire.cfm?chap=57&art=3&section=10#3
West, S. R. (2011, April). Awakening the press clause. *UCLA Law Review, 58*, 1025–70. Retrieved from https://www.uclalawreview.org/awakening-the-press-clause-2/
Zelizer, B. (1993). Journalists as interpretive communities. *Critical Studies in Mass Communication, 10*, 219–37. https://doi.org/10.1080/15295039309366865
Zelnick, R. (2005). Essay on source confidentiality: Journalists and confidential sources. *Notre Dame Journal of Law, Ethics & Public Policy, 19*, 541–789. Retrieved from http://scholarship.law.nd.edu/ndjlepp/vol19/iss2/10

Chapter Four

The History of Liveness and Mass Shootings

Adapting to Social Media

Chelsea Daggett

Author's Note: This chapter contains personal accounts from individuals directly affected by mass shootings. It also contains vivid descriptions of video footage from these events.

Liveness has always presented various ethical dilemmas to the journalists who cover mass shootings. Twenty years ago, when the Columbine Massacre (April 20, 1999) launched mass shootings into the center of public consciousness, liveness was a central value driving the media coverage. News organizations broadcasted the 911 calls made by students inside the school who had cell phones to keep in touch with parents, and many news organizations broadcasted from the lawn of the high school's campus as the shooting was taking place. This added layer of immediate communication acted as a precursor to issues of liveness that inflect incidents like the Christchurch, New Zealand, shooting (March 15, 2019). The live stream of this mass shooting notably lay within the control of the shooter, filmed from his perspective, and drew attention to the increasing struggle with social media liveness in media coverage of these incidents.

In the short time since the March 15, 2019, Christchurch attack that left 51 dead, other notable mass shootings, like the Poway Synagogue Shooting (April 27, 2019), were live streamed by the shooters. These incidents represent a new iteration of already existing ethical issues in covering mass shootings. While new forms of live media today appear to present a redefinition of the ethical struggles in covering mass shootings, they largely require a re-evaluation of preexisting ethical dilemmas. By outlining the tension between positive beliefs about liveness and the ethical issues that come with utilizing social media sources created by shooters, victims, and official sources in journalistic coverage of mass shootings, this chapter will discuss how ethical norms around liveness were created in the pre-social media era and how social media complicate those norms.

This chapter analyzes the evidence and news articles regarding a half dozen events that represent this evolution in liveness from the Columbine Massacre to the Poway Synagogue shooting. This analysis highlights the way that liveness has been perceived in relationship to mass shootings over time. I gathered this evidence through previous interviews with individuals who have used their expertise in response to mass shooting incidents in the past. I interviewed information gatekeepers like Steve Davis, the primary Public Information Officer (PIO) in the Columbine Massacre, and Ryan Huff, the PIO for AJ Boiks, a victim of the Aurora Theater Shooting (July 20, 2012). Both men are members of the Emergency Service Public Information Officers of Colorado (ESPIOC). I also interviewed advocates Sandy and Lonnie Phillips, founders of Survivors in Power and parents of Jessica Ghawi, a victim of the Aurora Theater Shooting, and Tom Mauser of Colorado Cease-fire and father of Daniel Mauser, a victim of the Columbine Massacre. Steve Davis and these other interviewees offered many thoughtful reflections on their personal experiences with mass shootings as well as the impact of social media in responding to these events during our 2017 interviews. Their comments connected to many recent mass shooting events and spoke to the journalistic values that contribute to decision-making in the media coverage of these incidents. Liveness maintains an increasingly complicated relationship to values of accuracy, speed, public safety, transparency, privacy, and respect in the era of live streaming that should be examined through a historically conscious lens of journalistic practice.

LIVENESS AND JOURNALISTIC VALUES IN THE ERA OF SOCIAL MEDIA

The current research on mass shootings and journalism primarily focuses on print and television media, which have also been more thoroughly theorized in terms of liveness. Building on these ideas requires a consideration of the ethical framework and values that transfer from these more traditional media to social media, as well as a discussion of how newer forms of media are commonly integrated into journalistic reporting on mass shootings today.

Most researchers highlight the need for journalists to use an Ethics of Care framework in decision-making on reporting about mass shootings. This perspective highlights the need to protect those that are weaker in the situation. In the case of mass shootings, this perspective focuses on the victims—their politics, the reporting norms they advocate for, and their stories. Walsh-Childers, Lewis, and Neely (2011) outline this approach for journalists stating that interviewees "reacted positively to journalists who treated them with compassion, showing concern for their well-being, managing interviews to accommodate sources' physical and emotional needs, and giving sources an opportunity to express what they wanted to say" (p. 199).

However, the use of victims' social media posts, videos, and photographs holds a complicated position within this perspective because social media blur the lines between public and private. Does the victim sharing this information in the form of videos, posts, and pictures during an intensely traumatic event indicate they want that information to be a part of the story later? In summary, should social media be understood as inherently public? While the Ethics of Care perspective largely dismisses the value of broadcasting or reporting that uses shooter created material, the position of using victim created material has yet to be decided and largely depends on how supportive of values like privacy and respect the use of these materials can be.

Many values shape the way television, print, and online news reports use or exclude "live" material of mass shootings culled from social media. The key values highlighted in previous research on reporting norms in traditional media appear in the research on social media as well. These values include the tension between the speed of reporting and accuracy, how that tension affects credibility, issues of privacy, and issues of public safety. The tensions of speed versus accuracy have been addressed in response to various live incidents that resulted in immediate inaccuracies, like the Sandy Hook Elementary School Shooting (December 14, 2012). Berkowitz and Liu (2014) summarize the dynamic that pushes journalists to resort to using social media sources rather than more credible or authoritative sources. They state that "lacking official sources . . . journalists rely on online media forms such as blogs and social media as information collection tools" (p. 157). Police and other official sources often withhold details until they are confirmed, preferring accuracy to speed in opposition to journalistic sources. Speaking on the reporting mistakes around the Sandy Hook Shooting, Berkowitz and Liu highlight that depending on these social media sources to fill in details while police and investigators withhold them can lead to an undermined sense of journalistic authority or credibility that then requires paradigm repair.

Practitioners remain divided on whether maintaining credibility should be privileged above speed or whether this perspective rejects the reality of social media dominance in the current information landscape. Some journalists believe that "without ironclad corroboration, reliance on social media 'is to play with fire' [asking] whether the real meaning falls on the issue of boundary work as a means of retaining authority for news media" (Berkowitz & Liu, 2014, pp. 161–62). While others have pointed to the use of transparency in information collection to offset speedy judgments of inaccuracies, inaccuracies have always existed in initial reporting on "live" events (Berkowitz & Liu, 2014). Surely, as the public fills in the lack of "official" information themselves with rumors and inaccuracies, as happened with the reporting of the Sandy Hook shooting, this boundary becomes more complicated, and more difficult for waiting to report information from any source infinitely. The complicated boundary between what information should be reported with caution, and which sources are considered credible in the initial stages of reporting on a "live" or developing story, remains unclear and situational in current journalistic practice.

Social media posted by victims during the shooting itself come with their own ethical limitations and baggage around the value of privacy. Deciding whether to use these highly personal forms of media depends primarily on issues of privacy weighed against the automatic perception that these media are both credible and public, unlike blogs or forums. Cumiskey and Hjorth (2018) completed an excellent study on media content produced at the scene of the Orlando Pulse Nightclub Shooting (June 12, 2016) through mobile communications. This study effectively surveyed the complicated relationship between victims and their phones. They argue that mobile devices serve an important social function for victims during the incident but comment little on what should be done with these media *after* the event is over or in future reporting. However, they do highlight important dilemmas contingent on the perceived "bleeding of boundaries between the public and the private" (Cumiskey & Hjorth, 2018, p. 414). Using the terms "presence bleed" and "context collapse" from Gregg (2011) and Boyd (2014), they comment on how the intention of mobile communication, whether it is meant to be public or private, becomes more difficult to determine in our current social media landscape. They state, "The enmeshment of social media posts, direct messages, text messages, the exchange of photos, video telephony and live broadcasting generates a context collapse in that the 'where' of where communication is occurring is not easily, defined, bounded or controlled" (Cumiskey & Hjorth, 2018, p. 415). In the case of journalists attempting to quickly report on a developing story, like a mass shooting, social media exist in the public eye despite also functioning as a private representation of the victims' grief and experiences. There are certain types of transient, private media, more clearly delineated from journalists' reach such as the temporary nature of the Snapchat story or text messages. However, the question remains whether Facebook posts, Facebook live stories, Tweets, and many more forms of social media should be understood as public statements made by victims during these crises.

Additionally, the difficulties media face when presenting credible, factual stories about mass shootings complicate decisions to use victim created media. Issues with these values are especially fraught in the current controversies around "fake news." Journalists using victim created media operate from the presumption that these media possess an aura of authority, one that the types of information culled from online forums and blog posts might lack. This belief stems from a strong historical basis in the televisual theory of liveness building from the ritual understanding of live events established by Daniel Dayan and Elihu Katz (1992). Mimi White (1999) elaborates on the ideological function of this assumed accuracy or fact. She states that "Ideologically, 'liveness' encourages us to accept what we see on television as . . . accurate—'real' because it is 'really' happening—rather than elaborately constructed and mediated" (p. 44). This perceived objectivity is more about the authority and credibility of the source than any inherent quality in the images or posts themselves. At the same time, liveness insulates those that use on-scene footage from accusations of inaccuracy while also filling time, what White calls "vamping." Liveness provides the illusion of new information as reporters wait for public officials and investigators to fill in the blanks. Cutting away from an on-scene broadcast to a loop of various social media posts that show different angles of the same event may not add new information, but they at least provide the illusion of movement and protect the media-makers from accusations of inaccuracy. In this way, using victim-created media helps media-makers preserve their credibility. The use of this practice gives an example of paradigm repair meant to protect against a history of media inaccuracies in reporting on mass shootings.

The other ethical dilemma presented by using this "live" media relates to public safety. Posting these media in the immediate aftermath of an event can encourage chaos within the scene as the victims experience the event, and officials receive contradictory information. As Cumiskey and Hjorth (2018) explain, the use of mobile devices by the victims and shooter caused miscommunication on site. Regarding the Pulse Night Club Shooting (June 12, 2016), they state, "it is also important to investigate the ways in which the presence of devices might have impeded the rescue and escape of many. . . . The shooter himself was complicit in spreading misleading information and confusion over the phone" (Cumiskey & Hjorth, 2018, p. 422). Not only should newsmakers pause to question the assumption of accuracy tied to "live" and on-scene images, but they should also consider the public safety cost of broadcasting those images as well as the private function they play for scared victims on-scene. Under the ethics of care model that many researchers have advocated for, in reporting on mass shootings, victim-created media should be treated carefully and only used when there is proper consideration of its potential to harm victims.

LIVENESS AND THE ILLUSION OF MEDIUM SPECIFICITY

Underlying all these news values are the history of liveness as a concept and its connection to newsworthiness, primarily developed out of television theory. According to the ritual view of media, Daniel Dayan and Elihu Katz (1992) differentiated between media events and news events. They state that "the messages of these two broadcasts are different, their effects are different, they are presented in quite a different tone. Great news events speak of accidents, of disruption; great ceremonial events celebrate order and its restoration" (p. 9). Despite Dayan and Katz's insistence on the differences between media events and news events, they do share one commonality, ideological implications due to their opposing relationship to the social order. A mass shooting plays the ideological role of disrupting the social order in order to enable the status quo through emotions of grief and fear. This perspective has been expanded on in other ritual perspectives of liveness. White (1999) acknowledges this ideology of liveness and its relationship to a variety of television news stories, ranging from the *Challenger* Explosion to the Persian Gulf War, to highlight how various forms of "liveness" are part of the "modes of production, rhetoric, and address prevalent on television" (p. 43). These perspectives elaborate on how liveness is specifically expressed through style in television. Yet these ideological functions extend to other live forms of media as well.

Early theory about how liveness occurs in online spaces is focused on the differences between television and the Internet, differentiating them based on theories of medium specificity. Nick Couldry (2004) coined the term *online liveness* to discuss the specific mode of live address in online space. He states that online liveness provides "social co-presence on a variety of scales from very small groups in chat rooms to huge international audiences for breaking news . . . made possible by the Internet as an underlying infrastructure. Often, online liveness overlaps with the existing category of liveness" (pp. 356–57). Couldry acknowledges the strong preexisting relationship between televisual and online liveness. Yet, the distinction between online and televisual liveness is even less relevant and clear in the current media environment. This era is dominated by streaming and fragmented viewing patterns where some viewers may get their news from social media, YouTube, online media outlets, cable television, and more. However, the continued blurring of lines does confirm his observation that online there is no true "center of transmission," as individuals learn about media events at staggered moments across many platforms. Couldry (2004) also highlights the importance of liveness as an ideological category. He believes this category is "put into use in various forms of structured action that naturalize wider relationships" (p. 354). This observation connects the ideological function of liveness to audience behaviors such as fact-checking and participating in online forums related to mass shootings. The Internet has only amplified the importance of these responses to news events because they offer a place for citizens to openly criticize more traditional media makers about inaccuracies or evolving ethical issues.

However, not every news event gains the attention that leads to an observable audience reaction, and some mass shootings receive very little attention. This situational aspect of covering mass shootings also differentiates them from one another and can do so along the lines of how much social media presence an event has. The question of what makes some mass shootings more newsworthy than others relates to crime reporting more generally. Schildkraut, Elsass, and Meredith (2018) produced a content analysis of mass shooting news coverage based on the five factors of newsworthiness outlined by Chermak. They summarized,

> Chermak (1995) has suggested that newsworthiness may be assessed based on five criteria—the violent nature of the crime, demographic characteristics of the victim and offender (such as age, gender, race, and occupation), characteristics of the news agency, the uniqueness of the event, and the event's saliency. Greater values of newsworthiness regularly are assigned to the most serious or violent crimes—those that are statistically rare, have atypical elements or [have more than one victim]. (p. 225)

The study of Schildkraut and associates (2018) on mass shooting coverage confirmed that some of these factors influenced how prominent those mass shootings had been covered respectively. They concluded that the number and age of victims, whether the shooter lived or died, and whether the shooting took place in a school, defined the amount of coverage or newsworthiness of the shooting.

These patterns appear in many of the most notable mass shootings. They explain what leads news coverage to focus on events such as the Sandy Hook Shooting, which victimized elementary-aged children and resulted in 26 deaths; the Aurora Theater Shooting that had a surviving shooter and 12 deaths and 76 injuries; and the Las Vegas Shooting that resulted in 59 deaths. All of these incidents gained much attention due to the age of the victims, the perpetrator's status, and the large number of deaths, respectively. However, the shootings discussed in this chapter diverge from the pattern of newsworthiness. Schildkraut and associates (2018) observed the differences of mass shooting media coverages, in part, due to the increased presence of social media in reporting on these events. For example, the content analysis found that mass shootings in public places were less newsworthy, and yet, all the shootings analyzed here were both newsworthy and occurred in public places. What makes them unique is that they primarily occurred in environments such as clubs, restaurants, and airports where individuals are likely to use their devices, unlike schools. The focus on these events helps to show

how liveness plays a role through the publication of social media by victims, especially in more public incidents of mass violence.

SHOOTINGS THAT FEATURED SOCIAL MEDIA ARTIFACTS

Liveness has been a feature of mass shooting media coverage since the days of the Columbine Massacre in 1999. News vans cluttered the surrounding park and parking lots for weeks and captured various incidents featuring victims as the police searched the school. One notable example of a live broadcast incident centered on the injured boy, Patrick Ireland, who fell out of the library window on live television. According to Steve Davis, 911 calls from students and teachers trapped inside were broadcast on television, and in some cases, reporters spoke with victims while they were trapped inside the school. Later, surveillance videos of the event were broadcast repeatedly in news programs describing the shooting. The media's use of these types of found footage set the stage for the intrinsic value attributed to liveness during mass shooting events. The trouble official sources reported in managing the impact of these live broadcasts has only increased in the age of social media. Steve Davis, the PIO on the site, reflected on this development during an interview in 2017. He stated, "I think a lot about the same exact situation, the same set of circumstances today, what it would be like to try and stay on top of things—Twitter going, Facebook going, Instagram, I can't even imagine" (S. Davis, Personal Interview, September 22, 2017). Using further reflections from Steve Davis and others involved in high profile incidents and mass shooting responses, this analysis examines how liveness has changed or stayed the same in media coverage today.

To begin with, there are several tiers of media incorporated in "live" coverage of events, and all these tiers receive different treatment by journalists. Both the Fort Lauderdale Airport Shooting (January 6, 2017) and the Sutherland Springs Church Shooting (November 5, 2017) included what was essentially surveillance footage, like footage broadcast of Eric Harris and Dylan Klebold walking through Columbine High School released after the shooting. Importantly, the Sutherland Springs Church Shooting footage is in custody of the police and has never been released (Blinder, 2017). However, the footage of the Fort Lauderdale Airport shooting was leaked to *TMZ* (Thirty Mile Zone, tmz.com) and subsequently broadcast on several major news outlets (Spencer, 2017). Coverage of the Borderline Bar and Grill Shooting (November 7, 2018) and the Orlando Pulse Night Club Shooting (June 12, 2016) included a wide variety of social media created by the victims including Instagram Stories, Snapchats, private text messages, and various other social media posts (Cumiskey & Hjorth, 2018; "Video shows inside bar during shooting," 2018). These forms of media present the biggest ethical challenge to journalists because of their highly personal quality, and subsequent public distribution differentiates them from pre-Internet era media sources. As such, the standards and practices developed around talking to victims face-to-face have little to no applicable value when discussing social media.

The type of live media that has garnered the most attention is, ironically, the least new or surprising, live media created by the shooters themselves. Mass shooters have often created media in the form of manifestos and video diaries leading up to the shootings, and some, like Elliot Rodger, have posted them to YouTube and online forums in the past (Branson-Potts & Winton, 2018; Paton, 2012). Journalists have consistently limited or refused to broadcast those media artifacts because they are perceived as valorizing the shooters (Moritz, 2011). The same remains true for the live footage of the Christchurch, New Zealand shooting, and the Poway Synagogue shooting, both of which were live streamed by the perpetrator. The difference now seems to be that these shooters can access social media networks, such as Reddit and 4Chan, to broadcast their streams without worrying about the authority granted by mainstream media in broadcasting their messages. All three of these scenarios complicate existing journalistic norms around values of accuracy, speed, public safety, credibility, privacy, and respect in media coverage of mass shootings.

STREAMING BY THE SHOOTERS: PUBLIC SAFETY, SPEED, AND CREDIBILITY

The perpetrators of mass shootings have always engaged in various forms of media creation. Eric Harris and Dylan Klebold recorded "The Basement Tapes" as a manifesto of sorts to be released after their deaths, and Sueng Hui-Cho, the Virginia Tech shooter, sent his manifesto to NBC prior to committing his act (Johnson, 2007). Elliot Rodger released both a written and video manifesto using a YouTube account, and YouTuber Nasim Aghdam even committed a shooting at the company's headquarters, supposedly over "demonetization" of her content and policy changes (Chen, 2018). These individuals all sought a platform to broadcast their beliefs and ideas. What makes the issue of live streaming mass shootings, such as Christchurch and Poway, unique is less the shooter's desire for a platform and more the ease and accessibility to their audience through any given platform. Decisions by media makers evaluating how necessary shooter-created media is to the story have typically revolved around the values of public safety, speed versus accuracy, and the credibility of the press.

As the accessibility of media that shooters use to express their beliefs and publish their acts increased, the gatekeeping practices around those media have also intensified and worked to evolve. While the Columbine shooters and the Virginia Tech shooters relied on the decisions of officials and media sources to disseminate their message, current shooters do not have to go through mainstream channels of law enforcement and journalism to publish their manifestos or broadcast their actions. For instance, the Jefferson County Sheriff's Department decided, after completing the investigation into Columbine, how much of "The Basement Tapes" would be released to journalistic media. They never released the entirety of the tapes to anyone and only provided a private, in-office viewing of the tapes for the immediate family members of the victims and selected media, allegedly with the understanding they would not directly quote the tapes (Kass, 2009). NBC decided to air a two-minute and twenty-five second segment of Sueng Hui-Cho's tape at least once, a decision which was reexamined on a later episode of *Oprah Winfrey Show* (Tragedy at Virginia Tech, 2007). The value of public safety is tied to the need for accuracy and maintaining credibility when more official gate-keepers have control of the decisions about what should and should not be shown of the perpetrators' message. These gatekeepers can choose respon-sible inclusions and exclusions, as well as limit the way those messages are broadcast if they even choose to broadcast them at all. While mainstream media have increasingly limited the broadcast of these messages, media ca-pabilities have evolved to create more media makers, which complicates this gatekeeping dynamic.

Mainstream media, more and more, have resisted showing any shooter-created material, but the evolution of the Internet created many more outlets for these materials. These new outlets can be harder to limit and control than in the past. The loss of media authority that comes with shooters posting information through outlets such as YouTube, Reddit, and 4Chan, all chan-nels that have been used to distribute shooter-created livestreams or manifes-tos, gives the impression that this trend is specific to new forms of media. For instance, by the time the original forum for the live stream removed the footage of the Christchurch shooting, other users had already recorded the footage and redistributed it across several other platforms, including You-Tube (Timberg et al., 2019). Each time that material was removed, it simply appeared elsewhere. In this way, the gatekeepers of journalism and official sources, such as law enforcement, no longer maintain control of this material and struggle to respond quickly enough to limit its distribution. However, in an interesting opposition, because the Poway Synagogue shooter posted his manifesto a few minutes prior to committing and streaming his terrible act, the police received a warning about the perpetrator and responded with far better speed to the incident as a result (Reinstein, 2019).

These cases lead to a renegotiation of the relationship between public safety, on the one hand, and accuracy and credibility on the other. The reporting of shooter-created material can act as an early warning provided through social media, which has both benefits and drawbacks. For instance, the benefit of exposing the crime more quickly also results in a record that more people will be affected by. Later, this record becomes harder to erase due to the permanence and proliferation of online media. In this way, shooters expressing their beliefs or plans online can potentially provide fast and accurate information relevant to public safety during a mass shooting while also negatively impacting witnesses, victims, and communities.

The media's loss of control and inability to limit exposure to shooter-created material has led the mainstream media to engage in a high level of paradigm repair, especially in response to these two live streamed shootings. Countless news articles criticized those users reposting the live stream of the incidents while also attacking the social media platforms used by the shooters. Many outlets have followed up on the legal consequences, e.g., the user Philip Neville Arps faced 21 months in jail for his role in this process of sharing the Christchurch New Zealand live stream (Hollingsworth, 2019). These criticisms were similarly directed at media outlets that broadcast short clips of the footage themselves despite these outlets suffering no legal consequences for their contribution to the dissemination of the videos (Meade, 2019). These varying responses represent the dynamic of paradigm repair after a breach of ethical boundaries. Berkowitz and Liu (2014) say the process of paradigm repair is triggered in situations "that breach the boundaries of practice. . . . Something must be done to assure society that professional practice remains viable although boundaries have temporarily been crossed" (p. 158).

These incidents presented the mainstream media with a new boundary to negotiate in their decision-making about whether shooter-created material should be shown. Some news outlets transgressed the boundary, and therefore threatened the credibility of mainstream media. As a result, those media-makers that used the footage became collapsed with individual users who made the questionable decision to share the footage independently. While paradigm repair is not at all new, the process of negotiation takes place in front of the media audience, which draws attention to the unique aspects of each new dilemma. Ultimately, while there has been a notable shift in the relationship between public safety and accuracy as a result of social media content created by shooters, the mainstream media's negotiation of their credibility in reporting on mass shootings remains the same.

SOCIAL MEDIA OF VICTIMS; SPEED, RESPECT, AND PRIVACY

While the media focus more and more on victims over shooters, the practices around victims have changed greatly over time, evolving more toward respect and privacy and away from speed. Social media potentially offer a new outlet for gathering information about victims quickly while still respecting the victims and allowing them more privacy. The interviews conducted with those who had experience with victims after Columbine included Steve Davis and Tom Mauser, who shared several very difficult stories about the media's conduct in response to that incident. According to Steve Davis, several KOA radio interviews were conducted with students in the school over cell phones as the incident occurred, and one journalist stole a badge to pose as a victim's advocate to speak with victims in the hospital (S. Davis, Personal Interview, September 22, 2017). Tom Mauser recounted how his neighbors formed a barrier within their community cul-de-sac to block news vans from approaching his premises (T. Mauser, Personal Interview, September 6, 2017).

Additionally, national networks conducted many live interviews with students still in shock at the scene, and ABC even interviewed victim Mark Taylor on-camera in his hospital bed (Wounded Columbine student Mark Taylor, 2010). This series of intrusive practices has drawn much criticism in the long term from those within the media as well as researchers applying the Ethics of Care framework to media behaviors following mass shootings. These violations of respect and privacy are notable and egregious, but also, less relevant today due to the coevolution of reporting norms around mass shootings and the use of victim-created social media in reporting.

Barriers between media and victims have increased in the two decades since the Columbine shooting. According to interviews with Sandy and Lonnie Philips and Ryan Huff, all three of whom had experience with the victims of the Aurora Theater Shooting, the media process has become less intrusive over time. The primary barrier to protect victims from intrusive media is PIOs like Huff and Davis, who also spend their free time volunteering with local branches of groups like the ESPIOC as media liaisons for individual families. Interestingly, Tom Mauser, who worked for the Colorado Department of Transportation at the time of the Columbine Massacre, had a media liaison, unlike many of the victims' families in that incident. Ryan Huff explained the process by which PIOs insulate victims and their families from media requests after a mass shooting. He stated,

> There was an e-mail from our leadership of that group that said, you know we have 12 families that have lost loved ones, and they're getting inundated by international media, morning talk shows, national networks, etc. and they've never done a simple newspaper interview in their lives. So, we're putting the call out for PIOs who do this all the time to serve as liaisons to these families so that their phones aren't blowing up with requests so that if they need some advice, you are there to give it. We were not to serve as spokespeople to talk on behalf of the family. However, we were that go-between between the media and these families. Some families did every interview, some did none, some did a few. (R. Huff, Personal Interview, September 8, 2017)

Huff's comments again reflect the need for professional gatekeepers, this time between victims and the media. Huff also discussed the process of working alongside the media to film AJ Boiks's funeral ceremony and complimented their respectful nature and cooperation. This approach of providing PIO support to victims and their families has subsequently been applied to the scene of other shootings, like the Sandy Hook School Shooting. While this process protects victims during the initial shock after a shooting, there remain open questions about how much help victims can provide journalists following a shooting in their heightened emotional state.

The Ethics of Care model of journalism prioritizes victims controlling their story and having a platform for their own beliefs. The slow adoption of "No Notoriety," or practices that include limiting images of the shooter and stating their name as little as possible in news reports, represents one example of journalists adapting to the victims' platform and beliefs. These values of respect and privacy help to support victims emotionally at a difficult time. However, asking for interviews and press coverage generally does not acknowledge how hard it can be for victims to make clear-headed decisions about how to interact with media during the aftermath of a shooting. Sandy Phillips described this period stating,

> Chaos, absolute chaos, people wanting interviews. And because Jessie was in journalism and had done internships in San Antonio, all those media folks were over at the house as friends, not as media. And of course, they also needed to get a story . . . we just did the best we could with what we had. (S. Phillips, Personal Interview, September 4, 2017)

This sense of overwhelming and conflicting needs and motivations was similarly echoed by Tom Mauser. He stated,

> before I had the PR person from CDOT . . . the people who were there in the house with us, family, neighbors, friends helping us out—They would take most of the phone calls, and they would say, Tom, this is so and so, do you want to talk to them? Almost always, it was no, I didn't want to talk to anybody. (T. Mauser, Personal Interview, September 6, 2017)

In both cases, these families' narratives included reflections on their high level of distress and grief that led to a need for isolation in the face of media demands. Even though these interviewees now interact with the media regularly as advocates, they remember that immediate aftermath as a moment when they needed privacy and respect. The role of social media produced by victims today, as opposed to 1999 or even 2012, presents both new solutions and problems for those journalists engaged in the Ethics of Care practice who want to grant that moment of respect and privacy. Do these sources help to limit the need for media interviews with and access to victims, or do they further violate the privacy of victims?

Using social media produced by victims poses interesting questions about the definition of privacy, while also potentially facilitating greater respect for victims by using secondary sources, instead of making more intrusive requests. Social media sources are largely viewed as public information, readily accessible. When a victim captures live video of a shooting through Instagram, as was the case at the Borderline Bar and Grill Shooting, the appropriateness of broadcasting the victim's video is not nearly as cut and dry as the media's decision not to use shooter-created material ("Video shows inside bar during shooting," 2018). However, this undecided status raises a variety of questions. Do you ask for permission to use this video in your newscast? If you receive permission, does this video provide vital information worth risking the mental health of other victims and viewers? Is a graphic content warning enough to justify using the material in a newscast? For instance, in the case of the Borderline Bar and Grill Shooting, CNN utilized the footage to discuss the investigation process and forensics of the scene with an expert interviewee. Could this information have waited for an official source, or was this vital information to release quickly? The speed and accessibility of information when official sources are slow to respond, due to the constraints of the investigative process, seems less of a problem when there are social media sources to draw upon. However, these sources also inhabit a grey area between public and private.

Some of these questions depend heavily on the context of each case. Shootings that occur in schools or other spaces where cell phones are less prolific rarely produce such footage. Whereas those that take place in public spaces such as malls, restaurants, or other large events almost always produce some social media presence even if the videos are captured accidentally. For instance, during the Pulse Night Club shooting, many victims used their phones to produce various formats of social media. Some of these media were as clearly private as text messages and unposted cell phone videos to other variations such as Snapchat stories, which are temporary and often shared only with a small group of followers (Cumiskey & Hjorth, 2018). Are Instagram stories, like those shared after the Borderline Bar and Grill Shooting, acceptable to use as public sources while text messages or Snapchat stories require the permission of both the sender and receiver of the exchange? Aside from questions about the line between public and private, the potential benefits of using secondary sources like social media may be offset by journalists making insistent requests to victims for permission to use those posts. While these requests remain less intrusive than requests for statements or interviews, there may be a benefit to applying a standard definition of which sources count as public to future incidents.

Another complication in assessing the ethical boundaries of using victim-created media involves the balance of public safety, in opposition to the potential emotional catharsis victims experience by having the option to document the moment. Steve Davis mentioned this issue of safety and liveness during Columbine as well. He stated,

> The news had one particular video of the SWAT team; they were moving behind a firetruck for cover that was being shown live. To make a long story short, the issue is if you've got suspects on the inside with a TV, you're showing them . . . and they're students in the school, so they know exactly where that is. (S. Davis, Personal Interview, September 22, 2017)

While the media agreed not to show footage like this live in the future, victims do not have the same awareness of these gatekeeping practices and may not be thinking beyond the immediate emotional need for catharsis during these events. Indeed, Davis recounted several other incidents where the information about victim's identities or suspect apprehension was documented by citizens through social media, and subsequently, leaked to journalists early enough to compromise the police response and subsequent investigation.

This issue of public safety complicates the role of victim-created material as well despite the highly personal function of mobile devices during a crisis. Cumiskey and Hjorth (2018) point to the cathartic value of being connected through mobile communication for victims while also acknowledging the problem of crosstalk and how it affected those victims of the Pulse Night Club shooting. They refer to these technologies and social media as a potential "witness and companion in tragedy and as a potential vehicle for connection with remote loved ones at the moment of death" (Cumiskey & Hjorth, 2018, p. 415). Cumiskey and Hjorth (2018) also recount several stories of victims clinging to their devices during the crisis as a sort of lifeline and argue for the catharsis this access provided. Steve Davis spoke similarly about the few students who had cellular phones during the Columbine shooting. These stories show that victims naturally reach out with their devices during a crisis, creating another layer of practical difficulty around public safety.

This emotional function cannot erase the dangers that come with liveness in mass shootings. In addition to spreading misinformation and creating crosstalk between officials, suspects, and victims, dependence on these live media can inhibit victims at the scene. Cumiskey and Hjorth (2018) caution, "One must question whether club goers' reliance on their mobile devices impeded their ability to accurately assess the situation and affected their ability to connect and work together with each other to ensure their safety" (p. 9). Some individuals even searched for stories about the shooting as it unfolded. Did these actions increase the danger to victims in any meaningful way? These questions again vary greatly on a case-by-case basis and primarily matter to journalists' using the Ethics of Care model that focuses on the victims' emotional state and looks to support their story and intention. These statements indicate that the use of social media in these situations is less intentional and more emotional, which suggests media should be cautious in their approach to even the most seemingly public posts of mass shooting footage. Journalists could violate the privacy of victims and disrespect a traumatic, highly personal experience if they do not stop to consider the victims' mentality in the moment of creating these social media.

Finally, on top of considering these case-by-case questions of privacy and respect, journalists should consider what these videos add to their newscasts and whether there are alternative "official" sources. Steve Davis points to the advantage of the speed that social media posts about developing events can provide for media-makers. He stated about a situation on a recent homicide,

> I hadn't even sent a news release out yet. Granted, there was some media out on the scene, and I did talk to them a few times . . . but you've got neighbors shooting video, shooting photos, talking to the media, sending in information, tweeting their stuff . . . the newscast, they had the whole story. (S. Davis, Personal Interview, September 22, 2017)

Yet, in the same case, the victim had been incorrectly identified by that newscast. The advantage of the speed that comes from using these citizens as sources can add context to a story, but it can also tend toward "vamping," especially in the case of mass shootings, which are often large media events. Rather than risk broadcasting inaccurate information, this decision leads to the constant repetition of potentially traumatic and graphic content for viewers without adding information or context to the story. In this case, the media place their sense of credibility on speed without considering the consequences. This trap can be tempting when media makers consider using victims' social media, which seem to be inherently public sources of information without considering the victims' emotional state or intention for creating them.

OFFICIAL SOURCES: PROTECTING THE COMMUNITY THROUGH SPEED, TRANSPARENCY, AND ACCURACY

The clearest cut and adaptive uses of social media for reporting and managing the situation after a mass shooting emerged from the ongoing work of PIOs who act as liaisons between official agencies and the public. Steve Davis offered a broad view of the drawbacks of social media, as well as their advantages while acknowledging how these capabilities would further complicate something on the scale of the Columbine Massacre today. He stated,

> At Columbine, some kids had cell phones, and they were calling from inside
> the school. Then we had people that were calling that weren't but they told the
> media that they were a student at Columbine . . . but that's how it would be
> like today with every student having a phone, every student tweeting, I mean,
> taking pictures. I can't imagine. (S. Davis, Personal Interview, September 22,
> 2017)

While schools often limit student use of mobile devices during class time
even today, the risks associated with uncontrolled information after any mass
shooting affect these gatekeepers more than others. Even during the Columbine Massacre, the sheer number of media descending on the town and the
constant flow of rumors from media-makers tainted the official story in ways
that still resonate today. Tom Mauser discussed how he still receives letters
from young people who believe the rumor that the perpetrators were part of
the group the "Trench Coat Mafia," a rumor corrected within 72 hours of
coverage (Wilogren, 1999). Steve Davis advocated for the use of staggered
news conferences to aid in rumor control but cautioned, "I personally don't
know how you could completely control rumors and speculation. I think you
can do what you can . . . those news conferences being so often gave me that
opportunity to say no, that's not true" (S. Davis, Personal Interview, September 22, 2017).

Maintaining constant contact with the media gave Davis a chance to
address their information directly and limit rumors, especially those that
could affect the credibility of the investigation, a key value of PIOs. Social
media affect the roles of these gatekeepers in various positive and negative
ways, but ultimately, these new media sources simply exacerbate problems
that have always existed while acting as a potentially constructive tool for
PIOs.

Social media can play a key role in preserving the credibility of official
sources by providing information after an event like a mass shooting, consolidating the voice of the investigating agencies, and clearly demarcating the
official story from rumors and speculation. Steve Davis discussed the issue
of attribution during Columbine, stating,

> I cautioned everybody quite often. You've got a lot of people out there asking
> questions just like we are. So, you may hear something that we aren't aware of
> yet. Be careful. Please attribute it to where you got it and not as the official
> word. (S. Davis, Personal Interview, September 22, 2017)

Davis had little control over whether the media took that proper step and
often faced the problem of conflicting information coming from the Sheriff
himself. Social media present an opportunity to differentiate what one individual from an organization states in an interview from the organizational
word. Ryan Huff, who must coordinate over 1,000 social media accounts on

the University of Colorado campus, emphasized the importance of identifying the primary voice and message of the organization ahead of time. He stated that "You have to speak with one voice, especially when you have multiple agencies involved" (R. Huff, Personal Interview, September 8, 2017). Both examples emphasize how social media can provide a primary outlet of information for official sources. When properly managed as part of a media strategy, social media provide tools that these agencies can use to maintain their credibility in the face of misinformation or conflicting information from other sources.

Social media can also potentially reduce the impact of media presence on a community after a mass shooting occurs. At Columbine, the sheer number of individual journalists and police officials using mobile devices overloaded the phone lines. Steve Davis summarized in detail the difficulties of managing the physical presence of the media. He states that "At the height of this thing, we literally had a small city of media in Clement Park" (S. Davis, Personal Interview, September 22, 2017) and estimated that there were over 60 television cameras and an additional 60 satellite vans in the park after the shooting. The physical burden of the sheer number of media intruding into a small, local community during a time of grief cannot be overestimated. Social media, at least to some extent, present an alternative to intrusive media behaviors. These more secondary sources reduce the burden of on-scene reporting to some extent. Ryan Huff stated that

> But you know on the outbound side, on the accounts that we control, [social media's] extremely helpful . . . the call volume is down, they're not calling dispatch as much . . . we can push out message and it's not, we're not just relying on traditional media. Anybody can see this information. (R. Huff, Personal Interview, September 8, 2017)

These media are good for communicating in emergencies while reducing the need for other forms of media. Steve Davis spoke of this benefit to the community in more mundane, everyday events as well, such as traffic jams or amber alerts, where information can be shared among thousands of people in minutes. Overall, the benefits to the community and public safety for law enforcement show that social media have not categorically complicated or disadvantaged gatekeepers after these events. Just as using social media can mitigate media intrusion into victims' lives, these media can aid officials in protecting their communities.

Yet Steve Davis's comparisons to problems with Columbine twenty years ago largely hinges on one important factor, the increasing speed of social media and its impact on inaccuracies in reporting. Even as Davis praised the abilities of social media to connect him and his office with their constituents, he highlighted how his department had been cut out of reporting routines in some ways by the advent of social media. In response to that homicide in which the media collected their information from alternative sources, he explained that they misreported the victim's name by relying on neighbors' accounts. He stated,

> The name they had was wrong . . . the guy that was shot and killed didn't live there . . . That's the gamble that the media takes, and I always caution them, you're not hearing it from me. . . . There's a big risk in trying to be fast. (S. Davis, Personal Interview, September 22, 2017)

This incident echoes many examples, past and present, of inaccurate reporting about other mass shootings, from body counts at the Columbine Massacre to misidentifying Adam Lanza and his mother's relationship to Sandy Hook Elementary School (Berkowitz & Liu, 2014). However, these practitioners expressed their belief that inaccuracies are simply part of fluid situations, not specific to any sort of social media presence or mass shootings, even if the speed of social media can exacerbate these problems. For instance, Ryan Huff stated,

> There's always going to be some inaccuracies in the first moment of an incident . . . if you have injuries and deaths, in those first few moments, don't say a number because it's always going to change . . . and there's always going to be rumors on social media too. (R. Huff, Personal Interview, September 8, 2017)

He finds inaccuracies to be inherent to the situation itself, although he also believes that PIOs acting as gatekeepers have the potential to mitigate the impact of these inaccuracies. Social media increase the volume and frequency of inaccuracies but do not present a new ethical struggle in reporting on mass shootings.

Social media enable certain best practices in rumor control by creating a new outlet to help negotiate the boundary between official sources and potentially inaccurate reporting. Using social media on the scene does not entirely supplant more traditional reporting routines, but can be used to compliment them. For instance, Steve Davis compiles all his Twitter updates into press releases for ease of access. He states,

> a lot of it, I just use Twitter. . . . That doesn't mean I don't come back and summarize everything into a news release. . . . They use it as a reader on the news. . . . I see my news releases copied and pasted verbatim into websites. . . . I'm sure it's quick, they can do it quickly. I don't know. I'm not sure what the drawback would be. (S. Davis, Personal Interview, September 22, 2017)

By providing up to date information on-scene, Davis can disincentivize rumors while also gathering information that he can release in a complete form later. This complete form also helps to disincentivize rumors by providing an easy statement that may not need much additional context. Both of these practices make journalists' jobs easier and support the value of speed. When social media work as a tool to support the speed of reporting, these sources can act as a reinforcement of the official narrative to fight against inaccuracies.

Another potential downside of social media for official sources includes the ways that leaked material can harm the investigative process. Steve Davis discussed the way that liveness can worsen a situation as it develops. He described a situation in which someone filmed a SWAT team gearing up and sent it to the suspect as well as the news media. Again, this issue of liveness has less to do with social media itself and more to do with the struggles of gatekeepers in a world of citizen journalists. Steve Davis's final note on the question of social media highlighted this danger to the role of a PIO as the number one change. He stated,

> Another Columbine today, think of the students that could snap a photo of a deceased person . . . those pictures could be out to the world in a matter of seconds. And with that many students . . . today. It would be almost expected . . . it can make a case in court difficult. That's probably the biggest goal of a person in this role, is the protection of the integrity of a case. (S. Davis, Personal Interview, September 22, 2017)

He did state that this issue of protecting the case represents another highly contextual issue, as 53 percent of the perpetrators of mass shootings have committed suicide and therefore do not go to trial ("Ten years of mass shootings in the United States," 2019).

Recently, the Fort Lauderdale Airport shooting (2017, January 6) demonstrated the problem of leaked official sources. A security guard leaked footage of the shooting to *TMZ*, compromising the investigation into the shooting, and he was subsequently charged with violating Florida public records law (Spencer, 2017). Even as Ryan Huff stated that having multiple angles of video can help the investigation, he cautioned that the decision on how to use that footage had to be made through the coordinating agency or agencies. For instance, Cumiskey and Hjorth (2018) used publicly released bodycam footage of the Pulse Night Club shooting to analyze the incident. Overall, the speed and access of citizen journalists can compromise investigations and lead to a higher volume of inaccuracies and rumors. However, these issues again relate to proper information gatekeeping rather than anything specific to social media. For official sources, the value of public safety often becomes entangled in issues of speed versus accuracy, and they view their decisions as successful when then insulate the community and victims.

FUTURE RESEARCH

This chapter primarily gathered evidence of how various stakeholders respond to the ethical dilemmas related to media coverage of mass shootings in the age of social media. These stakeholders include victims and public information officers but exclude the most important group, journalists. Decision-making for media-makers often occurs behind closed doors. Transparency has increased about these processes through the development of online journalism and the publication of Standards of Practice by journalism Ethics groups such as the Poynter Institute (McBride, 2017). However, future research may want to include the voices of journalists who have covered mass shootings to gain their perspective on using public forms of social media. The question of what journalists consider public versus private in the case of grey areas like Snapchat and other applications with similar privacy settings remains opened. The question of how journalists negotiate the risk of inaccuracies and intrusion while maintaining their credibility also requires more in-depth interviews with those individuals. This chapter takes a first step toward posing the ethical questions that journalists and researchers should consider in their continually evolving discussions of how technology changes media coverage of mass shootings.

Another area of consideration is the fact that Standards and Best Practices cannot adequately account for the contextual or situational factors of reporting on various mass shootings ahead of time. The difficulties summarized in this chapter reflect how complicated it is for media-makers to handle the myriad of different social media sources and assess their status properly. Victims can be more or less open to the media, while also suffering from varying states of distress, and the Ethics of Care framework advocates for responding to individual victims' desires. Some victims might view care as using their social media without bothering them to ask for permission, while others may view the media they created during the incident as highly personal and cathartic, rather than something to be shared for public consumption. Using official sources can also present contextual dilemmas as media makers may not be aware of the status of the shooter or other investigations that could be underway. Future studies may want to consider better ways to account for or anticipate these situational aspects of covering mass shootings. Most material discussing Standards and Practices of covering these incidents focuses on settled issues such as how much coverage to give the shooters and how to interact with victims while limiting intrusion (McBride, 2017). These same sources have yet to address the ethical difficulties of using social media sources in general reporting, let alone the various complexities related to other stakeholders like victims and official sources.

CONCLUSION

This chapter proceeds from a reexamination of the presumption that social media and live streaming have totally shifted journalistic practice in covering mass shootings. Using examples from earlier events such as the Columbine Massacre and the Aurora Theater Shooting, the chapter examined the ways that technology exacerbates, rearranges, and occasionally reprioritizes the same values that have always been central to issues of media coverage about mass shootings rather than shifting the paradigm to "new media." Through interviews with various stakeholders, some of whom have been involved with mass shooting response or advocacy for over twenty years, and others who entered the situation only seven years ago, we can track the progression of these ethical issues. The overwhelming censure of media makers who create a platform for shooter-created material and broadcast these perpetrators' manifestos or livestreams suggests these media sources represent the boundary of respectable practice. Indeed, the use of paradigm repair to reflect on this media practice expresses growing anxieties that media-makers and officials have about the lack of control they maintain as gatekeepers in the social media era. Social media have helped redefine the boundaries of practice while also presenting some unique dilemmas related to other stakeholders.

Practices of gatekeeping have become more complicated in the age of social media for both victims and PIOs. PIOs often insulate victims in the current media landscape, which has helped to improve gatekeeping for them overall. Yet the assumption that social media represent public statements from the victims on these incidents threatens to cut short the process of getting permission from victims in potentially harmful ways that violate values of privacy and respect. PIOs working with official agencies still struggle against the speed of reporting and can be similarly cut out of reporting routines if they do not adapt social media as a tool to provide information quickly. Instead, citizen journalists often provide faster information that can violate the values of public safety and accuracy. This new role for citizens and victims, as media-makers, is the most unique aspect of the problem of social media in mass shooting coverage and cuts across all three stakeholders discussed here.

However, as this historically aware analysis shows, focusing on what makes the issue of social media unique dismisses the reality of mass shootings as media events rooted in the value of liveness from the beginning. To privilege the problems around gatekeeping, accuracy, and credibility over the potential benefits of social media in a crisis misses out on the opportunity to develop new Standards of Practice. Social media function as a tool, one that can increase a sense of privacy and respect for victims or help officials maintain a strong, unified voice that combats inaccuracies. How one uses the tool defines how beneficial or harmful that tool might become. Even as mainstream media criticize and rail against the use of social media as a function of paradigm repair, practitioners do see potential benefits in using social media for reporting on mass shootings.

REFERENCES

Berkowitz, D., & Liu, Z. M. (2014). Media errors and the "nutty professor": Riding the journalistic boundaries of the Sandy Hook shootings. *Journalism, 17*(2), 155–72. https://doi.org/10.1177/1464884914552266

Blinder, A. (2017, November 9). Texas church shooting video raises an unsettling question: Who should see it? *The New York Times.* Retrieved from https://www.nytimes.com/2017/11/09/us/texas-shooting-video-devin-kelley.html

Boyd, D. (2014). *It's complicated: The social lives of networked teens.* New Haven, CT: Yale University Press.

Branson-Potts, H., & Winton, R. (2018, April 26). How Elliot Rodger went from misfit mass murderer to "saint" for group of misogynists—and suspected Toronto killer. *Los Angeles Times.* Retrieved from https://www.latimes.com/local/lanow/la-me-ln-elliot-rodger-incel-20180426-story.html

Chen, A. (2018, April 6). Nasim Aghdam, the YouTube shooting, and the anxiety of demonetization. *The New Yorker.* Retrieved from https://www.newyorker.com/tech/annals-of-technology/nasim-aghdam-the-youtube-shooting-and-the-anxiety-of-demonetization

Chermak, S. M. (1995). *Victims in the news: Crime and the American news media.* Boulder, CO: Westview Press.

Couldry, N. (2004). Liveness, "reality," and the mediated habitus from television to the mobile phone. *The Communication Review, 7*(4), 353–61. https://doi.org/10.1080/10714420490886952

Cumiskey, K., & Hjorth, L. (2018). "I wish they could have answered their phones": Mobile communication in mass shootings. *Death Studies, 43*(7), 414–25. https://doi.org/10.1080/07481187.2018.1541940

Dayan, D., & Katz, E. (1992). *Media events: The live broadcasting of history.* Cambridge, MA: Harvard U.P.

Gregg, M. (2011). *Work's intimacy.* Cambridge, MA: Polity Press.

Hollingsworth, J. (2019, June 18). Man who shared New Zealand mosque shooting video online jailed for 21 months. *CNN.* Retrieved from https://www.cnn.com/2019/06/18/asia/christchurch-livestream-sentence-nz-intl-hnk/index.html

Johnson, A. (2007, Apr. 19). Gunman sent package to NBC News. *NBC News.* Retrieved from http://www.nbcnews.com/id/18195423/ns/us_news-crime_and_courts/t/gunman-sent-package-nbc-news/#.XjNoA2hKiM8

Kass, J. (2009). *Columbine: A true crime story.* Denver: Ghost Road Press.

McBride, Kelly. (2017, October 2). Best practices for covering mass shootings. *Poynter.* Retrieved from https://www.poynter.org/news/best-practices-covering-mass-shootings

Meade, A. (2019, July 11). No media penalty over Christchurch shootings live stream, watchdog says. *The Guardian.* Retrieved from https://www.theguardian.com/media/2019/jul/12/no-media-penalty-over-christchurch-shootings-live-stream-watchdog-suggests

Moritz, M. (2011). From Columbine to Kauhajoki: Amateur videos as acts of terror. In K. Andén-Papadopoulos & M. Pantti (Eds.), *Amateur images and global news* (pp. 143–56). Chicago, IL: University of Chicago Press.

Paton, N. (2012), Media participation of school shooters and their fans: Navigating between self-distinction and imitation to achieve individuation. In G. Muschert & J. Sumiala (Eds.), *School shootings: Mediatized violence in a global age (Studies in Media and Communications, Vol. 7)* (pp. 203–29). Bingley, UK: Emerald Group Publishing Limited. https://doi.org/10.1108/S2050-2060(2012)0000007014

Reinstein, J. (2019, April 29). Someone found the Poway Synagogue shooter's manifesto and called the FBI minutes before the attack began. *Buzzfeed News*. Retrieved from https://www.buzzfeednews.com/article/juliareinstein/8chan-poway-synagogue-shooter-manifesto-fbi

Schildkraut, J., Elsass, H. J., & Meredith, K. (2018). Mass shootings and the media: Why all events are not created equal. *Journal of Crime and Justice, 41*(3), 223–43. https://doi.org/10.1080/0735648X.2017.1284689

Spencer, T. (2017, August 16). Deputy charged with leaking airport shooting video to TMZ. *AP News*. Retrieved from https://www.apnews.com/7ff2fb9dfdb84352b3a48e4b9da216fe

Ten years of mass shootings in the United States (2009–2020). (2019, November 21). *An Everytown for Gun Safety Support Fund*. Retrieved from https://everytownresearch.org/reports/mass-shootings-analysis/

Timberg, C., Harwell, D., Shaban, H. Tran, A. B., & Fung, B. (2019, March 15). The New Zealand shooting shows how YouTube and Facebook spread hate and violent images—yet again. *The Washington Post*. Retrieved from https://www.washingtonpost.com/technology/2019/03/15/facebook-youtube-twitter-amplified-video-christchurch-mosque-shooting/

Tragedy at Virginia Tech. (2007, April 16). [Oprah Winfrey Show]. *Oprah.com*. Retrieved from http://www.oprah.com/oprahshow/tragedy-at-virginia-tech_2/4

Video shows inside bar during shooting. (2018, November 8). [Video File]. *CNN*. Retrieved from https://www.cnn.com/videos/us/2018/11/08/thousand-oaks-shooting-instagram-video-blitzer-mudd-tsr-vpx.cnn

Walsh-Childers, K., Lewis, N. P., & Neely, J. (2011). Listeners, not leeches: What Virginia Tech survivors needed from journalists. *Journal of Mass Media Ethics, 26*(3), 191–205. https://doi.org/10.1080/08900523.2011.581976

White, M. (1999). Television liveness: History, banality, attractions. *Spectator. 20*(1), 39–56. Retrieved from https://cinema.usc.edu/assets/099/15896.pdf

Wilogren, J. (1999, April 25). Terror in Littleton: The group; society of outcasts began with a $99 black coat. *New York Times, Section* 1, p. 30. Retrieved from https://www.nytimes.com/1999/04/25/us/terror-in-littleton-the-group-society-of-outcasts-began-with-a-99-black-coat.html

Wounded Columbine student Mark Taylor. (2010, February 26). [Video File]. *YouTube*. Retrieved from https://www.youtube.com/watch?v=YCO0AN8PJmA

Chapter Five

Research Ethics of Live Streaming Data

Nicolas M. Legewie and Anne Nassauer

Video live streaming on websites such as Facebook Live, Weibo, YouTube Live, iQiyi, Twitch, Mixer, Periscope, Earthcam, Ustream, and YouNow, allows researchers to gain easy and unobtrusive access to real-life situations, processes, and events. Live streaming is part of a greater technological and societal change that is marked by a proliferation of cameras in devices such as web cameras, mobile phones, Closed Circuit Television (CCTV), or body-worn cameras, and the information technologies that enable people to share such content online. This dual development leads to a sharp increase in video recordings of human behavior which are available online. Among other fields, video data are especially fruitful for researchers interested in analyzing situational dynamics and patterns of violence, and have been increasingly used in studies on brawls, violent crime, or mass violence. Yet, while holding great potential for social science research, live streaming videos raise crucial questions of research ethics. Under what circumstances are live streaming videos "fair game" for research? Should researchers refrain from using footage of violent incidents in their research? How should perpetrators' and/or victims' privacy rights be taken into consideration? What about bystanders and people participating in the comments thread during the live streaming? Do researchers need to acquire informed consent before using live streaming videos for research? Existing guidelines and publications only provide partial answers to such questions.

In this chapter, we aim to address this gap and evaluate live streaming videos as a data source from a perspective of research ethics. We draw on existing ethical discussions and reflect on collecting, storing, analyzing, and presenting live streaming data in social science research based on five ethical key areas: informed consent, unique analytic opportunities, privacy, transparency, and potential harm to participants. We suggest a framework to assess issues of research ethics for live streaming videos and other online video data, with the goal to help researchers, reviewers, and readers engage in a systematic reflection of research ethics. We apply this framework to a study of the Christchurch terror attack that took place in New Zealand on March 15, 2019. As a widely debated and extreme example of live streaming, it illustrates the needs and challenges in weighing different areas of research ethics against each other to assess ethics in live streaming.

LITERATURE REVIEW

Novel Types of Video Data

The Internet creates ever-new opportunities for researchers to observe human behavior and interactions. One key area that has profited from this development is research using video data. An ever-expanding pool of visual data (i.e., moving or still images) is being produced with webcams, mobile phone cameras, CCTV, body cameras, and drones. The simultaneous advent of user-generated-content websites made many of these data easily accessible. For example, in 2013, 31 percent of online adults posted a video to a website, and on YouTube alone, more than one hundred hours of video material are uploaded every minute (Anderson, 2015). Many of these videos document real-life social situations and interactions. Thus, online video research can be an attractive, time- and cost-efficient alternative to self-recording videos (Kissmann, 2009; Knoblauch, 2012; Tuma, Schnettler, & Knoblauch, 2013) and to accessing video data through third parties such as police or courts (Levine, Taylor, & Best, 2011; Lindegaard, Vries, & Bernasco, 2018). This development continues to fuel an already vital field of social science research that employs video data, for example, to study violent altercations (Collins, 2008), atrocities (Klusemann, 2009), protest violence (Nassauer, 2016, 2018b), street fights (Levine, Taylor, & Best, 2011), human-machine interaction (Anthony, Kim, & Findlater, 2013), robberies (Lindegaard, Vries, & Bernasco, 2018; Nassauer, 2018a), or education and learning (Elsner & Wertz, 2019; Goldman, Pea, Barron, & Derry, 2007). The potential of online video research has also spurred methodological development-focused on the analysis of behavior, interactions, and situational dynamics (e.g., Derry et al., 2010; LeBaron, Jarzabkowski, Pratt, & Fetzer, 2018; Nassauer & Legewie, 2018, 2019, 2020; Legewie, Naussauer, & Stuerznickel, 2019).

Data from live streaming videos fit this type of novel video data. Live streaming videos are defined as,

> live broadcasts of audio-visual content on the web in which several forms of interactive media like chatrooms, webcam video, twitter feeds, and more converge into a continuous stream of content [. . .] creat[ing] "synthetic situations"

(Cetina, 2009) which stretch over spatial, temporal and social boundaries. (Woermann & Kirschner, 2015, p. 439)

Beneath this broad definition of live streaming lies extensive variation. Live streaming may describe broadcasts of sporting events, broadcasts from individuals who earn an income through their streams (e.g., gamers broadcasting on platforms such as Twitch or influencers providing product reviews as a form of marketing), broadcasts from amateurs who wish to share an experience with the online community, or broadcasts directly from CCTV cameras around the globe. In addition to such everyday examples, a small but significant number of live streaming videos show criminal and violent behavior such as the Christchurch terror attack of March 15, 2019.

Analyzing live streaming videos for social science research, live and/or at a later point in time, can provide numerous advantages. It can allow observing an event unobtrusively, without being influenced by the filming person later deciding whether to post it or not, or editing the footage. It can enable studying the mutual influence between people filmed in the live streaming video and viewer reactions on the comment or Twitter feeds. And, in the case of some live streaming videos of criminal and violent behavior, it affords researchers the extremely rare possibility to analyze behavior, interactions, and situational dynamics during events for which often no other form of first-hand video footage exists. Despite these potentials, uses of live streaming data have been limited so far: for instance, Woermann and Kirschner (2015) conduct a consumer analysis of a live streaming site; and Ringer, Walker, and Nicolaou (2019) use live streaming videos for multimodal player emotion and game context recognition in computer vision. Despite this sparse use of live streaming data, the continuous proliferation of live streaming videos and parallel increase in video-based social research suggest live streaming data will see growing use in the near future. As a result, it becomes necessary to include live streaming data into our reflections of and guidelines on research ethics.

Research Ethics in Online Video Research

Research ethics concern the application of ethical principles to the research process as a reflection of moral rules and values (von Unger, 2014). Core goals are to protect participants from harm, avoid conflict of interest and misrepresentation, respect common laws, and adhere to standards such as professional competence and nondiscrimination (e.g., American Sociological Association [ASA], 1999; British Psychological Society [BPS], 2014; British Psychological Association [BSA], 2017b). General ethical principles and issues are discussed in numerous publications (e.g., Mauthner, Birch, Millner, & Jessop, 2012; von Unger, Narimani, & M'Bayo, 2014) and official guidelines (e.g., [for the field of sociology], ASA, 1999; BSA, 2017b; Deutsche Gesellschaft für Soziologie [DGS] & Bund Deutscher Soziologinnen und Soziologen [BDS], 2017). These provide the overall frame of reference for reflections on online video research.

In a paper on research ethics in online video research, Legewie and Nassauer (2018) distill five ethical areas from the research ethics literature and apply them to online video research: (1) informed consent; (2) privacy; (3) unique opportunities; (4) minimizing harm; and (5) transparency. These five areas derive from four basic ethical principles (Salganik, 2018): (1) beneficence means that a study's benefits should outweigh its risks and that researchers should always try to minimize the risks involved for participants or research subjects; (2) respect for people refers to acknowledging peoples' rights to self-determination, personality, and privacy; (3) justice refers to a fair distribution of a study's risks and benefits; and (4) respect for law and public interest refers to compliance with existing law and transparency-based accountability of research.

There are two further general points to make. First, these ethical areas and principles always have to be evaluated in relation to each other and weighed against each other in the context of a specific study (von Unger, 2014), in what the British Sociological Association calls "situational ethics" in their guidelines for digital research (BSA, 2017a, p. 3). Second, research ethics are continuous, not binary, meaning a study is usually not entirely ethical or unethical but has certain characteristics that fall on a continuum between the two extremes. As Salganik (2018) points out, "binary thinking polarizes discussion, hinders efforts to develop shared norms, promotes intellectual laziness, and absolves researchers whose research is labeled 'ethical' from their responsibility to act more ethically" (p. 324). To avoid antagonistic discussions, it helps to adopt such a continuous understanding and weigh a study's benefits against ethical challenges and risks when assessing research ethics. Of course, an outcome of such an assessment may very well be that a study is too unethical to be implemented, or requires substantial revisions.

Building on this work, we aim to contribute to the field of research ethics in two ways in this chapter: first, we discuss notions of research ethics in the special context of live streaming data; and second, facilitate a transparent, situational, and non-binary discussion, suggests a framework for assessing research ethics for studies with live streaming or other online video data. The framework offers a set of continuous dimensions for the five areas of research ethics introduced above can serve as assessment criteria for researchers to compile a balanced picture of research ethics for a given study. We provide guiding questions for each area. The areas and dimensions are not exhaustive, and future research or specific projects may add additional elements. Further, they do not provide quick rules that offer unambiguous answers to complex ethical questions. Rather, we aim to provide a basis for an informed and transparent discussion about ethics for live streaming and other online video research. To illustrate our framework, we apply it to the case of a study using the live streaming video produced during the Christchurch terror attack that took place in New Zealand on March 15, 2019.

RESEARCH ETHICS AND THE
CHRISTCHURCH TERROR ATTACK

The Christchurch terror attack was committed on March 15, 2019, by a 28-year-old male who was an active contributor to right-wing Internet forums.[1] He entered Al Noor mosque in Christchurch, New Zealand, and shot dead 42 people in a racist hate crime. Upon exiting the mosque, he allegedly shot another person and then drove to nearby Linwood mosque, where he killed another six people. Police rammed the perpetrator's car and detained him while he allegedly was en route to a third target. Two more victims would die of their wounds (Macklin, 2019).

The alleged attacker (in the following "perpetrator") had announced his attack on a right-wing Internet forum and started streaming a video of himself using a helmet-mounted GoPro camera and Facebook Live. The live streaming lasted 17 minutes before cutting off while the perpetrator was driving, at 1:50 p.m. (Macklin, 2019). Thus, digital technology was an important part of the perpetrator's plan and a goal in itself. The live streaming created the grimmest of examples of Cetina's (2009) notion of "synthetic space," with about 200 spectators watching live and commenting on the stream. However, the attack does not stand alone; a 2016 jihadi terrorist attack in France was also partially live streamed. The video also spurred copycats; in the United States, a 19-year-old male allegedly attempted but failed to live stream his attack on a synagogue in Poway, California (Macklin, 2019). Beyond terror attacks and mass shootings, live streaming is also used to broadcast other violent content, such as murder, rape, and suicide.

Before assessing the research ethics of the Christchurch terror attack live streaming video, it should be stressed that there is a fundamental legal barrier to its use which would have to be addressed in a study. New Zealand authorities classified the raw 17-minute live streaming video as "objectionable," making its possession or dissemination a criminal act. People who shared the video without knowing its status were fined up to $10,000, while people who did so when being aware of its status could receive up to 14 years in prison (Macklin, 2019). Hence, it would seem that the best and possibly the only legal way to access the raw live streaming footage is through collaboration with New Zealand authorities. Assuming for now that researchers receive permission to use the video, the key ethical question is: Should they do so?

Informed Consent

A first ethical challenge to live streaming videos, such as the Christchurch video, concerns informed consent. Informed consent pertains to the ethical principle of respect for people and aims to ensure that a person's personality rights and rights to informational self-determination are guaranteed (Gebel et al., 2015). In practice, this means that people should know when they are being researched, they should receive relevant information on the planned research in a comprehensible format, and should then voluntarily agree to participate or decline to do so (Sumner, 2006).

When assessing issues of informed consent, we suggest asking three questions of the data (see Figure 5.1): Does the space filmed require informed consent? If not, was the focus on the space or on the people? And if the space filmed requires consent, did the people give consent? The first relevant question is what type of space was filmed. Public spaces are characterized by unrestricted access, relative cultural and social heterogeneity, and the co-presence of strangers. Private spaces are characterized by restricted access, relative cultural and social homogeneity, and absence of strangers. For instance, spaces such as town squares or public transport are regarded as public, whereas people's homes are regarded as private. Between these poles lies a continuum (Pauwels, 2006); for example, restaurants can be regarded as semi-public spaces because access is usually only lightly restricted. If a video shows a public space, it is usually regarded as permissible to use video data (or collect data) without consent. In contrast, filming private spaces calls for informed consent of the people depicted in the live streaming, and semi-public spaces often require permission by the owner(s). Hence, all things being equal, if a live streamed video was filmed in public space, this makes its use without consent less problematic than if the video was filmed in a private space (Knoblauch, Schnettler, & Raab, 2006; Wiles, Clark, & Prosser, 2011).

A related question is whether the focus of the video was on the space itself, or whether specific people were filmed and followed around in that space. Laws differ on this issue between national contexts; for instance, in the United States, it is permissible to film any person without consent, as long as they move in a public space. In Germany, it requires consent to film specific people, even if they move through a public space (Knoblauch, Schnettler, & Raab, 2006; von Unger, Dilger, & Schönhuth 2016). Hence, researchers should reflect on this issue, as well, and keep in mind the legal and cultural context which the video stems from.

If a video shows a private space or specific people in a public space, it becomes relevant whether people in the live streamed video gave consent to being filmed and to the footage used for research. If all people visible in a video gave informed consent, this shifts the perspective on many, though not all, of the other issues of research ethics, discussed below. It also makes void the other dimensions of informed consent. Due to the often awareness-raising nature of many live streaming videos, either for notoriety, as in violent behavior against oneself or others, or for raising awareness, such as in the Philando Castille shooting on July 6, 2016, in Falcon Heights, Minnesota, many live streaming videos film public spaces, but focus on specific people, and, due to the context of the situation they film, do not ask for consent. Researchers can usually not ask for consent in live streaming videos as it is difficult to track down people visible in a video. If, for such reasons, it is impossible to receive consent, researchers should reflect with extra care about potential ramifications, should they decide to go ahead with their research.

Informed Consent and the Christchurch Live Streaming Video

Most of the live streamed footage of the attack takes place in private and semi-public spaces (e.g., perpetrator's car, two mosques), and the video shows specific people (e.g., the perpetrator, victims).[2] Both aspects call for informed consent. Not asking for, or not receiving, consent would cast doubt on a study from a research ethics standpoint. In the Christchurch attack, it is actually possible to contact victims who have survived (e.g., through author-

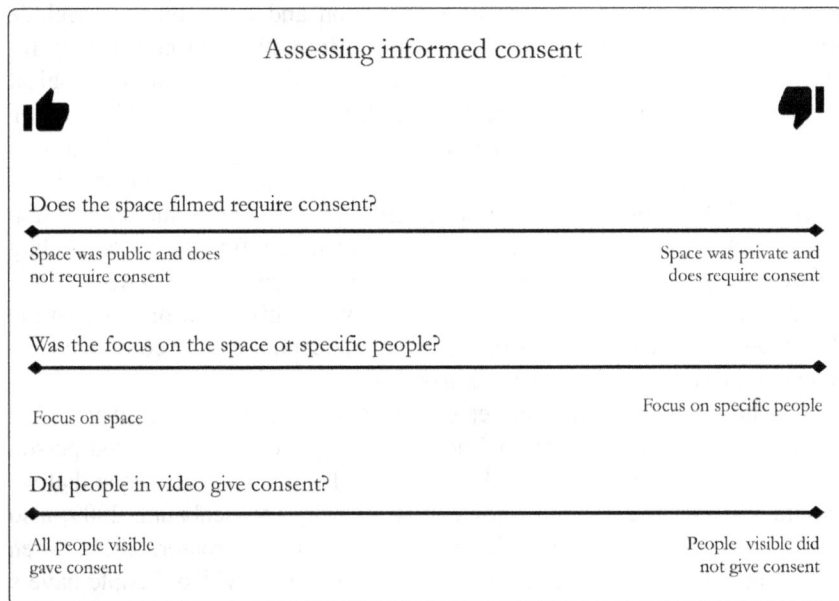

Figure 5.1.   Informed Consent Assessment Sheet. *Source:* **Created by the authors.**

ities or groups), but it entails a further ethical question: could contacting lead to further harm for potentially traumatized individuals (see below)? A further fundamental question is whether to consider the consent of the perpetrator? First, currently, the legal proceedings against the defendant in the Christchurch attack have not been completed. But even if he was, is it the researcher's position to decide when the perpetrator's right to control over the flow of information is forgone?

Using the above suggested assessment sheet shown in Figure 5.1 as a guideline, the Christchurch terror attack would place close to the right pole, regarding space filmed and people visible. Moreover, victims of the shooting can be regarded as a vulnerable group that warrants additional care and protection. Lacking informed consent would move the placement on the third dimension to the right, indicating a problematic position on consent overall in terms of research ethics. On the other hand, asking directly for consent may cause harm to victims and their families, for example, in the form of re-traumatization (BSA, 2017a); potentially more harm than using the video. An alternative may be to ask New Zealand authorities and victim support organizations such as Victim Support (2020) for their assessment.

Privacy

A second challenge for ethical assessments concerns privacy, meaning to respect filmed individuals' private information and allow them to seclude such information. This concerns particular information the person may regard as private. The code of ethics approved by the American Sociological Association membership in June 1997, states, in section 11.01 *Maintaining Confidentiality*, "(g) . . . information is private when an individual can reasonably expect that information will not be made public with personal identifiers" (ASA, 1999, p. 12). Information from public records and information that is not provided under an understanding of confidentiality (including behavior in public places) does not fall under privacy concerns (ASA, 1999, in *11.02 Limits of Confidentiality* (c)). Following this logic, one may argue that people depicted in videos uploaded online cannot expect confidentiality or claim the right to privacy (Bruckman, 2002).

On the other hand, people depicted in a video may not be aware of or agree to a video being posted online. Moreover, even if the depicted person has uploaded the video or agreed to the upload, some scholars argue that we should consider the notion of contextual integrity (Nissenbaum, 2009; also see Pauwels, 2006; Salganik, 2018; Wiles, Clark, & Prosser, 2011) when assessing whether to use data such as a live streaming video. People have a right to control the flow of information on their person, and researchers should reflect on whether there is an appropriate and inappropriate flow of information depending on the context the information originates from (Nissenbaum, 2009; Pauwels, 2006). From this perspective, even information freely accessible online might be considered off-limits because using it would disrupt a person's control over the flow of information.

To assess issues of privacy in live streaming and online video research, we suggest a series of questions around the online and situational context and the content of the live streaming video (see Figure 5.2).[3] To assess the online and situational contexts, we suggest three questions. First, researchers should reflect on users' expectations of the used platform's purpose. Tilley and Woodthorpe (2011) show that the users of some platforms share information with a clear expectation of communicating with a limited group of people. As an example, the authors describe participants in an online support group who posted comments online but still expected to be talking only among others affected, not the general public.

In contrast, on platforms such as YouTube, maximum visibility, at least as a possibility, can be expected to be either the users' explicit goal or an accepted fact. Due to their nature as an awareness-raising medium, we can assume most live streaming videos are filmed for a broader audience, e.g., to show a crime happening. The live streaming may be filmed by the perpetrator (e.g., live streaming videos showing perpetrators rape or murder), or by the victim (e.g., live streaming videos showing someone being shot by police); in both cases, the expectations are to share information with a wide audience. In contrast, the person being filmed might usually not be aware of or expect broad public distribution.

Second, a further important aspect is how access to the platform is organized. On one side are open access platforms such as YouTube and Live-Leaks, open-access forums, and open-access Facebook and Instagram accounts. On the other side are restricted-access platforms such as private Facebook and Instagram accounts or membership-only forums. For instance, users may share information with their circle of Facebook friends, but do not expect this information to be accessible publicly (Zimmer, 2010). Thus, accessing live streaming data on such a restricted-access platform takes it beyond its intended audience.

Third, researchers should reflect on the nature of the social context filmed. For instance, demonstration marches are events with the purpose to achieve visibility and communicate grievances or needs to the public. Similarly, videos of professional YouTubers are usually intended to reach as large an audience as possible, even though they are often filmed in a private space. In contrast, a video of a family dinner may well be intended for a very small audience of family and friends, even if it is live streamed online (Wiles, Clark, & Prosser 2011). Assuming all things being equal, if a video depicts a situation or event that has the purpose or entails the expectation of public visibility, this makes its use despite lack of consent less problematic than if the video depicts a context that was meant for a limited audience or that people expect to be private.

When assessing video content regarding privacy, the first question to consider is whether the video contains private and person-specific information, such as faces, voice, attire and personal belongings, and information transmitted verbally. Such information can be used for de-anonymization and, therefore, may clash with privacy rights. In some videos, the characteristics of people will be easy to discern, while in others, it will be more difficult or even impossible. For instance, faces may not be visible because a person has the back turned toward the camera, the resolution of the video is too poor, or the scene has been filmed from too great a distance. Voices may not be audible because a person does not speak or the video does not contain audio. Bodies and clothing may not be visible because the video shows a crowd and people in the foreground block most bodies from view.

Second, in some cases, non-video data may provide additional information on the people shown in a video. For instance, if a live streaming video shows an altercation between citizens and police officers, newspaper articles may be available to provide additional information on both parties. Together with the personal information from the video, researchers may have quite detailed information on a given person, together with personal identifiers such as the person's face and voice. In other cases, obtaining such additional information may not be possible, for example, the situation or event shown in the video has not received public attention.

In a similar vein, researchers can reflect on available information on the location and context shown in a video. The main concern, again, is confidentiality and the danger of de-anonymization. If a video or easily accessible non-video data provides information on the geographic location from which the live streaming was broadcast, the name of the event, or the date it took place, this contextual information may facilitate de-anonymization and thus challenge confidentiality. For instance, if a student live streams a video from her or his school, the name of the school may be visible on a building façade, a door sign, or a banner, and may thus provide additional personal information on the student.

Privacy and the Christchurch Live Streaming Video

Regarding online and situational context, the Christchurch video was originally streamed via Facebook Live and was later disseminated via YouTube and Facebook, and presumably further sites. The audience was hence general, although only about 200 people watched the initial streaming video (Macklin, 2019). Access to the platform was open, but the social context filmed was not aimed toward public visibility. Hence, a study using the live streaming data would score toward the unproblematic pole on the first two

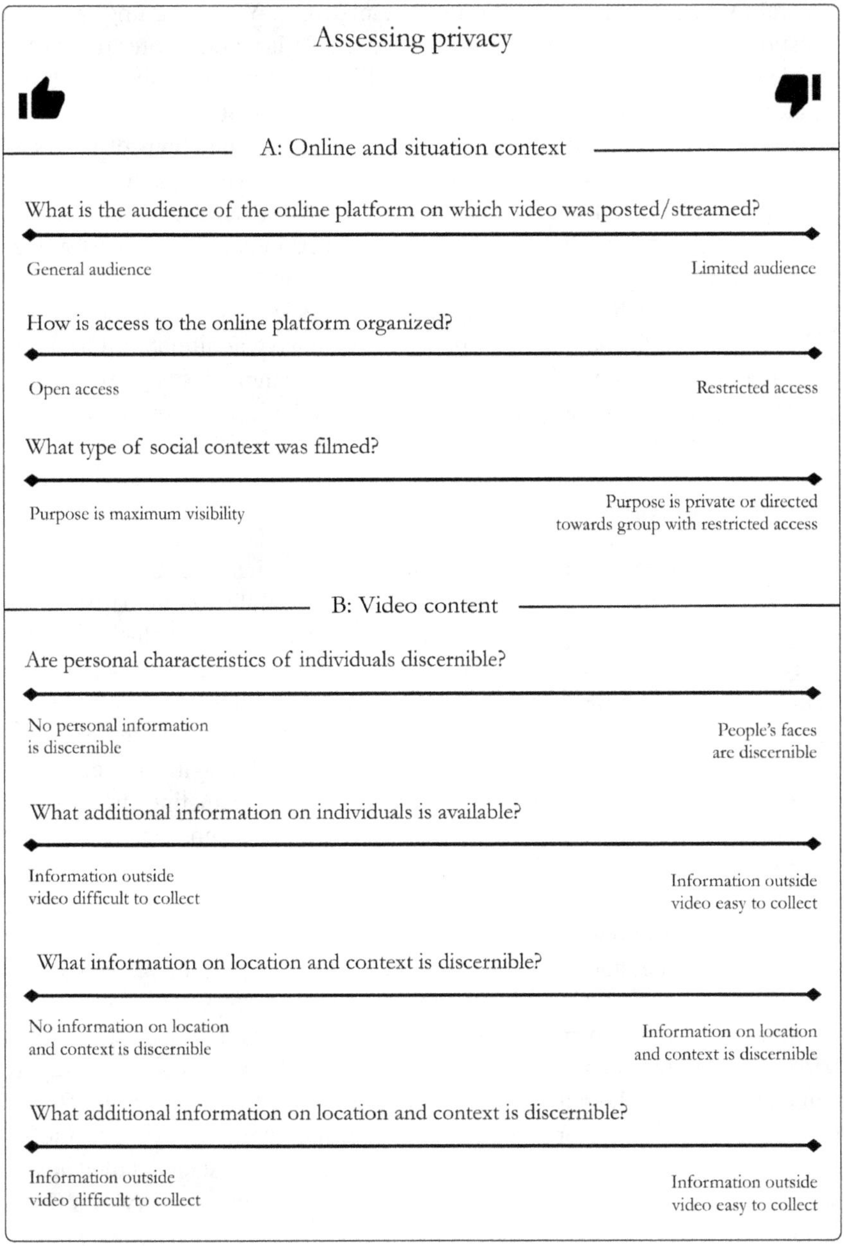

Assessing privacy

A: Online and situation context

What is the audience of the online platform on which video was posted/streamed?

General audience   Limited audience

How is access to the online platform organized?

Open access   Restricted access

What type of social context was filmed?

Purpose is maximum visibility   Purpose is private or directed
                                                towards group with restricted access

B: Video content

Are personal characteristics of individuals discernible?

No personal information   People's faces
is discernible   are discernible

What additional information on individuals is available?

Information outside   Information outside
video difficult to collect   video easy to collect

What information on location and context is discernible?

No information on location   Information on location
and context is discernible   and context is discernible

What additional information on location and context is discernible?

Information outside   Information outside
video difficult to collect   video easy to collect

Figure 5.2.   Privacy Assessment Sheet. *Source*: Created by the authors.

questions regarding online audience and platform, due to its vast intended general audience and organization of the platform. Yet, regarding the third question in the privacy heuristic (see Figure 5.2) it would score toward the problematic pole regarding social context filmed, because the footage shows a place of worship, which does not aim at maximum visibility.

Much more important in this example, however, are questions of the video content. We know that the alleged perpetrator's face is visible, and we have to assume that the victim's faces are discernable. Moreover, since the attack received extensive media attention, additional information on the event, as well as people involved in it, is easily available. The same is true for the location and social context in which the attacks took place. We have to assume that the video contains information about both, and extensive additional information is available from non-video sources. Hence, a potential study of the live streaming video would fall on the problematic end of the spectrum on all four video-content-related dimensions of privacy (see Figure 5.2).

Unique Opportunities

Does a study offer unique potential for scientific insights and/or real-life benefits, and could other data replace the video fully or in parts of the analysis? The underlying notion of unique opportunities is that even if a study may be problematic in some area of research ethics, the better-safe-than-sorry approach of dropping a project, e.g., due to a lack of consent, is not always the most ethical choice (Salganik, 2018). Reflecting the principle of beneficence (Gebel et al., 2015; Salganik, 2018), if studying a live streaming video promises the best insights into an issue, conducting the research despite it not meeting other ethical criteria may be the more ethical option, the potential benefits outweigh possible risks.

Figure 5.3 illustrates three questions we suggest asking in the context of assessing unique opportunities in live streamed video data. First, what unique potential does the study offer for scientific insight? In general, video data may provide unique analytic potential for studying micro-situational processes or dynamics of social events (e.g., Collins, 2008; Nassauer, 2018a). Videos enable researchers to study captured events frame-by-frame, replay situations, observe them in slow-motion, focus on different actors at different replays, examine behavior and emotion expression that only last very briefly, and meticulously focus on temporal dynamics of events. Such detailed analyses are virtually impossible with participant observation or interviews (Nassauer & Legewie, 2018).

Online video research, in particular, may offer unique opportunities to study rare events. Data on events such as mass panics are often readily available online. Moreover, they often entail little reactivity, which is a desirable data characteristic and crucial for the valid analysis of social situations

(Nassauer & Legewie, 2018). Live streaming data may offer a further unique potential because they comprise a synthetic situation in which streamer and commenters can interact in real-time. This may allow new ways of studying phenomena such as social influence and pressure in real-life settings. Researchers should reflect whether a given study exhibits one or several of these unique opportunities and, crucially, whether this allows for better scientific analyses that promise to answer meaningful theoretical and empirical questions.

Second, what unique real-life benefits could the study provide? Based on the potential characteristics just described, online video data may offer new real-life benefits. Hence, just as with scientific insights, researchers should reflect whether a given study exhibits one or several of the characteristics and whether this helps us solving real-life problems. For instance, given that a number of recent live streaming videos feature never-before documented criminal or violent behavior, their analysis might allow for finding patterns that can help avoid or stop such events.

Third, could other data replace video data fully or in part? This question serves as a double-check, especially if a study fails to meet other criteria of good practice in research ethics. If less problematic data could be used to replace the video in question fully or partially, that video provides less unique opportunities. In such cases, if a study shows problematic aspects of research ethics because of its use of a live streaming video, other data means should be used.

Unique Opportunities and the Christchurch Live Streaming Video

The Christchurch terror attack exemplifies an extremely rare event. Accordingly, the live streaming footage of the attack comprises unique data. There is a scientific approach and a productive field of research that study interactional sequences in violent situations (e.g., Collins, 2008; Levine, Taylor, & Best 2011; Nassauer, 2016; among many others). Hence, from an academic perspective, the live streaming video offers unique opportunities to study situational dynamics during terror attacks as a special case, but also as an example of lethal violence in general. A potential study of the Christchurch terror attack live streaming video would hence score positively on the first question raised and provide unique opportunities for scientific insights.

More importantly, analyzing the video could promise insights into developing options for behavior during attacks (run, fight, hide?), and possible measures to stop them when underway. The analysis might thus provide real-life benefits by informing law enforcement and citizens in similar situations how to minimize harm/the impact of such an attack, stop an attack underway or guarantee their safety. While such findings are never a guarantee, there is a clear possibility that research on live streaming data could help us move

Assessing unique opportunities

What scientific insights does the study promise?

Important new insights   No new insights

What real-life benefits could the study provide?

Research promises to benefit   No benefit of research to
study group and/or society   study group and/or society

Could other data provide the same insights?

No other data could provide insights   Other data could provide insights

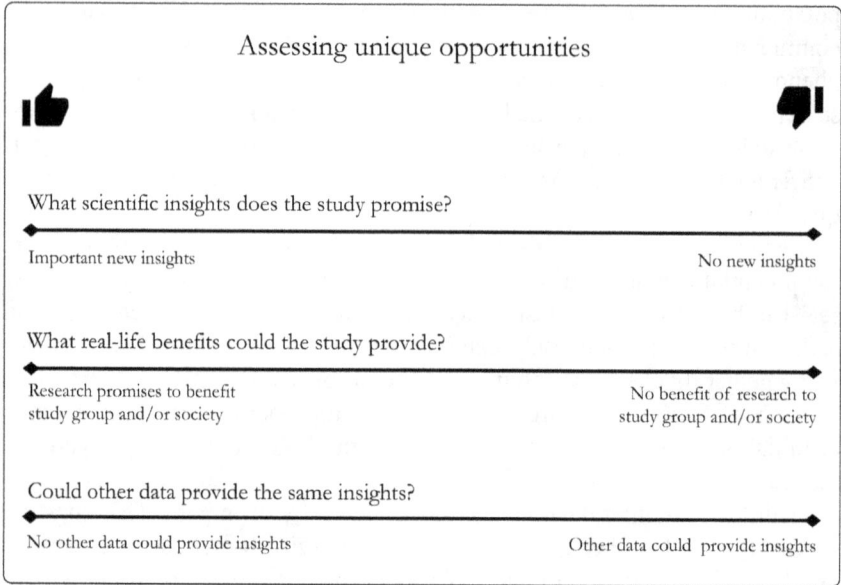

Figure 5.3.   Unique Opportunities Assessment Sheet. *Source:* **Created by the authors.**

toward such options and measures. For instance, Nassauer's (2015) research on situational dynamics during protest marches using online video data (among other data types) resulted in guidelines for protesters and police on how to keep protests peaceful. Hence, there is a clear possibility of real-life benefit of studying the Christchurch live streaming footage, which suggests a study score toward the positive, left-hand pole on this dimension.

Lastly, past research suggests that no other type of data can provide the above insights. For instance, ex-post testimonials from perpetrators and victims could be an alternative, but research suggests they are very unreliable as data sources on what happened when and how (Nassauer & Legewie, 2018). In a somewhat similar event, the terrorist attack on the Westgate Mall in Nairobi, Kenya, in 2013, which left 67 dead and 175 wounded, evaluations of CCTV footage showed that accounts shoppers who managed to escape the mall while the attack was underway were wildly inaccurate, despite the witnesses' best intentions (Gatehouse, 2013; Krulwich & Abumrad, 2014). Hence, a study of the Christchurch video would be positioned close to the positive pole regarding alternative data sources. Overall, an analysis of the attack would thus score very favorably in all ethical aspects concerning unique opportunities.

Potential Harm

Potential harm refers to possible ways in which a study may hurt the study subjects, researchers, or third parties. Since one of the main goals in research ethics is to minimize harm, a rigorous assessment of potential harm is essential for any study. Figure 5.4 collects three guiding questions we suggest for assessing potential harm specific to video research: (1) What kind of behavior is depicted? (2) Could data harm people or groups depicted in the video? (3) How publicly available is the video prior to research? First, asking about the behavior and interactions depicted in videos, the main concern is whether depicted behavior and interactions may risk harm to people shown in a video if it is used in a scientific study and possibly shared with reviewers, readers, and conference audiences. Such harm can be social (e.g., embarrassment), mental (traumatization or re-traumatization), economic (e.g., losing jobs), or legal (e.g., criminal prosecution) (see Legewie & Nassauer, 2018). While people may differ in what kinds of behavior and interactions they regard as embarrassing, common sense suggests that some behavior is more likely to be unproblematic (e.g., everyday behavior such as talking to each other or playing sports) whereas other behavior may be regarded as embarrassing (e.g., bullying or being bullied). Special caution should be taken when considering using videos that depict criminal behavior or behavior that may be regarded as deviant (e.g., assault, drug use, protesting in some political contexts).

Second, researchers should reflect on whether third-party actions may harm people as a result of the study, for example, by being prosecuted. If the behavior and interactions depicted are potentially harmful and potential third-party threats exist, a further question is how meaningful the information and captured behavior is to parties that may inflict harm. For instance, in Nassauer's (2018b) robbery study, filmed perpetrators might later be subject to prosecution. However, it seems highly unlikely that law enforcement did not have access to better and more complete video footage of the robberies, as well as further information on these events. Moreover, it seems highly unlikely that the risk of police becoming aware of a robbery through the study is comparable to the everyday risks of being prosecuted based on standard police investigations because of a committed robbery. In the case of live streaming videos particularly, several videos of violent or criminal behaviors are uploaded by the perpetrator, thus making an audience aware of their behavior and making it unlikely that a study would risk prosecution that is not already happening. However, a study might expose a person filmed by the perpetrator to harm by third-parties, such as shaming or threatening a filmed victim.

Third, a question connected to the first two points is how visible a given video is at the point a researcher considers it for inclusion in the study. Videos streamed through well-known platforms such as Facebook Live,

Weibo, YouTube Live, or iQiyi usually have more views than videos posted to smaller platforms or forums. Some videos are also featured in TV news coverage, and others are posted multiple times by multiple users, further adding to the video's dissemination. The total number of views and TV coverage a video receives should impact the assessment of potential harm entailed in the study. All things being equal, using videos from platforms with more traffic should be regarded as less ethically problematic than using videos from platforms with less traffic, because potential additional exposure due to research is small relative to prior visibility.

Potential Harm and the Christchurch Live Streaming Video

The first aspect we suggested to consider when assessing potential harm is what is shown in the video. The events visible in the Christchurch terror attack live streaming video are brutal, violent, and shocking. The content, therefore, qualifies as potentially traumatic, embarrassing, deviant, and criminal, placing the video at the far-right end of this dimension's continuum.

A second aspect is considering if analyzing the data could potentially harm the people or group depicted, or others not visible in the video. Using the video for research may potentially harm victims and their families, who may be re-traumatized by the knowledge of a study being conducted, or the

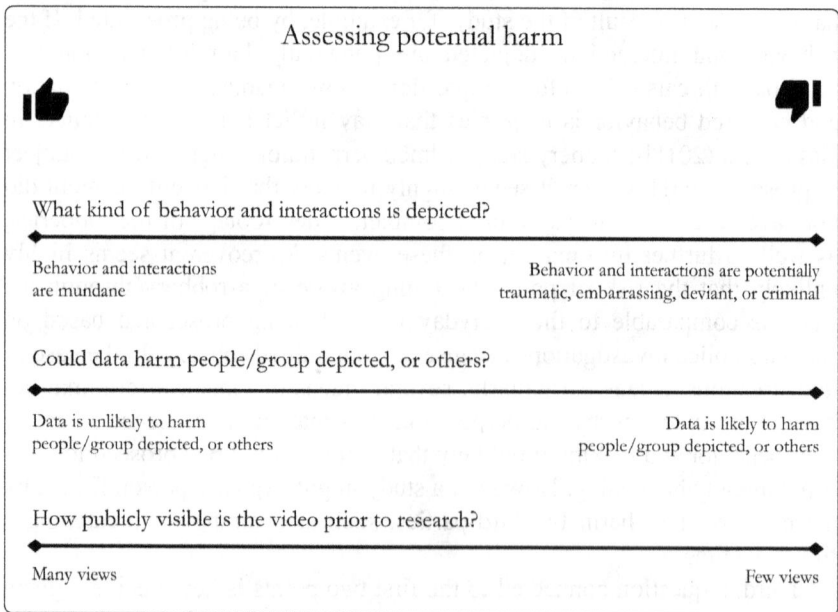

Figure 5.4. **Potential Harm Assessment Sheet.** *Source*: Created by the authors.

mere request for consent a researcher may send, directly or through intermediaries. However, so would any other type of research on the topic; for
instance, a study using newspaper reports or interviews with survivors could
remind them of the event. This factor would thus ethically question any type
of study on any event that was traumatizing for individuals. But a large part
of the research is especially interested in such events to be able to understand
and avoid them in the future (see benefits discussed above). Using videos or
live streaming of such events might overall even be ethically favorable, since
it would not directly involve potentially traumatized survivors to recall the
event, in contrast to, for example, retrospective interviewing.

We also suggest considering potential harm to the alleged perpetrator. In
the Christchurch example, further harm to the perpetrator due to the footage
being studied by scientists seems unlikely, since he is already being prosecuted, and law enforcement is already aware of the footage. But there is an
additional consideration to be made connected to the perpetrator. Conducting
research on the event may afford further prominence to the perpetrator and
could contribute to more copycat attacks. One way to address this may be not
to mention the perpetrator's name, an approach we take here.

As we discussed above (unique opportunities), studying the video may
allow researchers to identify patterns in which the attack unfolds and might
help law enforcement and victims react more effectively during future events
of this nature. But on the flip side of this coin, the same study may also be
used by future copycat attackers during their preparation for an attack (e.g.,
some school shooters have been found to read research on previous shootings). We can, however, assume that the real-life benefits of preparing law-
enforcement may outweigh the less-frequent use of a study by future attackers to maximize harm.

Viewing video content can also potentially be harmful to the researchers
involved in the study, as well as attendees at workshops and conferences if
they are shown parts of the footage. Special consideration should be given to
scholars paid or requested to analyze such footage, such as hired research
assistants or students under supervision, who may be less likely to express
their discomfort with watching the footage because of their dependency on
the professional relation to the PI or supervisor. Thus, without a doubt, the
Christchurch live streaming video exemplifies the problematic extreme pole
of behavior and interactions depicted in a video, and the potential it has to
hurt people.[4]

The third question we suggest to ask is how publicly visible the video is
prior to a potential study. The Christchurch live streaming was viewed by
about 200 people and received around 4,000 views in total before it was
taken down the Facebook website. It saw much broader dissemination
through mirror uploads on YouTube, Facebook, and other websites; Facebook removed a total of 1.5 million videos of the attack within the first 24

hours. On YouTube, one copy per second was uploaded in the hours after the live streaming. In addition to the videos, the live streaming received attention through comment threads on Discord, 8chan, and Reddit, among many other sites (Macklin, 2019). The event itself saw a global echo, too, with virtually every news outlet reporting on it. This substantial dissemination suggests placing a potential study on the unproblematic end of the spectrum for additional exposure since further dissemination through research would be minimal compared to already existing dissemination.

Overall this assessment on potential harm places the Christchurch attack on the problematic ends of the spectrum in the first two dimensions and the unproblematic end of the spectrum in the third dimension.

Transparency

Transparency refers to making goals, procedures, and data as accessible to the public as possible, thereby improving traceability and openness of scientific processes and findings (ASA, 1999, in *13.05 Data Sharing*; Salganik, 2018). Video data holds unique potential for transparency in research. Because videos can capture situations precisely as they happened, multiple researchers can analyze the same raw data.[5] This fosters cooperation and exchange on research projects and allows testing inter-coder reliability, if desired. Moreover, it facilitates traceability of research processes and findings (Heath, Hindmarsh, & Luff, 2010). Online video data such as live streaming takes this potential one step further because sharing videos with reviewers and readers is incredibly easy. Authors need only provide a list of links or compile a playlist of relevant videos, and any reader with Internet access will be able to inspect the researcher's raw data. This potential of online video research to offer maximum transparency through easy access to primary data is a giant step forward for the ideal of making research reliable through the traceability from the raw data to the conclusions drawn from research findings (Lincoln & Guba, 1985). However, concerns such as ownership, consent, anonymity, and sensitivity of information have to be factored into the consideration when deciding whether data can and should be published. Hence, other characteristics of online video data may limit the extent to which researchers can realize the transparency potential.

Figure 5.5 collecting questions we suggest can guide the assessment of transparency issues in online video research: Can permanent access to the video be assured? Can the researcher share the data with reviewers? Can the researcher share the data with the broader research community? Can the researcher share the data during talks at conferences or workshops? First, a basic concern is if researchers have the possibility to download or otherwise obtain a video file, for example, to archive and anonymize it. Downloading videos from YouTube and other platforms violates most platforms' terms of service (e.g., YouTube, 2019) as well as the uploaders' or creators' copy-right. Alternatives may be to contact people who uploaded a video to ask for a copy of the file. If no copy of the file can be obtained, it is still possible to share the primary data by providing links to all videos used in a study (Bramsen, 2017; Nassauer, 2018b). However, some links may be disconnected over time, which could lead to certain videos not being accessible anymore. It may, therefore, be useful to focus on videos that have been uploaded multiple times, or have been uploaded by larger providers (e.g., large news media outlets), which may be more likely to keep the account and footage online.

The first step toward transparency in video data is to be able to share the primary data with reviewers, should they raise questions about some aspect of data quality or the analysis. The next, and crucial, step is whether data can be shared with readers of scientific publications. Third, is it possible to show data at conferences and workshops? For each step, issues may arise which limit researchers in taking full advantage of the potential for transparency inherent in video data. In some cases, data ownership may limit the transparency potential of online video data. For instance, if the live streaming videos a researcher uses for a study are secondary data that are part of the data set another research team has invested time and resources to compile over time, that research team may not agree to the data being shared openly with all readers. In other cases, privacy protection may limit how freely researchers can share online video data (see above). For instance, if a researcher gathered video data from a closed forum on mental health support, that video data set would contain highly private information, as well as key personal identifiers (people's faces, possible their real names, among others). In such cases, it may not be possible to realize the full transparency potential of video data. Finally, researchers should consider video content when contemplating if and how to share data. The less the videos contain behavior and interactions that are potentially traumatic, embarrassing, deviant, or criminal, the more sharing the data is in line with minimizing the harm of study subjects. When sharing videos with the research community is possible in principle, but considerations of privacy or potential harm pose limitations, and it may be feasible to employ a "walled garden" approach in which data access requires signing a data protection agreement and/or is limited to researchers with specific research interests (Salganik, 2018, p. 313).

Transparency and the Christchurch Live Streaming Video

The Christchurch live streaming video is archived by New Zealand authorities and is thus, in principle, accessible to other researchers. However, there are heavy limitations on sharing it with reviewers and readers, both for reasons of privacy protection and potential harm (see above). Additionally, there are severe legal limitations on who can possess and share the footage.

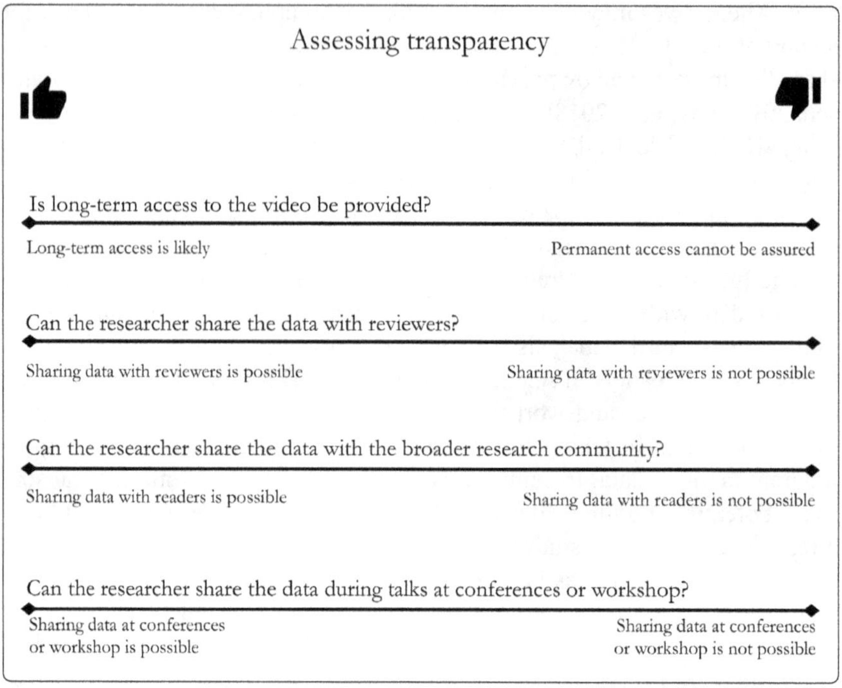

Figure 5.5.   Transparency Assessment Sheet. *Source*: **Created by the authors.**

Thus, the Christchurch live streaming video is an extreme case of great potential for, but ultimately limited room to realize, transparency. However, this is the only case of live streaming footage we are aware of which has been made illegal to possess or disseminate. Live streaming footage will usually be much less limited in its potential for transparent data sharing. Even violent live streaming videos, such as the aftermath of the shooting of Philando Castille by a U.S. police officer in 2016, are available online and can be transparently and openly shared with interested readers, researchers, and audiences.

Weighing Areas and Dimensions for Final Assessment

The areas introduced in the previous sections can help compile a profile of a study's ethical challenges and risks. For an assessment of the study, areas that pose challenges and risks have to be weighed against those that imply ethical benefits. The above assessment sheets can facilitate this process. By assessing where a study stands on each area discussed, and weighing areas against each other, researchers can assess a study in ethical terms. Researchers may also weigh specific aspects more or less strongly, or to consider a low score in one of the areas as a reason not to conduct the study, or a high score in other areas as a reason to conduct the study in any case. These choices are for each researcher, reviewer, supervisor, or review board member to make and justify, but it is fruitful to make such decisions based on an informed and transparent evaluation of ethical concerns, as presented here.

Following our assessment framework, a potential study of the Christchurch terror attack live streaming video faces the difficult task of weighing stark strengths and weaknesses in research ethics. Given that the Christchurch attack is, in many ways, an extreme example of live streamed video footage, it allows highlighting the broad range of options to assess such footage. Legal concerns taken aside, we argue that on the one hand, a study of this live stream could promise truly unique academic insights and real-life benefits, and the video and event have received global dissemination and attention. These aspects suggest that it would be ethically justified for researchers to analyze the footage. On the other hand, the video shows exceptionally brutal and potentially traumatic behavior and interactions and, thus, studying it is potentially harmful to researchers (and in this case, to a lesser degree to victims and the alleged perpetrator). Faces and locations are clearly visible in the footage, thus hindering privacy. It seems that a careful assessment of potential harm is called for, for example, by contacting authorities, victim support organizations, and/or mental health professionals to ask about possible ramifications of conducting the study and of contacting victims for consent (since asking for consent from victims might also harm them, as it reminds them of the traumatic experience).

As mentioned, the Christchurch attack is an extreme example. For other live streaming videos, we would rank potential harm and underline great transparency, as an aspect of research ethics commonly speaking for their use. Ultimately, our framework does not imply clear-cut, universally accepted decisions on research ethics for live streaming or other online video data. Rather, the idea is to provide a transparent basis for conversation and assessment that facilitates the work of researchers, reviewers, and review board members.

CONCLUSION

Live streaming videos will become increasingly common and will likely be used more frequently as data sources for social science research. But under what circumstances are live streaming videos "fair game" for research? What insights from existing work on research ethics can researchers apply to this new form of data? In this chapter, we addressed this gap by developing a framework that can be used to assess issues of research ethics for live streaming videos and other online video data that aims to help researchers, reviewers, and readers to engage in a systematic reflection of research ethics. We apply this framework to a study of the Christchurch terror attack that took place in New Zealand on March 15, 2019. As a widely debated and extreme example of live streaming videos, the attack illustrates the need to and challenges in weighing different areas of research ethics against each other in order to assess a study using live streaming videos.

In this chapter, we showed that using a framework with clear dimensions can help make the discussion systematic, transparent, and non-binary. Further, the example illustrates how in a given case one area of research ethics may outweigh other areas that may, in turn, become more relevant in a different research scenario. The suggested framework facilitates such "situational ethics" (BSA, 2017a, p. 3) by providing a basis for transparent assessment of specific studies.

NOTES

1. Since the defendant pleaded "not guilty" to the multiple charges of murder and attempted murder and one charge of carrying out a terrorist attack, the details from the event described here are treated as allegations taken from newspaper and scientific reports. Further, because perpetrators often aim to gain notoriety through their actions, we will refrain from using the alleged attackers name (see also https://www.dontnamethem.org).

2. In other similar cases, police officers or first responders may also be visible.

3. Of course, the first issue to consider is legality of access. Researchers should familiarize themselves with a platform's terms of service, for example, regarding how access to the platform is managed, who holds copyrights, and whether there are restrictions regarding use of the data.

4. To reduce some of this potential harm, researchers could receive supervision and mental health support, and researchers could only use transcripts, instead of real footage, at conferences and workshops.

5. In contrast, in participant observation—which also focuses on analyzing behavior and may focus on situational dynamics—readers must rely on a researcher's subjective perception of the situation and his or her accuracy in documenting and describing situations, which is necessarily limited by the human capacity to record situational details (LeCompte & Goetz, 1982; Lipinski & Nelson, 1974).

REFERENCES

American Sociological Association (ASA). (1999). *Code of Ethics and Policies and Procedures of the ASA Committee on Professional Ethics*. Retrieved from https://www.asanet.org/sites/default/files/savvy/images/asa/docs/pdf/CodeofEthics.pdf

Anderson, M. (2015, February 12). 5 facts about online video for Youtube's 10th birthday. *Pew Research Center* (blog). Retrieved from http://www.pewresearch.org/fact-tank/2015/02/12/5-facts-about-online-video-for-youtubes-10th-birthday/

Anthony, L., Kim, Y., & Findlater, L. (2013). Analyzing user-generated Youtube videos to understand touchscreen use by people with Motor Impairments. In J. A. Konstan, E. Chi, & K. Höök (Eds.), *Proceedings of the SIGCHI conference on human factors in computing systems* (pp. 1223–32). New York: ACM Press.

Bramsen, I. (2017). How violence breeds violence: Micro-dynamics and reciprocity of violent interaction in the Arab uprisings. *International Journal of Conflict and Violence, 11*, 1–11. https://doi.org/10.4119/ijcv-3094

British Psychological Society (BPS). (2014). *Code of Human Research Ethics.* Retrieved from https://www.bps.org.uk/sites/bps.org.uk/files/Policy/Policy%20-%20Files/BPS%20Code%20of %20Human%20Research%20Ethics.pdf

British Sociological Association (BSA). (2017a). *Ethics guidelines and collated resources for digital research: Statement of Ethical Practice Annexe.* Retrieved from https:// www.britsoc.co.uk/media/24309/bsa_statement_of_ethical_practice_annexe.pdf

British Sociological Association (BSA). (2017b). *Statement of Ethical Practice.* Retrieved from https://www.britsoc.co.uk/media/24310/bsa_statement_of_ethical_practice.pdf

Bruckman, A. (2002). Studying the amateur artist: A perspective on disguising data collected in Human Subjects Research on the Internet. *Ethics and Information Technology, 4* (3), 217–31. https://doi.org/10.1023/A:1021316409277

Cetina, K. K. (2009). The synthetic situation: Interactionism for a global world. *Symbolic Interaction, 32*(1), 61–87. https://doi.org/10.1525/si.2009.32.1.61

Collins, R. (2008). *Violence: A micro-sociological theory.* Princeton, NJ: Princeton University Press.

Derry, S. J., Pea, R. D., Barron, B., Engle, R. A., Erickson, F., Goldman, R., . . . Sherin, B. L. (2010). Conducting video research in the learning sciences: Guidance on selection, analysis, technology, and ethics. *Journal of the Learning Sciences, 19*(1), 3–53. https://doi.org/ 10.1080/10508400903452884

Deutsche Gesellschaft für Soziologie (DGS), & Bund Deutscher Soziologinnen und Soziologen (BDS). (2017). *Ethik-Kodex der Deutschen Gesellschaft für Soziologie (DGS) und des Berufsverbandes Deutscher Soziologinnen und Soziologen (BDS).*

Elsner, C., & Wertz, A. E. (2019). The seeds of social learning: Infants exhibit more social looking for plants than other object types. *Cognition, 183*, 244–55. https://doi.org/10.1016/ j.cognition.2018.09.016

Gatehouse, G. (2013, October 5). Kenya military names Westgate Mall attack suspects. *BBC News*.

Gebel, T., Grenzer, M., Kreusch, J., Liebig, S., Schuster, H., Tscherwinka, R., . . . Witzel, A. (2015). Verboten ist, was nicht ausdrücklich erlaubt ist: Datenschutz in qualitativen Interviews. *Forum Qualitative Sozialforschung / Forum: Qualitative Social Research, 16*(2). http://dx.doi.org/10.17169/fqs-16.2.2266

Goldman, R., Pea, R., Barron, B., & Derry, S. J., (Eds). (2007). *Video research in the learning sciences.* New York/London: Routledge.

Heath, C., Hindmarsh, J., & Luff, P. (2010). *Video in qualitative research: Analyzing social interaction in everyday life.* [*Introducing Qualitative Methods series*]. Los Angeles: SAGE.

Kissmann, U. T. (Ed). (2009). *Video interaction analysis: Methods and methodology.* Frankfurt/Main: Peter Lang.

Klusemann, S. (2009). Atrocities and confrontational tension. *Frontiers in Behavioral Neuroscience, 3*(42). https://doi.org/10.3389/neuro.08.042.2009

Knoblauch, H. (2012). Introduction to the special issue of qualitative research: Video-analysis and videography. *Qualitative Research, 12*(3), 251–54. https://doi.org/10.1177/ 1468794111436144

Knoblauch, H., Schnettler, B., & Raab, J. (2006). Video analysis. Methodological aspects of interpretative audiovisual analysis in social research. In H. Knoblauch, B. Schnettler, J. Raab, & H.-G. Soeffner (Eds.), *Video-analysis: Methodology and methods. Qualitative Audiovisual Data Analysis in Sociology* (pp. 9–28). Frankfurt/Main: Peter Lang.

Krulwich, R., & Abumrad, J. (2014, November 29). Outside Westgate. *Radiolab.* Retrieved from https://www.wnycstudios.org/podcasts/radiolab/articles/outside-westgate

LeBaron, C., Jarzabkowski, P., Pratt, M. G., & Fetzer, G. (2018). An introduction to video methods in organizational research. *Organizational Research Methods, 21*(2), 239–60. https://doi.org/10.1177/1094428117745649

LeCompte, M. D., & Goetz, J. P. (1982). Problems of reliability and validity in ethnographic research. *Review of Educational Research, 52*(1), 31–60. https://doi.org/10.3102/00346543052001031

Legewie, N. M., & Nassauer, A. (2018). YouTube, Google, Facebook: 21st century online video research and research ethics. *Forum Qualitative Sozialforschung / Forum: Qualitative Social Research, 19*(3). http://dx.doi.org/10.17169/fqs-19.3.3130

Legewie, N. M., Nassauer, A., & Stuerznickel, M. (2019). Opportunities for analyzing visual data in the 21st century. Report on the 2019 blankensee-colloquium on capturing and analyzing social change. SSRN working paper. https://ssrn.com/abstract=3489981.

Levine, M., Taylor, P. J., & Best, R. (2011). Third parties, violence, and conflict resolution: The role of group size and collective action in the microregulation of violence. *Psychological Science, 22* (3), 406–12. https://doi.org/10.1177/0956797611398495

Lincoln, Y. S., & Guba, E. G. (1985). *Naturalistic inquiry.* Newbury Park: SAGE.

Lindegaard, M., de Vries, T. D., & Bernasco, W. (2018). Patterns of force, sequences of resistance: Revisiting Luckenbill with robberies caught on camera. *Deviant Behavior, 39*(4), 421–36. https://doi.org/10.1080/01639625.2017.1407100

Lipinski, D., & Nelson, R. (1974). Problems in the use of naturalistic observation as a means of behavioral assessment. *Behavior Therapy, 5*(3), 341–51. https://doi.org/10.1016/S0005-7894(74)80003-1

Macklin, G. (2019). The Christchurch attacks: Livestream terror in the viral video age. *CTC Sentinel, 12*(6), 18–29. Retrieved from https://ctc.usma.edu/christchurch-attacks-livestream-terror-viral-video-age/ or https://ctc.usma.edu/app/uploads/2019/07/CTC-SENTINEL-062019.pdf

Mauthner, M., Birch, M., Millner, T., & Jessop, J. (Eds.). (2012). *Ethics in qualitative research.* London: SAGE.

Nassauer, A. (2015). Effective crowd policing: Empirical insights on avoiding protest violence. *Policing: An International Journal of Police Strategies & Management, 38*(1), 3–23. https://doi.org/10.1108/PIJPSM-06-2014-0065

Nassauer, A. (2016). From peaceful marches to violent clashes: A micro-situational analysis. *Social Movement Studies, 15*(5), 515–30. https://doi.org/10.1080/14742837.2016.1150161

Nassauer, A. (2018a). Situational dynamics and the emergence of violence during protests. *Psychology of Violence, 8*(3), 293–304. http://dx.doi.org/10.1037/vio0000176

Nassauer, A. (2018b). How robberies succeed or fail: Analyzing crime caught on CCTV.

Nassauer, A., & Legewie, N. M. (20202). Methodologische Entwicklungen in der Gewaltforschung: Videodatenanalyse, mixed methods und big data. In A. Braun & T. Kron (Eds.), "Bestandsaufnahme soziologischer Gewaltforschung," Special Issue, Österreichische Zeitschrift für Soziologie.
Journal of Research in Crime and Delinquency, 55(1), 125–54. https://doi.org/10.1177/0022427817715754

Nassauer, A., & Legewie, N. M. (2018, May 17). Video data analysis: A methodological frame for a novel research trend. *Sociological Methods & Research.* https://doi.org/10.1177/0049124118769093

Nassauer, A., & Legewie, N. M. (2019). Analyzing 21st century video data on situational dynamics—issues and challenges in video data analysis. *Social Sciences, 8*(3), 100. https://doi.org/10.3390/socsci8030100

Nissenbaum, H. (2009). *Privacy in context: Technology, policy, and the integrity of social life.* Stanford: Stanford University Press.

Pauwels, L. (2006). Ethical issues of online (visual) research. *Visual Anthropology, 19*(3–4), 365–69. https://doi.org/10.1080/08949460600656691

Ringer, C., Walker, J. A., & Nicolaou, M. A. (2019). Multimodal joint emotion and game context recognition in league of legends livestreams. *ArXiv:1905.13694 [Cs].* Retrieved from http://arxiv.org/abs/1905.13694

Salganik, M. J. (2018). *Bit by bit: Social research in the digital age.* Princeton, NJ: Princeton University Press.

Sumner, M. (2006). Ethics. In V. Jupp (Ed.), *The SAGE dictionary of social research methods* (pp. 96–97). Thousand Oaks: SAGE.

Tilley, L., & Woodthorpe, K. (2011). Is it the end for anonymity as we know it? A critical examination of the ethical principle of anonymity in the context of 21st century demands on the qualitative researcher. *Qualitative Research, 11*(2), 197–212. https://doi.org/10.1177/1468794110394073

Tuma, R., Schnettler, B., & Knoblauch, H. (2013). *Videographie: Einführung in die interpretative videoanalyse sozialer situationen.* Wiesbaden: Springer VS.

Victim Support / Manaaki Tāngata (2020). Standing Together. Our Response to the Christchurch Terror Attacks. Retrieved May 29, 2020 (https://www.victimsupport.org.nz).

Von Unger, H. (2014). Forschungsethik in der qualitativen forschung: Grundsätze, debatten und offene Fragen. In H. von Unger, P. Narimani, & R. M´Bayo (Eds.), *Forschungsethik in der qualitativen forschung: Reflexivität, perspektiven, positionen* (pp. 15–40). Wiesbaden: Springer VS.

Von Unger, H., Dilger, H., & Schönhuth, M. (2016). Ethics reviews in the social and cultural sciences? A sociological and anthropological contribution to the debate. *Forum Qualitative Sozialforschung / Forum: Qualitative Social Research, 17*(3). http://dx.doi.org/10.17169/fqs-17.3.2719

Von Unger, H., Narimani, P., & M´Bayo, R. (Eds.). (2014). *Forschungsethik in der qualitativen forschung: Reflexivität, perspektiven, positionen.* Wiesbaden: Springer VS.

Wiles, R., Clark, A., & Prosser, J. (2011). Visual research ethics at the crossroads. In E. Margolis, & Luc Pauwels (Eds.), *The SAGE handbook of visual research methods* (pp. 685–706). Los Angeles: SAGE.

Woermann, N., & Kirschner, H. (2015). Online livestreams, community practices, and assemblages. Towards a site ontology of consumer community. *Advances in Consumer Research, 43*, 438–42. Retrieved from http://acrwebsite.org/volumes/1019801/volumes/v43/NA-43

YouTube. (2019, December 10). Terms of service 2018. Retrieved from https://www.youtube.com/static?template=terms

Zimmer, M. (2010). "But the data is already public": On the ethics of research in Facebook. *Ethics and Information Technology, 12*(4), 313–25. https://doi.org/10.1007/s10676-010-9227-5

Chapter Six

Fixed? The Law of Live Streaming

Brian N. Larson and Genelle I. Belmas

INTRODUCTION

Much of the law and ethics of live streaming can be seen to revolve around the question of *fixation*. The English verb "to fix" can mean to concentrate one's attention, and it is this characteristic of streaming video that draws our attention to it and holds it there. It can mean to secure from change or put in a quasi-permanent form, and it is this sense in which copyright law generally considers streaming video "fixed in a tangible medium of expression" (Copyright Law of United States, 2016, Section 102 (a)), contrary to the suggestion of transitoriness in the medium's name. "To fix" can also mean to make or to repair something, and it is in this sense that we can hope that ethics and law might fix some of the harms that live streaming may cause.

In this chapter, we explore the U.S. law regarding live streaming, with some references to laws of other jurisdictions. We talk about the contexts and technologies involved in streaming and live streaming, the law of streaming generally, and then the law of live streaming specifically. As we shall see, a legal analysis generally turns on one or more of the following questions: Was the videographer or person(s) depicted engaging in illegal activity on the scene? Was the videographer present lawfully on the scene with a legal right to record the activity? Did the videographer have the right to distribute it? Does the videographer have rights in the resulting media, such as copyright, that others must respect? Were the media processor or content delivery network legally responsible for the consequences of the video's distribution? Is anyone else responsible for the consequences of the video's distribution? How may researchers use the video arising from live streaming, if at all?

Our discussion of the law is grounded, naturally, in the world before COVID-19. We have tried, however, to note ways that it might change in response to the most significant worldwide pandemic in a century. Along the way, we also discuss the ways in which U.S. law does and does not take account of concerns raised in other chapters of this volume. The central challenge here is that there is only an oblique connection between law and ethics. The law does not fix ethical problems because ethics and law are not directly fixed to each other. The law is not a floor or ceiling for ethical principles, just as ethics are neither floor nor ceiling for legal rules. In simpler terms, the law outlines what *must* happen, while ethics is concerned with what *should* happen. While lawmakers may take into consideration ethical norms and concerns when drafting statutes, they need not do so, and courts are under no obligation to temper their interpretations of legal doctrine with ethical principles, as Ken Zeran (*Zeran v. America Online*, 1997) and Matthew Herrick (*Herrick v. Grindr LLC*, 2019), discussed later, found to their dismay.

We conclude with a discussion on Section 230 of the Communications Decency Act (1996), which immunizes social media and other internet platforms from liability in the United States for the actions of their users. Section 230 illustrates the challenges of the scale of the internet: at the one end, individuals and groups that are sometimes terribly traumatized and harmed by the conduct of users of social media, including live streamers; at the other end, social media and similar platforms that we instinctively understand are unable to police all the content that flows through them. Supporters of Section 230 fix on the extent to which it may be "the twenty-six words that created the Internet" (Kosseff, 2019). Critics of Section 230 fix on its function in creating a "moral hazard" (Franks, 2019, p. 166) that allows social media platforms and internet service providers to shift the social costs of their users' misconduct onto other users and disincentivizes the platforms and providers from acting to protect their users.

Our goal has been to provide a fairly comprehensive overview of the laws affecting live streaming, but of course, we cannot, in this brief essay, hope to summarize or even identify *all* the aspects of the law that intersect with live streaming. We hope instead to provide a foundation on which other scholars may ground their own efforts.

THE CONTEXT AND TECH OF STREAMING

As Christians (2020) notes in the introduction of this volume, "Theorizing live stream communication and seeking a pathway forward requires a competent understanding of the larger technological framework that live streaming represents." We also believe it is helpful to offer some description of the context and technology before trying to explain its legal implications. 'Streaming' is usually used to refer to a service where a media consumer with a player (computer, smartphone, etc.) simultaneously downloads and plays audio or video over the internet on the player. When the consumer selects the media, it begins downloading, but before the file has been fully downloaded, it begins to play on the player after some of the content is buffered on it (Miller, 2018). The result is services like Spotify, Hulu, Netflix, and so on. In these cases, the media have already been produced, recorded, and saved on the applicable service's content servers. In the case of live streaming, events are being recorded and transmitted to consumers as they are happening. According to *The Guardian*, sports network ESPN was the first to *live stream* an event on the internet, a baseball game in 1995 (Zambelli, 2013). Since then, many other services have engaged in live streaming events. So live streaming is, in that sense, not a new phenomenon.

From a legal perspective, distributing media—audio, video, or both—on the internet in live streaming form functions much the same as delivering it in a streaming form generally and requires quite-similar technology. Except where noted, the following summary of the process relates to both streaming and live streaming but refers only to "video"—though largely the same issues surround audio streaming—and we italicize the terms that we will use here for standard roles on their first use. At the *scene* of the events, *subjects*—often, but not always human beings—engage in some kind of *activity*, and a *videographer* records the activity with a camera or other device capable of capturing video and converting it to a digital signal. High-end video devices can generate vast amounts of data per second, so it is generally encoded in compressed form, and the videographer transmits it to a *media processor* (Miller, 2018). The media processor may then operate on the video in a variety of ways: for example, transizing the media to optimize it for different player displays; transrating the media for different speeds of data transmission; and transmuxing, to package the media in different technical protocols.[1] The media processor then delivers the video over the internet using a *content delivery network*, often involving multiple copies of the media on different servers, sometimes in different parts of the world. Finally, the *media consumer* uses some kind of *player*, which downloads data from the content delivery network, decodes and decompresses it, and displays it to the consumer.

All the segments of the streaming process could be part of the same business enterprise. Consider a corporation live streaming an address from the CEO to its employees. All the people involved are employees of the corporation. In practice, the corporation may hire contractors for some or all of the videography, media processing, and content delivery, but the corporation remains in control. In this scenario, the media consumers are also the corporation's employees.

Most often, however, we imagine that the media consumer will be outside that enterprise. For example, perhaps employees of the sports network

ESPN—a subsidiary of Disney—perform before cameras operated by other ESPN staff, sending data over a proprietary network to Disney media servers, which then transize, transrate, transmux, and distribute them over a proprietary content delivery network to Disney's customers. Here, the media consumers are not part of the Disney enterprise, but every other segment of the process is under Disney's control. In news reporting using streaming media, the subjects (other than news reporters) and activity at the scene are generally not under the control of the videographer, but the videographer and other production segments remain under the news outlet's control.

Finally, in the social-media context, one more segment of the production and distribution falls outside control of the owner of the media servers and content delivery network: that of the videographer. So, in this instance, the subject at the scene engages in an activity, and the videographer (who may be the same person—video "selfie" is common) transmits it to the media processor, which has little control or even awareness of its content. For example, one report claims that as of May 2019, users of YouTube uploaded 500 *hours* of video every minute (Clement, 2019). At that rate, it would take more than 130,000 employees, working fulltime, viewing eight hours of video a day, to review the material appearing on YouTube alone. Instead, as mentioned in the introduction by Christians (2020), we have "the world of machineness behind machines" that efficiently bureaucratizes this process, making it financially possible for YouTube to operate.

What has changed in the last four to five years is the availability to consumers generally of the ability to *live stream* over social media platforms like Facebook[2] and Twitter, though Amazon subsidiary Twitch.tv made such options available at least for some as early as 2011, and Twitch's predecessor justin.tv as early as 2007. A consequence of this development is that some videographers, who are often subjects on the scene, can engage in criminal or shocking acts and transmit them simultaneously. For example, generally, a person committing suicide on camera or a person recording himself engaged in a shooting spree at a mosque might not be expected to survive the incident on the scene, go home, and upload the video to YouTube or the like. Live streaming makes it possible for the videographer to distribute media of those shocking events without taking any additional steps, while they are happening.

As we shall see, the law has something to say about every stage of the live streaming process.

THE LAW OF STREAMING

Whether we are speaking of streaming generally or live streaming more particularly, the law is concerned with many of the same questions: Was the subject engaging in illegal activity on the scene? Was the videographer present lawfully on the scene with a legal right to record the activity? Did the videographer have the right to distribute the video? Does the videographer have rights in the resulting media, such as copyright, that others must respect? Were the media processor or content delivery network legally responsible for the consequences of the video's distribution? Is anyone else responsible for the consequences of the video's distribution? How may researchers use the video arising from live streaming?

Other chapters in this volume have approached these questions from an ethical perspective. For example, Christians (2020), in the introduction of this volume, places the ethics of live streaming, and all the segments in the streaming process, in a broader context of electronic communication. Corr and Michaels (2020), in Chapter 2, address all the segments of the streaming process in relation to the streaming of suicides, though their focus is perhaps best seen as falling on the media processor, content delivery network, and media consumer. Weinhold (2020), in Chapter 3, addresses the presence of journalists on the scene and as videographers, both in ethical and legal dimensions. Finally, Legewie and Nassauer (2020), in Chapter 5, consider ethical implications of the downstream use by researchers of live streamed video.

This chapter describes the legal dimensions of some of these same questions in more detail, focusing first on questions about the creation of the media, then on its distribution, and finally on its impact on the media consumers or consequences for those involved.

Creation

Legal questions surrounding the creation of media begin with the subjects and their activity, and proceed to the videographer's right to be present on the scene and to make a video of it. Assuming the creation of the media is lawful, there is also some question regarding the videographer's legal rights, particularly copyright, in the resulting media.

Some activities are illegal, and making media of those activities is also illegal. For example, sex with minors is illegal in most jurisdictions (see, for example, Texas Statutes, Penal Code § 22.01 [Assault], 2019), and the production of video involving sex with minors—child pornography—is also illegal (see, for example, United States Code, 2020, Title 18 § 2251(a), pp. 813–22).[3] Note that streaming, whether of the live variety or not, always involves making a recording. The digital signal created by the camera or recording device is reduced to a digital file or files on the recording device, and there are often many digital intermediary copies of the recording during the streaming process on the way to the media consumer. Thus, it is not necessary from the live streaming perspective for the child-pornography statute to make a distinction between "producing any visual depiction" and "transmitting a live visual depiction"[4] (United States Code, 2020, Title 18 § 2251(a), p. 813).

In other cases, whether the videographers may legally record a video depends on whether they are legally present in the place where they record. A videographer is thus not entitled to trespass on private property to make a video, and if the videographer is on a property with the owner's permission—called a "license"—the owner may still withhold the permission to record. For example, when concert-goers buy their concert tickets, they obtain a license to enter the concert venue, which is typically limited to prevent the concert-goers from making video recordings of the concert. If they make a video during the concert in violation of these limitations, they may be liable to the venue for damages, though these are hard to calculate (Franchim, 2017). Government regulations may also limit the ability to make video recordings in some spaces under government control. For example, U.S. Customs and Border Protection advises travelers not to use cameras in passport control (2007). Generally, however, "filming of government officials engaged in their duties in a public place, including police officers performing their responsibilities," is protected by the First Amendment (*Glik v. Cunniffe*, 2011, p. 82).

Even in public spaces, though, the making of certain kinds of recordings is prohibited. So, in many courtrooms, it is not permitted to use a camera. Even in those courtrooms that permit cameras, as Weinhold (2020) has noted in her chapter, sometimes only those the court has credentialed as journalists are permitted to use them.[5] Restrictions exist in less formal public spaces, too. For example, the Massachusetts Supreme Judicial Court ruled in March 2014 that the State could not use existing laws to punish a man using public transit who "aimed his cellular telephone camera at the crotch area of a seated female passenger and attempted secretly to photograph or videotape a visual image of the area" (*Commonwealth v. Robertson*, 2014, p. 372). The Massachusetts legislature promptly passed a statute to prohibit the practice, called by some "up-skirting" (Massachusetts General Laws Ch. 272 § 105, 2019; Ravitz, 2014).

In many cases, the consent of a subject will make it permissible to make video, and in the case of private conversations, the consent of one or all of the subjects may be necessary. So, a video made with the subject's knowledge and consent would not be a violation of the Massachusetts up-skirting statute. In some states, a private conversation can be recorded if any of the participants in it consents (see, for example, Minnesota Statutes § 626A.02 Interception and Disclosure of Wire, Electronic, or Oral Communications Prohibited, Subd. 2(d). Exemptions, 2019). In others, every participant in a private conversation must consent to the recording (see, for example, Maryland Statutes, Courts & Judicial Proceedings § 10-402 (c) (3), 2019, p. 611).

A series of legal questions quite apart from whether the videographer has the right to make the recording is whether the videographer *acquires* any rights—particularly copyrights—in the recordings they create. The owner of a copyright has exclusive rights to duplicate and distribute their copyrighted work (Copyright Law of United States, 17 U.S. Code § 106, 2016). A copyright springs into being the moment that the author's original work is "fixed in any tangible medium of expression" (Copyright Law of United States, 17 U.S. Code § 102 (a), 2016). Recording of images and sounds in digital form counts as fixation (*Midway v. Strohon*, 1983). It is worth noting that live streaming always creates a digital recording, and indeed, often many digital intermediary copies of the recording, on the way to the media consumer. This is true even if the recordings are later deleted. So, a videographer who is not making the video in the course of employment for someone else probably owns copyrights in the resulting video.[6]

Even if the streamed video is subject to copyright, others may still use it under certain circumstances. So, for example, in the case of *Kanongataa v. A.B.C.* (2017), the videographer live streamed his partner giving birth to their child on Facebook. Several media outlets posted images and excerpts from the video with stories that commented on the social phenomenon of live streaming, especially in the context of such a personal moment (Mullin, 2017). The court concluded in that case that the copies of Kanongataa's work were fair use under the Copyright Law (Copyright Law of United States, 17 U.S. Code § 107, 2016).

Distribution

In the previous section, we considered whether a videographer had the right to create media and, if so, whether they held copyrights in it. Here, we consider whether the videographer, media processor, and content delivery network are permitted to distribute the media. There are, first, some public interests to consider, and then, the private, reciprocal interests of these parties.

Some laws that prohibit the creation of certain types of video also criminalize their distribution by videographers, media processors, and content delivery networks. Thus, the U.S. statute that prohibits making child pornography also prohibits its distribution, the Massachusetts law that prohibits making "up-skirting" videos also makes it criminal to distribute those videos, and the Maryland statute (2019) that prohibits recording private conversations without consent makes it criminal to distribute those recordings. In most cases, though, those laws criminalize distribution only where the distributor is aware of the unlawful circumstances of the videos' creation. Consequently, it is unlikely that YouTube or Facebook is going to be held criminally accountable for distribution unless they have been informed of a video's criminal nature.[7]

In other cases, distribution might be prohibited on other grounds in some countries but not others. So, for example, several European countries, including France and Germany, have public laws prohibiting Holocaust denial (Bazyler, n.d.). Assuming that a video fits that definition, Facebook would likely suppress it at least in those countries to satisfy their governments (Stampler, 2014; Facebook Transparency, 2020). Similarly, as Daggett (2020) notes in Chapter 4, white supremacist Phillip Neville Arps was convicted under New Zealand's Films, Videos, and Publications Classification Act 1993 (2018) for "distributing objectionable content" (see also Bayer, 2020). The Act defines a publication as objectionable "if it describes, depicts, expresses, or otherwise deals with matters such as sex, horror, crime, cruelty, or violence in such a manner that the availability of the publication is likely to be injurious to the public good" ([New Zealand] Films, Videos, and Publications Classification Act 1993, 2018, Section 3 Meaning of objectionable, (1), p. 13). The statute further calls on judges to weigh heavily the issue of whether the publication "represents (whether directly or by implication) that members of any particular class of the public are inherently inferior to other members of the public by reason of any characteristic of members of that class" (Section 3(3)(e), p. 15), an assessment clearly implicated in the Christchurch mosque shootings.

Such a statute would not, however, pass constitutional muster in the United States, which permits content-based restriction of free speech only in limited circumstances: for example, obscenity and child pornography. Such laws must withstand a searching constitutional review called *strict scrutiny*. For example, the state may punish physically violent crimes and crimes against property more aggressively when the offender utters hate speech in conjunction with them (*Wisconsin v. Mitchell*, 1993). Speech—and other expressive conduct, like videos, whether live streamed or not—by itself cannot, however, be punished. This long-standing constitutional rule has been applied in hundreds of cases when laws that single out speech for what it conveys are challenged. A good example dates from 1972 when the Supreme Court declared that the First Amendment, coupled with the Fourteenth Amendment's Equal Protection Clause, prohibited an ordinance that exempted *peaceful labor* picketing from a ban on *all* picketing around schools (*Police Dept. of Chicago v. Mosley*, 1972). As the Court put it, "the First Amendment means that government has no power to restrict expression because of its message, its ideas, its subject matter, or its content" (p. 95).[8]

Media processors and content delivery networks like Facebook usually retain broad discretion to suppress or ban content for a wide variety of reasons and could, in theory, be held legally accountable for the distribution of materials. As private actors, they are not bound in the United States by the free-speech provisions of the First Amendment: "It is, of course, a commonplace that the constitutional guarantee of free speech is a guarantee only against abridgment by government, federal or state" (*Hudgens v. N.L.R.B.*, 1976, p. 513). Nevertheless, the Communications Decency Act (1996), discussed below, excuses most media processors and content delivery networks from liability in these cases in the United States, unless they play an active role in creating or editing the content.

Most of the remaining legal issues associated with distribution arise from bilateral relations among the parties involved. So, for example, under a Missouri statute, the subjects of a video might consent to a videographer making it for private use, but the videographer would not be allowed to distribute it without further consent from the subjects (Missouri Rev. St. §573.110, 2020). Such a distribution could also result in civil liability in states, such as Minnesota, that recognize the privacy tort of publication of private facts (*Lake v. Wal-Mart*, 1998). Publication of private facts is an invasion of privacy when one "gives publicity to a matter concerning the private life of another . . . if the matter publicized is of a kind that (a) would be highly offensive to a reasonable person, and (b) is not of legitimate concern to the public" (p. 231). Violation of this right gives the person whose private life was publicized a right to damages against the infringer.

Assuming the videographer and the media processor are not under the control of the same entity, their relationship will probably be bound by some kind of contract. Facebook users, for example, are bound by its terms of use and community standards, with the latter prohibiting posts (including video) that depict hate speech, violent conduct, and sexual activity ([Facebook] Community Standards, 2020). Thus, even a videographer who has the consent of subjects to distribute a video of their sexual activity may not be able to do so on Facebook.

Of course, assuming the videographer has copyright in the video produced, they may also impose limits on the distribution of their video (Copyright Law of United States, U.S. Code §106, 2016). Media processors and content delivery networks like Facebook usually secure a license from the videographer, permitting them to make quite-broad use of uploaded media according to their terms of use. Facebook's terms of use say that the videographer, for example, grants Facebook "a non-exclusive, transferable, sublicensable, royalty-free, and worldwide license to host, use, distribute, modify, run, copy, publicly perform or display, translate, and create derivative works of" uploaded content, including media ([Facebook] Terms of Service, 2020, 3/3/1. "Permission to use content you create and share," para. 4). Given the nature of Facebook as a platform where folks share content—with the service and with each other, it does not seem unreasonable for the platform to demand this license. It does not claim to limit any other uses that the videographer might make of their own copyrights.

Impacts or Consequences

Even assuming that media are lawfully recorded and that the videographer is within their rights to distribute, we can ask to what extent the videographer is liable for direct effects of video/distribution. In the United States, there are some bases upon which governments have considered punishing or been able to punish the producers of videos. A pending bill in Massachusetts, for example, would, under certain circumstances, charge with a felony someone who "intentionally coerces or encourages [a] person to commit or attempt to commit suicide" if the person then attempts suicide (Mass. Senate Bill S.2382, 2019, An Act Relative to Preventing Suicide, p. 3). Government restrictions of this kind in the United States may run up against constitutional limitations under the First Amendment, which generally protects free speech. In fact, this Massachusetts statute is a response to a case where teenager Michelle Carter encouraged her boyfriend, Conrad Roy III, to commit suicide; a jury convicted her of manslaughter in that case, and she appealed both to the Massachusetts Supreme Judicial Court and to the U.S. Supreme Court on First Amendment grounds, both without success (*Carter v. Massachusetts*, 2020).

Other consequences may be a civil liability to the videographer if the media contain defamatory remarks—false remarks that cause damage to their subject—about a third party in social media (*Walsh v. Latham*, 2014).

In fact, any generally applicable law that targets certain kinds of speech as either criminal or subject to civil liability is quite likely to apply if the speech appears in media that streams live or in social media. It is difficult to see how courts would distinguish such speech from the traditional means of communicating.

Note that in the United States, media processors and content delivery networks, provided they meet certain statutory requirements, are not themselves generally liable for the content that their user's post. This is a result of immunity under Section 230 of the Communications Decency Act (1996), which we discuss further below.

Another impact or consequence of distribution is how academic researchers may or may not use live streamed video. Legewie and Nassauer (2020), in Chapter 5, raise one area where the law and ethics are, to some extent, congruent in the United States. As Larson (2017) noted: "As a practical matter, most research universities in the United States require that all research involving human participants be subject to IRB review" (p. 32). This requirement arises from what is sometimes known as the "Common Rule," a U.S. federal regulation that requires certain practices in federally funded research involving human subjects or participants (Protection of Human Subjects, 45 CFR, Part 46 § 102, 2009). As a legal matter, though, this requirement is limited to "human subjects," which the regulation defines as an "individual about whom an investigator . . . conducting research [o]btains information . . . through intervention or interaction . . . or [o]btains, uses, studies, analyzes, or generates identifiable private information" (45 CFR, Part 46 § 102, 2009, p. 4).

As Legewie and Nassauer (2020) point out in Chapter 5, much of the video that might be of interest to researchers is available online and where materials and data are available publicly and thus require no intervention or interaction with the subjects and no access to private information; consequently, they are probably not the "research involving human subjects" in the sense of the Common Rule. Scholarly societies like the ones Legewie and Nassauer (2020) identified (and the journals those societies publish) may have more stringent ethical requirements, but they are not the law. Several scholars have urged researchers to see the law as a floor upon which greater ethical standards should be built. Fiesler and Proferes (2018), for example, explored Twitter users' perceptions of research ethics on the platform, suggesting several "best practices," including asking users for permission before using their content, despite the fact that the law for researchers does not require it (p. 10).

Recent changes to the Common Rule in 2018 have been criticized as "increasing access to identifiable private information under broad consent and . . . limiting oversight, [so that] the Final Rule alleviates administrative burdens for both researchers and the IRB" (Azim, 2018, p. 1724). It is perhaps too early to assess empirically what the effects of the new Common Rule have been. The 2018 amendments came nearly 30 years after the previous version, and further amendment is unlikely in the near future (Evans, 2013).

At least in the United States, researchers probably do not need to worry about one other issue that Legewie and Nassauer (2020) raise: Making copies of videos from online that have been live streamed by the videographers for purposes of conducting research is almost certainly fair use under U.S. copyright law. Research is one of the activities singled out in the statutory definition of fair use (Copyright Law of United States, 17 U.S. Code § 107, 2016), and there is a "strong presumption" that research use of a copyright-protected work is the kind of use the fair-use doctrine is meant to protect (*Wright v. Warner Books*, 1991, p. 736). The researchers might not be able themselves to *distribute* the videos upon which their research is based because the fair-use analysis permits only the amount of copying necessary to achieve the purpose for which the fair use is being made. For example, the Second Circuit in *Authors Guild v. Google* (2015) concluded that Google Books could make complete copies of books because that is the only way that it could index them online. But the court took notice of the fact that a reader could not actually read all the consecutive pages of the copyright-protected books using the Google Books tool. This implicates Legewie and Nassauer's

(2020) goal of transparency. Hosting whole copies of videos used in research on the researchers' or a journal's site permits those sites to function as a substitute for the site where the videographer originally posted the video, a factor often held against fair use; and merely linking to the original site arguably provides the same benefits for transparency. On the other hand, while researchers would be on firmer fair-use ground if they merely linked out to videos being hosted elsewhere, link-rot is a common problem, and a content delivery network might take down a video if local law or its own policies require it. The ethical goal of researcher transparency thus might find itself in tension with the law of copyright fair use.

The previous section described the technical process of video live streaming, and this one has considered the law of video streaming generally. Legal questions arise regarding the scene of the events where a video is created, including the subjects and activity going on there. They arise regarding videographers, their right to be present, to make a video, and to distribute it. And they arise from public policies relating to distribution and its consequences, matters of concern to media processors, and content delivery networks. The law here also governs relationships among these parties, often through the license agreements that accompany most computers, software, and online services. We turn now to a consideration of how the shift from just streaming to live streaming affects the legal analyses.

THE LAW OF LIVE STREAMING

To reiterate, live streaming is subject to most of the same laws as streaming generally, principally because each technology requires the making of recordings of the media in question. The only difference is that the digital signals associated with live streaming become available over content delivery networks to media consumers immediately, theoretically *simultaneously* with the activities that are taking place in the scene. There are, however, legal developments in the last couple years that address live streaming particularly. They have so far related primarily to trial and court proceedings, deliberations of other government bodies, and road safety, with some other contexts also addressed.

Trial and Court Proceedings

One of the first reported court decisions relating to live streaming was from the U.S. Supreme Court. In *Hollingsworth v. Perry* (2010), the Supreme Court prevented a local rule of a California federal trial court from going into effect that would have permitted live streaming of the testimony in a high-profile case involving California's Proposition 8, which had banned same-sex marriage in the state. The proposed rule would have allowed transmission to other federal courthouses, where it was expected there would be interested audiences. The Court founded its decision on the argument that the California court had adopted the local rule, which varied from long-standing federal court preferences for no video in courtrooms, hastily and in a manner inconsistent with law. It also concluded that the presence of cameras in the courtroom might intimidate witnesses. In dissent, Justice Stephen Breyer excoriated the majority's argument that the local court adopted its rule inappropriately and that any harm would result from the "broadcast."

In one case, a trial-court judge did not permit the live streaming of the deposition of a witness to persons not otherwise expressly permitted by the federal rules of civil procedure to be present at the deposition (*National Railroad v. Cimarron*, 2017).[9] Another court used the availability of live streaming technology to conclude that a case involving facilities in many states could be adjudicated in a Rhode Island Court (*Downs v. 3M Co.*, 2010). The defendants had argued that "personally viewing the workplaces, homes, and other locations where the alleged exposures to asbestos [occurred] . . . would be nearly impossible without bringing the action in the respective alternative states" (*Downs v. 3M Co.*, 2010, III. B. 2. Private Factors for Consideration, para. 11). In contrast, the court concluded that "given the sophistication of modern technology—photography, video, *live streaming*, webcams— . . . a sufficient view of the property would be possible from a Rhode Island courtroom" (para. 11, emphasis is added).

One ethico-legal concern that arises regarding the live streaming of trial and court proceedings is the question of who controls production of the live stream. In *Hollingsworth* (2010), for example, the Court considered a court-organized live stream. Many appellate courts in the United States have moved their oral arguments to online streaming, though the U.S. Supreme Court has continued to resist that trend (Barnes, 2020).[10] Even if courts organize live streaming of their proceedings, allowing them to supervise the live streaming—in effect, to "direct" the videos—allows them to control, to a great extent, the message of the resulting live streams, because courtrooms are not simple tableaus. As Mulcahy (2007) explains:

> The suggestion that space is fundamental in any exercise of power by ensuring a certain allocation of people in space and coding of their reciprocal relations is a compelling one. . . . Viewed in this way, space is very far from being a flat, immobilized surface. The subject is a particularly interesting one for legal systems which rely on oral testimony and adversarial procedure. In these jurisdictions performance is all. The courtroom is converted into a stage in which space, sight lines and acoustics are critical in assessments about the credibility of the speaker and the statement they are making. (p. 385)

If we understand the video "as the product not only of mechanical reproduction, but also of a dynamic field of aesthetic and social relations and contestations" (Eileraas, 2003, p. 810), we can begin to understand the ways in which permitting journalists and lay people—to the extent they can be distinguished (noted in Chapter 3 by Weinhold, 2020)—can change the narrative of what happens in the courtroom.

The concept of the camera's gaze being violent or oppressive or requiring resistance is especially appropriate when the videographers are official operatives (court employees, for example) or representatives of a powerful elite (large media companies). Many judges in the United States are elected and are therefore politicians. But as Strachan and Kendall (2004) have noted, "Politicians usually construct images that reflect core political values because embodying exalted American values . . . enhances their status, legitimizes their claim to wield power and justifies their policy preferences" (p. 136). In the courtroom context, the judge already benefits from the rhetorical construction of the space, and being able to direct the video adds another layer of message control. This is particularly true where, as White notes, "'liveness' encourages us to accept what we see on television as . . . accurate—'real' because it is 'really' happening—rather than elaborately constructed and mediated" (1999, p. 44, quoted by Daggett, 2020, in Chapter 4). But imagine freelance videographers in the courtroom could focus on judges as they fidget, sleep, or engage in other distractions; in this case, the media consumer would derive a quite different message from the proceedings, one that challenges the political image the judge seeks to portray. Many courts, however, continue to permit only their official live streams, not these other views.

The courts' power to rhetorically construct the courtroom and its power dynamics have at least temporarily been disrupted by the COVID-19 pandemic. Many courts throughout the United States have held proceedings via Zoom and other technology platforms that permit live video (and have the ability to record all persons present in a court case), with judges attending hearings from home. In fact, the Supreme Court of the United States announced that it would allow oral arguments to take place by telephone in spring of 2020, allowing the public to listen to a live audio feed (Liptak, 2020). For a body as tradition-bound and mysterious to the public as the High Court, this announcement is momentous, since the Court has never allowed live video or audio during its sessions (and only rarely even permitted the release of audio recordings the same day). In these cases, the courts have still made decisions about when and how their proceedings are live streamed, but it is more difficult for them to enjoy the power dynamics of the physical structure of the traditional courtroom, and—like the rest of us—they run the risk of unexpected appearances by 'coworkers' like children and pets.

Government Deliberating Bodies

Many jurisdictions have requirements that certain deliberations of legislative and executive bodies must be recorded and the recordings made available. A Montana statute requires that recordings of certain bodies be made available within "1 business day" after the meetings, and it permits the video to be made available via live streaming (Montana Code Annotated, § 2-3-214 Recording of meetings for certain boards, 2019). Beginning March 2020, the City Council of New Castle County, Delaware, must make a video of its meetings available via live streaming (New Castle Code of Ordinances, Section 2.02.501-502 [county council meetings; public access by audio and video means], 2019). Similarly, a municipal ordinance in Palmetto Bay, Florida, provides that "(b) Live streaming and a video recording of each board or committee meeting shall be taken" (Palmetto Code of Ordinances, Section 2-70. - Records, 2019).

This is an area where a pandemic like COVID-19 raises ethico-legal concerns. Unlike the court proceedings described above, city council and county board meetings are often bidirectional communication channels between officials and their audiences. The parties in the court proceedings, the only ones normally permitted to speak in the courtroom, can speak in the live video conference call. If citizens who might otherwise be able to attend a council or board meeting and get in line at the microphone to be heard and hold politicians accountable are now constrained to watching the proceedings unfolding from home, live streaming does little to bring the democratic process to them. Governments may need to strive toward technology approaches that allow remote citizens to "appear" before decision-making bodies on an impromptu basis. Even after the pandemic subsides, a move to remote attendance would make the democratic process more accessible to more people, particularly those unable to attend in person because of medical issues or disability. At the same time, reform proposals must be conscious of the fact that Zoom meetings can be "zoombombed," with unauthorized individuals taking control or broadcasting messages that are offensive to all. Some organizations, including Google and NASA, have identified security and encryption problems in Zoom that have caused them to abandon the app for others they consider more secure (Vigliarolo, 2020). Hackers will likely be able to exploit those in the future as well—the security arms race will continue.

Road Safety

At least one state and one municipality have taken live streaming into account in apparent concerns over road safety. Minnesota adopted a statute prohibiting the use of mobile devices while driving, but the statute has an exception for using such devices in hands-free mode (Minnesota Statutes, §

169.475 Use of Wireless Communications Device, 2019). The exception itself has an exception, which makes use of the device, even in hands-free mode, prohibited for "accessing nonnavigation video content, engaging in video calling, engaging in live streaming, accessing gaming data, or reading electronic messages" (Minnesota Statutes, § 169.475. Subd. 3. Exceptions. (6) (b), 2019). This would seem to prohibit the driver from sending or receiving live streaming signals while driving.

A municipal ordinance in Stillwater, Oklahoma, provides that business signs in the city that use "changing lights to display an electronic image, video, or text messages" must not display live streaming video (Stillwater Code of Ordinances, § 23-186.—General standards, (m) (7), 2019). This restriction probably has significant road-safety roots: Drivers watching video on a billboard are probably as distracted and dangerous as those texting while driving. Two questions, however, immediately arise. First, it is not entirely clear how live streamed video poses a greater danger than recorded video for distracting drivers or causing other potential social harms. Second, it is not clear whether a live video feed from inside a building's premises that did not go through the usual technological process for live streaming described above is live *streaming* as opposed to just live video *display*. In other words, can video from a camera directly wired to the sign be displayed as "live video" but not "live streaming"?

Other Contexts

At least one state, New Jersey, has provided that if schools have live streaming video surveillance, they must make access to it available to local police subject to limitations negotiated between them (New Jersey Statutes, § 18A:41-9 [Education] Access to school surveillance equipment by law enforcement authorities, 2019). Though the legislative history of the bill does not make its motivation clear, in the contemporary context of school shootings, it is at least possible that the legislature there wished to allow police to use live streamed surveillance video from schools as a means to assess the tactical situation in schools during an emergency. In any event, the statute provides for the school to reach an understanding with police that would determine who could access the stream and when and that would prevent "unauthorized access" to the video.

At least one court has concluded that the availability of live streaming technology should impact the way that auctioneers conduct business. In *In re Ollie William Faison* (2018), a federal bankruptcy judge upheld the results of an auction of a debtor's property but noted that auctioneers should take certain precautions to prevent bidders from colluding to suppress the final bid price. The court opined that "Bidders should never be allowed to leave the immediate auction area. In this day of cell phones, live streaming, email, and text communication, no one should ever have to leave an auction room to get instructions from a client or from a superior" (In re Ollie William Faison, Discussion, 2018. para. 5).

In this section, we have considered legal developments focused particularly on *live* streaming, but we noted at the outset that streaming and live streaming are subject to many of the same laws. One law so far given little attention in this volume is Section 230 of the Communications Decency Act (1996). Section 230 raises significant legal and ethical issues, but as we show in the next section, resolving them likely requires judges and legislatures to shift the metaphors they use when thinking about how the internet works.

CDA SECTION 230: 26 WORDS' IMPLICATIONS FOR LIVE STREAMING

As the title of a recent book suggests, "the twenty-six words that created the Internet" (Kosseff, 2019) are indeed instrumental to the ways in which we use the web today. Simply put, Section 230 of the Communications Decency Act (1996), Protection for Private Blocking and Screening of Offensive Material, eliminates liability for online service providers who function as distributors of third-party content, as long as those providers do not exercise too much editorial control over that content.[11] Absent Section 230, social media channels and other internet "publishers" could be held legally accountable for distribution of defamatory, obscene, and confidential materials.

So, likely because of the protections Section 230 offers, we have the form and quantity of user-generated content on the internet represented by restaurant reviews on Yelp!, product and book critiques on Amazon, comments on articles on the *New York Times* and the *Washington Post*, and video uploaded and live streamed video to YouTube, TikTok, and other services. Absent Section 230, all those services might be considered publishers of the content on them and subject to the consequences of distributing those materials. It is unlikely they could afford to operate as we know them now in that environment. As Balkin (2008) succinctly put it, Section 230 "has been one of the most important guarantors of free expression on the Internet, at least in the United States" (p. 432). Without these 26 words, sites like YouTube, Facebook, and Twitter simply could not exist at their present scale. They would either be sued out of existence by plaintiffs seeking recovery from damages that they allege were created by third-party posters, or they would be forced to scale up their efforts to review content before distributing it, greatly increasing their costs and reducing the amount of content on the internet.

This section provides an overview of Section 230's function along with a case study of an early application. It then takes up the legal and ethical arguments for and against continuing Section 230 in its current form. In summary, critics of Section 230 illuminate its dark side: websites that refuse to intervene in cases of cyberstalking and cyberbullying (even when life and property are at risk); companies that hide behind the protection of the law to permit conclaves of racism, sexism, and hatred; and victims of online harassment who find that Section 230's protections for websites are perversely used against them in their search for justice. While the impetus for allowing websites to avoid liability for posts that they do not control may have been initially benign and have resulted in many positive outcomes, Section 230 critics are quick to point out that the law was passed in the internet's infancy. Certainly, the Congress of the mid-90s that passed this law could not have anticipated the ways in which it has been abused, and Section 230 is overdue for revision (see, e.g., Bolson, 2013). Even in 1997, the potential damage was probably foreseeable (Goldberg, 2019), as we shall see in the *Zeran* case study.

Operation of Section 230

As we noted above, Section 230 of the Communications Decency Act provides that "No provider or user of an interactive computer service shall be treated as the publisher or speaker of any information provided by another information content provider" (1996, (c) (1) Treatment of Publisher or Speaker, p. 101). We can translate this language into the language we have been using in this chapter: Section 230 provides that no media processor or content delivery network can be treated as the producer or distributor of content provided by its users. This provision extends legal immunity (under both federal and state laws in the United States) to media processors and content delivery networks, which includes social media platforms like Facebook, content portals like YouTube, and even the internet service providers who offer connectivity to homes and offices, all of whom might otherwise be liable for crimes and offenses based on content flowing through their systems.

Section 230 protects those providers as long as they do not exercise too much editorial control over that content. So, for example, the *New York Times* is still legally responsible for the stories its reporters write and that it publishes. It is, however, generally not liable for what online visitors to its site say in comments on those stories. A Good Samaritan provision in the law allows limited moderation for content that is hateful, libelous, obscene, or otherwise problematic without loss of immunity. The *Times* can, therefore, delete comments it deems objectionable without losing the Section 230 immunity.

As we have noted in so many other areas, the law here is not materially different for live streaming than it is for streaming or the internet generally. Section 230 contains no language about live streaming, and that should come as no surprise, as it was passed in 1996. However, given courts' willingness to extend its protection broadly, Section 230 likely eliminates liability for social media sites like Facebook and Twitter for third-party live streaming as long as those companies continue to act primarily as distributors of others' content.

Section 230 affects liability only in the United States. We are not aware of similar, sweeping legislation in any other country. Limiting liability for internet service providers is, however, not an issue only in the United States. For example, by its own terms, the New Zealand statute that resulted in Phillip Arps being sentenced to 21 months in prison does not impose liability on intermediaries like media processors and content delivery networks unless they are aware of the contents of the videos ([New Zealand] Films, Videos, and Publications Classification Act 1993, 2018, Section 122(3)-(4), p. 75).

Neither is the bar to liability under Section 230 absolute. We cannot discuss all the exceptions to Section 230 immunity. However, we will describe two briefly: cases where the internet service provider has made an enforceable promise to remedy some problems and cases involving communication that arguably encourages or supports sex trafficking.

Promissory estoppel is a doctrine of American contract law that requires those who make certain kinds of promises under certain circumstances to follow through on their promises, even if there is no contract. In one example, the plaintiff contacted Yahoo! to request that a fake profile of her be taken down, a request that Yahoo! repeatedly promised to honor (*Barnes v. Yahoo!, Inc.*, 2009). It never did so, and the plaintiff sued. Though the court concluded that Section 230 applied here, it also concluded that Yahoo! had sacrificed its immunity when it made the promise to remedy the problem. According to the Ninth Circuit, "once a court concludes a promise is legally enforceable according to contract law, it has implicitly concluded that the promisor has manifestly intended that the court enforce his promise" (p. 1108).

Another exception to broad Section 230 protections has been codified by statute. In 2018, Congress passed the Allow States and Victims to Fight Online Sex Trafficking Act (Public Law No. 115–164, H.R. 1865, 2017), often referred to by one of its earlier acronyms, FOSTA. A response to concerns raised over the deaths of sex workers, FOSTA removes Section 230 protections from websites that knowingly host content that supports sex trafficking.[12] Hailed by some as a necessary restraint on sites, like the former Backpage.com, that openly offer information useful in sex trafficking, the law has been challenged by a sexual freedom advocacy organization, Woodhull Freedom Foundation (*Woodhull v. United States*, 2020). According to Woodhull president Ricci Levy,

> FOSTA chills sexual speech and harms sex workers. It makes it harder for people to take care of and protect themselves, and, as an organization working

to protect people's fundamental human rights, Woodhull is deeply concerned about the damaging impact that this law will have on all people. (Malo, 2018)

Woodhull expressly raised concerns about liability it might face for live streaming from its conference, the annual "Sexual Freedom Summit," because it would be unable to edit or moderate the content before it appeared on the internet (*Woodhull v. United States*, 2018).[13]

As we noted above, the *Zeran v. America Online* case (1997) provides both an early and typical example of the application of Section 230.

Zeran as Early and Typical Case

Ken Zeran's experience is a painful example of how Section 230 can be used to protect online service providers at the expense of victims. *Zeran v. America Online* (1997) is one of the earliest applications of Section 230; the case was brought only months after its passage. The case demonstrates not just the breadth of protection the law provides to online service providers but the impact on the victim that critics decry; its outcome "turned Section 230 into a nearly impenetrable super-First Amendment for online companies" (Kosseff, 2019, p. 95).

In the wake of the 1995 bombing of the Alfred P. Murrah federal building in Oklahoma City, Zeran was "pranked" by an anonymous user of an America Online (AOL) message board who posted Zeran's phone number with the note to "ask for Ken" to buy memorabilia with offensive slogans about the bombing—resulting in hostile and threatening phone calls. Zeran contacted AOL and was told that the post would be removed but not retracted. The pranking continued, as did the threats, for four days, despite Zeran's numerous requests to AOL to remove the posts and to screen for new ones, and the fact that he "was receiving an abusive phone call approximately every two minutes" (p. 329), had increased police presence around his home, and suffered severe emotional distress. Zeran finally sued AOL for defamation. A district court found for AOL based on Section 230's protections for distributors of third-party content, and the Fourth Circuit affirmed.

Zeran's argument that Section 230 protection should be waived for online service providers who have received notice of defamatory content on their sites did not convince the judges. The Fourth Circuit said that Zeran asked too much of AOL:

> If computer service providers were subject to distributor liability, they would face potential liability each time they receive notice of a potentially defamatory statement—from any party, concerning any message. Each notification would require a careful yet rapid investigation of the circumstances surrounding the posted information, a legal judgment concerning the information's defamatory character, and an on-the-spot editorial decision whether to risk

liability by allowing the continued publication of that information. Although this might be feasible for the traditional print publisher, the sheer number of postings on interactive computer services would create an impossible burden in the Internet context. (1997, p. 333)

The Fourth Circuit said that Congress' reasons for passing Section 230 were to avoid the chilling effect of forcing online service providers to create heavy-handed posting restrictions to avoid tort liability and "to encourage service providers to self-regulate the dissemination of offensive material over their services" (p. 331). Forcing these providers to adhere to a notice-based liability scheme would discourage them from doing the self-policing that Congress hoped would happen.

Zeran's case has not been unique. In what he claims was the first empirical study of Section 230, Ardia (2010) analyzed 184 decisions in which federal and state courts applied the law. His findings point to the success of online service providers in using Section 230 to preempt liability for third-party content: in more than three-quarters of the cases, defendants won dismissal, although, in more than half the cases, plaintiffs succeeded in getting the offending content removed. Franks (2019) calls this level of defendant success a form of "super-immunity" for companies to continue to make money without regard to the harms that profit supports.

Ethico-Legal Status of Section 230

Is Section 230 defensible, from either a legal or an ethics perspective? Even as its critics (Franks, 2019; Goldberg, 2019) acknowledge the role the statute has played in the development of the internet as we currently experience it, they are quick to point out its deficiencies. As Franks (2019) writes, "While Section 230 has played a vital role in the growth and development of the Internet's positive potential, it has also incentivized powerful corporations to engage in increasingly risky conduct that inflicts massive harms to privacy, security, and democracy" (pp. 20–21). Put another way, for every honest negative or positive review that helps a consumer make a buying decision on Amazon, there is a victim of sexual harassment and stalking searching for help from Grindr or Instagram that may never (and is not required to) arrive.

Perhaps most poignant of these stories of need is when a suicide is live streamed. As Corr and Michaels (2020) note in Chapter 2, one of the earliest reported live streamed suicides, of a 19-year-old man streaming his overdose on justin.tv (now Twitch.tv), occurred in 2008. Sadly, the phenomenon is not rare: as Irby (2017) pointed out in January 2017, there had been at least three live streamed suicides (two of teenage girls) during that months' time. In one case, the 14-year-old victim's Facebook Live broadcast lasted for two hours, with thousands looking on as she hung herself with a scarf, while a series of "mishaps" (incorrect addresses and miscommunication) hindered rescue attempts (Miller & Burch, 2017).

Partially in response to this spate of live streamed suicides, Facebook CEO Mark Zuckerberg announced in May 2017 that it would hire 3,000 additional content moderators to monitor users, increasing the existing 4,500 moderators all over the world (Heath, 2017). How do these content moderators undertake the gigantic task of screening all that material? Klonick (2018) undertook an in-depth study on this question, and her findings revealed that not only is most content review done reactively—that is, moderators respond to content flagged as objectionable by Facebook users instead of seeking it out—but after this flagging results in a review, "the precise mechanics of the decision making process become murky" (p. 1639). The lack of transparency is not unique to Facebook (Facebook Transparency, 2020); Klonick notes that none of the major social media platforms has made its review and decision guidelines public.

The legal liability issue is clear: Facebook can, under Section 230, implement review guidelines and hire content monitors, but it does not have to. The fact that it does so, Klonick (2018) suggests, is a combination of "American free speech norms and corporate responsibility" and "the economic necessity of creating an environment that reflects the expectations of their users" (p. 1669). Legally, a social media platform such as Facebook is a private actor, not bound by the First Amendment to allow any particular speech on its site. However, Americans often do not comprehend the distinction. Raised on a steady diet of "the First Amendment guarantees us the right to say whatever we want to" exhortations, many Americans do not understand that Facebook, as a private company, can limit their speech rights on its platform much more than the government can with law. But Facebook, as a corporate entity, also relies on its users to generate content that advertisers want to support. It must act as a responsible corporation concerned with the well-being and happiness of its users. Thus, it makes good business sense to engage in acts that support a positive user experience, such as hiring additional content monitors and publicizing (to a limited extent) the handling of user concerns about harmful posts. Since Facebook is not required to engage in any content moderation, its perceived generosity in doing so might garner the company some ethical credibility.

In light of this, an incident like the 14-year-old's live streamed suicide can engender at least two reasonable reactions. On the one hand, proponents of Section 230 protection would point to the Good Samaritan clause and suggest that content policing, regardless of how it's done, is not legally required and is also precisely the kind of voluntary self-regulation that Congress hoped would happen (recall the *Zeran* court's assessment of Congress' goals). Section 230, then, is working as intended, and Facebook should suffer no legal liability for a user's harmful content as long as it continues its Good

Samaritan moderation. On the other hand, to critics such as Goldberg[14] (2019), the courts' expansive application of Section 230 "is the enabler of every asshole, troll, psycho, and perv on the internet" (p. 39). Section 230's lack of requirement to moderate content, coupled with courts' willingness to construe the law's protections broadly, has resulted in an untenable situation for victims of harassment and bullying. Unable to either rely on or force giant social media companies such as Facebook and Grindr to respond to their repeated pleas for help, they turn to the courts, who usually interpose Section 230 as a bar to their recovery.

While Facebook's legal liability might be clear, its ethical foundations are markedly less so. Christians (2020), in the introductory chapter, has already ably discussed a key ethics consideration in the live streaming of suicides: the sacredness of life. Facebook, then, should have a moral duty, separate from its legal requirements, to act to prevent both suicides themselves and their dissemination via live stream. Christians (2020) relies on Freire (1973) and his concern for *campesinos'* critical consciousness in his discussion of the importance of "the affirmation of people as persons." As an ethical actor, Facebook should heed Freire's call to consider its users as persons, not just abstract figures on a spreadsheet. To do this most effectively, Facebook should go beyond its legal requirements and engage in content moderation, which to some extent it has done.

However, Franks (2019) in her critique of Section 230, asserts that the statute is a "moral hazard," a term borrowed from economics that she defines as "the lack of incentive to guard against risk because one is protected from its negative consequences" (p. 166). As the law stands, Facebook is required to walk a fine line between "enough" moderation to satisfy its business and user demands and "too much" that would turn it into a publisher and eliminate its Section 230 protections. This line is the moral hazard—Facebook has no incentive to engage in more than the minimum amount of content moderation to quell user concerns, even if more moderation would serve a higher ethical principle (like honoring the sacredness of life by forbidding the live streaming of suicides). It would lose valuable legal protection if it does, opening itself up to increased liability by being considered a publisher rather than a distributor.

This conundrum is not entirely Facebook's fault. Courts bear the responsibility, starting with *Zeran*, for the broad protections that Section 230 has come to offer. Franks (2019) offers her own perspective on this problem; she believes that treating online service providers like "distributors" as understood in defamation law, would be a solution. In that context, a distributor faces liability only if she "knows or should have known of the unlawfulness" of the offending content (p. 171). But *Zeran* foreclosed that interpretation; as Franks put it,

> By completely immunizing AOL from liability, even when the company was made aware of the unlawful content and given ample opportunity to mitigate the harm, the [*Zeran*] court effectively eliminated incentives for intermediaries to address harmful and destructive uses of their services. (p. 173)

"There is not an easy moral answer to the Section 230 debate," Kosseff (2019) wrote in the introduction to his book (p. 7), adding that the book was also not a love story to the law. Still, it seems that Franks (2019) is correct: there are significant legal disincentives to the kind of moderation that might satisfy Freire's call to humanize the *campesinos* (or, in this case, social media users). Social media sites, like Facebook, and any other site that welcomes third-party content or commentary should balance those disincentives with a consideration of the real effects that harmful content, like live streaming of violence, can have on their users.

CONCLUSION

We have attempted in this chapter to provide a fairly comprehensive overview of the law that affects live streaming, keeping in mind the observations that other authors in this volume have contributed, and to delve fairly deeply into one issue not treated elsewhere in this volume, the ethico-legal status of Section 230 of the Communications Decency Act (1996). Because live streaming implicates so many aspects of the law (just as regular video streaming and indeed the internet itself do), we have certainly failed in the first task, and because so many thoughtful scholars in the legal literature have engaged meaningfully with the second task, we have likely failed in it as well. But in the present context, we felt our duty was to make a beginning so that readers could place the other chapters of this volume in a broader legal context and also recognize that significant bodies of the law raise ethical questions not otherwise treated here.

All the contributions to this volume invite further reflection on the intersection of law and ethics in communications generally, and live streaming more particularly. Though we have not proposed how to fix any of the problems described here, we believe we have explained the legal context to the extent that may help other scholars do that work.

NOTES

1. In the case of non-live streaming, the media processor may also be editing the video for content, cutting it, and so on.
2. Throughout this work, we will use Facebook as an example, but that does not mean that the law and ethics of live streaming apply solely to Facebook. We use this company because it is one of the most popular services that offer live streaming.

3. The Supreme Court held in *New York v. Ferber* (1982) that a New York child pornography statute did not violate the First Amendment.

4. The difference might still be important for other kinds of live broadcasts. Our only point is that live streaming probably violates any statute that prohibits either recording or transmitting live, or both.

5. Outside of those distinctions Weinhold has discussed, American law—especially under the First Amendment—makes very little distinction between journalists and non-journalists. In that sense, the U.S. legal answer to the question posed in her title—"Are we all journalists now?"—is "Yes, if we want to be." This answer does not conflict with Weinhold's views about the ethics of those who hold themselves out as journalists, that "good journalists are at their core engaged citizens," an appellation that fits few of the videographers of the kind of (live) streaming that typically gets into courts.

6. A videographer who makes a work within the scope of employment has created a work made for hire, and the employer owns the copyrights in it.

7. In any event, Section 230 of the Communications Decency Act (1996), discussed below, would probably insulate them from liability.

8. However, *content* neutrality is different from *viewpoint* neutrality. Viewpoint neutrality is a subset of content neutrality that singles out a particular viewpoint on a topic for disparate treatment. For example, in *Mosley* (1972), had the Chicago ordinance permitted only peaceful labor picketing *that supported unions* to occur around schools rather than just any labor picketing, regardless of message, it would have been a viewpoint-based regulation; as it was, the ordinance forbade all picketing except peaceful labor picketing (a content-based regulation).

9. A deposition is a formal interview in which one side in litigation interviews a witness from the other side (or a third party), under oath. The interviewer's side then uses a transcript or video recording to discover further evidence or to impeach the same witness's credibility at trial.

10. But see the update below in the context of COVID-19.

11. The 26 words are: "No provider or user of an interactive computer service shall be treated as the publisher or speaker of any information provided by another information content provider" (Communications Decency Act of 1996).

12. The operative language is: "Whoever, using a facility or means of interstate or foreign commerce or in or affecting interstate or foreign commerce, owns, manages, or operates an interactive computer service (as such term is defined in section 230(f) the Communications Act of 1934 47 U.S.C. 230(f))), or conspires or attempts to do so, with the intent to promote or facilitate the prostitution of another person shall be fined under this title, imprisoned for not more than 10 years, or both" (18 U.S. Code § 2421A(a), 2018).

13. The case is still pending. In January 2020, the D.C. Circuit remanded Woodhull's complaint to the lower court, which had dismissed it for lack of standing (*Woodhull v. United States*, 2020).

14. Goldberg represented Matthew Herrick in a bitter battle against Grindr, a dating app that caters to a gay clientele, in its refusal to remove fake profiles featuring Herrick that an ex-boyfriend had put up—profiles that resulted in over 1,200 men coming to Herrick's home in search of a hookup. The Second Circuit supported Grindr's Section 230 claims against Herrick's allegations that Grindr had not warned him that the app could be used to harm and harass him. The court was blunt: "Herrick's failure to warn claim is inextricably linked to Grindr's alleged failure to edit, monitor, or remove the offensive content provided by his ex-boyfriend; accordingly, it is barred by § 230" (*Herrick v. Grindr LLC*, 18–396, 2019, p. 6).

REFERENCES

18 U.S. Code § 2421A. (2018). Promotion or facilitation of prostitution and reckless disregard of sex trafficking. *Legal Information Institution, Cornell Law School*. Retrieved from https://www.law.cornell.edu/uscode/text/18/part-I/chapter-117

Ardia, D.S. (2010). Free speech savior or shield for scoundrels: An empirical study of intermediary immunity under Section 230 of the Communications Decency Act. *Loyola of Los*

Angeles Law Review, 43(2), 373–506. Retrieved from https://digitalcommons.lmu.edu/llr/vol43/iss2/1

Authors Guild v. Google, Inc., 804 F.3d 202 (2nd Cir.). (2015). *United States Court of Appeals for the Second Circuit.* Retrieved from http://www.ca2.uscourts.gov/decisions/isysquery/9ed12424-64b9-4a0d-949a-d64fff635132/2/doc/13-4829_opn.pdf

Azim, A. (2018). Common sense: Rethinking the new common rule's weak protections for human subjects. *Vanderbilt Law Review, 71*(5), 1703–37. Retrieved from https://vanderbiltlawreview.org/lawreview/2018/10/common-sense-rethinking-the-new-common-rules-weak-protections-for-human-subjects/

Balkin, J.M. (2008). The future of free expression in a digital age. *Pepperdine Law Review, 36*(2), 427–44. Retrieved from https://digitalcommons.law.yale.edu/cgi/viewcontent.cgi?article=1222&context=fss_papers

Barnes v. Yahoo!, Inc., 570 F.3d 1096 (9th Cir.). (2009). *United States Court of Appeals for the Nineth Circuit.* Retrieved from http://cdn.ca9.uscourts.gov/datastore/opinions/2009/06/22/05-36189.pdf

Barnes, P. (2020, March 10). Showdown brewing over live-streaming of U.S. Supreme Court proceedings. *Forbes.* Retrieved from https://www.forbes.com/sites/patriciagbarnes/2020/03/10/showdown-brewing-over-live-streaming-of-us-supreme-court-proceedings/#553a25fd5c7f

Bayer, K. (2020, January 29). Christchurch white supremacist Philip Neville Arps banned from mosques and contact with Muslims. *NZ Herald.* Retrieved from https://www.nzherald.co.nz/nz/news/article.cfm?c_id=1&objectid=12304328

Bazyler, M. J. (n.d.). Holocaust denial laws and other legislation criminalizing promotion of Nazism. *Yad Vashem: The World Holocaust Remembrance Center.* Retrieved from https://www.yadvashem.org/holocaust/holocaust-antisemitism/holocaust-denial-laws.html

Bolson, A. (2013, August 27). The Internet has grown up, why hasn't the law? Reexamining Section 230 of the Communications Decency Act. *International Association of Privacy Professionals (IAPP).* Retrieved from https://iapp.org/news/a/the-internet-has-grown-up-why-hasnt-the-law-reexamining-section-230-of-the/

Carter v. Massachusetts, denial of certiorari, 140 S. Ct. 910. (2020). *Supreme Judicial Court of Massachusetts.* Retrieved from https://www.supremecourt.gov/docket/docketfiles/html/public/19-62.html

Clement, J. (2019, August 9). Hours of video uploaded to YouTube every minute 2007-2019. *Statista.* Retrieved from https://www.statista.com/statistics/259477/hours-of-video-uploaded-to-youtube-every-minute/

Commonwealth v. Robertson, Massachusetts, 5 N.E.3d 522. (2014). *Supreme Judicial Court of Massachusetts, Suffolk.* Retrieved from https://scholar.google.com/scholar_case?case=17431626375901598207

Communications Decency Act of 1996, Public Law No. 104–104. (1996). A short title of Title V—Obscenity And Violence, Subtitle A—Obscene, Harassing, and Wrongful Utilization of Telecommunications Facilities, Telecommunication Act of 1996 (S652), (pp. 94–106). *The 104th Congress (1995–1996).* Retrieved from https://transition.fcc.gov/Reports/tcom1996.pdf

Copyright Law of United States. 17 U.S. Code (Title 17). (2016). Chapter 1: Subject Matter and Scope of Copyright. *U.S. Copyright Office.* Retrieved from https://www.copyright.gov/title17/92chap1.html

Downs v. 3M Co., R.I. Super., Providence. (2010). *Superior Court of Rhode Island, PROVIDENCE, SC.* Retrieved from https://scholar.google.com/scholar_case?case=11200256845580917060

Eileraas, K. (2003). Reframing the Colonial Gaze: Photography, Ownership, and Feminist Resistance. *MLN, 118*(4), 807–40. https://doi.org/10.1353/mln.2003.0074

Evans, B. (2013). Why the common rule is hard to amend. *Indiana Health Law Review, 10*(2), 365–414. https://doi.org/10.18060/18828

Facebook. (2020). Community Standards. *Facebook.* Retrieved from https://www.facebook.com/communitystandards/

Facebook. (2020). Facebook Transparency: Content restrictions based on local law. *Facebook.* Retrieved from https://govtrequests.facebook.com/content-restrictions

Facebook. (2020). Terms of Service. *Facebook*. Retrieved from https://www.facebook.com/terms.php

Fiesler, C., & Proferes, N. (2018). "Participant" perceptions of Twitter research ethics. *Social Media + Society, January–March 2018*, 1–14. https://doi.org/10.1177/2056305118763366

Films, Videos, and Publications Classification Act 1993, Public Act 1993 No 94. (2018). Administered by the Department of Internal Affairs, New Zealand (Reprint as at November 13, 2018). *Parliament Counsel Office, New Zealand Government*. Retrieved from http://www.legislation.govt.nz/act/public/1993/0094/latest/DLM312895.html

Franchim, S. C. (2017). It's a deal: Forging media rights deals in response to spectator live streaming. *Journal of Technology Law and Policy, 21*(2), 223–42. Retrieved from https://www.journaloftechlaw.org/issues/volume21-2/21-2-franchim/

Franks, M.A. (2019). *The cult of the constitution*. Stanford University Press.

Freire, P. (1973). *Education for critical consciousness*. Seabury Press.

Glik v. Cunniffe, 655 F.3d 78 (1st Cir). (2011). *United States Court of Appeals for the First Circuit*. Retrieved from http://media.ca1.uscourts.gov/pdf.opinions/10-1764P-01A.pdf

Goldberg, C. (2019). *Nobody's victim: Fighting psychos, stalkers, pervs, and trolls*. Plume.

Heath, A. (2017, May 3). Facebook will hire 3,000 more moderators to keep deaths and crimes from being streamed. *Business Insider*. Retrieved from https://www.businessinsider.com/facebook-to-hire-3000-moderators-to-keep-suicides-from-being-streamed-2017-5

Herrick v. Grindr LLC, 18-396 (Summary Order, 2nd Circuit). (2019). *United States Court of Appeals for the Second Circuit*. Retrieved from https://www.ca2.uscourts.gov/decisions/isysquery/98b17c25-bc0d-4f3b-9e58-78c4001094ec/2/doc/18-396_so.pdf#xml=https://www.ca2.uscourts.gov/decisions/isysquery/98b17c25-bc0d-4f3b-9e58-78c4001094ec/2/hilite/

Hollingsworth v. Perry, 558 U.S. 183. (2010). *Supreme Court of the United States*. Retrieved from https://www.supremecourt.gov/opinions/09pdf/09a648.pdf

Hudgens v. National Labor Relations Board, 424 U.S. 507. (1976). *Supreme Court of the United States*. Retrieved from https://scholar.google.com/scholar_case?case=16846166712547461971

In re Ollie William Faison, Chapter 11, Debtor, No. 14-00073-5-SWH. (2018, September 21). *United States Bankruptcy Court, E.D. North Carolina, Raleigh Division*. Retrieved from https://scholar.google.com/scholar_case?case=16719539039172849576

Irby, K. (2017, January 27). Why are people live-streaming their suicides? *Miami Herald*. Retrieved from https://www.miamiherald.com/news/nation-world/national/article129120064.html

Klonick, K. (2018). The new governors: The people, rules, and processes governing online speech. *Harvard Law Review, 131*(6), 1598–1670. Retrieved from https://harvardlawreview.org/wp-content/uploads/2018/04/1598-1670_Online.pdf

Kanongataa v. American Broadcasting Companies, Inc. et al, No. 1:2016cv07382 - Document 44 (United States District Court, Southern District of New York). (2017). *JUSTIA US Law*. Retrieved from https://law.justia.com/cases/federal/district-courts/new-york/nysdce/1:2016cv07382/463022/44/

Kosseff, J. (2019). *The twenty-six words that created the Internet*. Cornell University Press.

Lake v. Wal-Mart Stores, Inc., 582 N.W.2d 231. (1998, July 30). *State of Minnesota, in Supreme Court*. Retrieved from https://mn.gov/law-library-stat/archive/supct/9807/c797263.htm

Larson, B. N. (2017). Gender as a variable in natural-language processing: Ethical considerations. *Ethics in Natural Language Processing: Proceedings of the First ACL Workshop*, 1–11. Retrieved from https://www.aclweb.org/anthology/W17-1601/

Liptak, A. (2020, April 13). The supreme court will hear arguments by phone. The public can listen in. *New York Times*. Retrieved from https://www.nytimes.com/2020/04/13/us/politics/supreme-court-phone-arguments-virus.html

Malo, S. (2018, June 29). U.S. online sex trafficking law challenged in court. *Reuters*. Retrieved from https://www.reuters.com/article/us-usa-cyber-trafficking/us-online-sex-trafficking-law-challenged-in-court-idUSKBN1JP1D2

Maryland Statutes. (2019). Courts & Judicial Proceedings § 10-402 (c) (3). *Maryland General Assembly*. Retrieved from http://mgaleg.maryland.gov/2020RS/Statute_Web/gcj/gcj.pdf

Massachusetts General Laws. Part IV, Title I, Chapter 272 § 105. (2019). Photographing, videotaping or electronically surveilling partially nude or nude person or the sexual or other intimate parts of a person around the person's clothing; exceptions; punishment. *The 191st General Court of the Commonwealth of Massachusetts* (2019–2020). Retrieved from https://malegislature.gov/Laws/GeneralLaws/PartIV/TitleI/Chapter272/Section105

Massachusetts Senate Bill S.2382. (2019). An Act Relative to Preventing Suicide [Conrad's Law]. *The 191st General Court of the Commonwealth Massachusetts (2019–2020)*. Retrieved from https://malegislature.gov/Bills/191/SD2505

Midway Manufacturing Co. v. Strohon, 564 F. Supp. 741. (1983, June 1). *United States District Court, N.D. Illinois, E.D.* Retrieved from https://scholar.google.com/scholar_case?case=13362028579102752809

Miller, C.M., & Burch, A.D.S. (2017, January 24). Another girl hangs herself while streaming it live—This time in Miami. *Miami Herald*. Retrieved from https://www.miamiherald.com/news/local/article128563889.html

Miller, J. (2018, December 5). Live video streaming: How it works. *WOWZA Media Systems*. Retrieved from https://www.wowza.com/blog/live-video-streaming-how-it-works

Minnesota Statutes. (2019). *Minnesota Legislature*. Retrieved from https://www.revisor.mn.gov/statutes/

Missouri Revisor Statutes. (2020). Chapter 169. Traffic Regulation. *Missouri Constitution Committee Publications*. Retrieved from https://revisor.mo.gov/main/Home.aspx

Montana Code Annotated. (2019). *Montana State Legislature*. Retrieved from https://leg.mt.gov/bills/mca/index.html

Mulcahy, L. (2007). Architects of justice: The politics of courtroom design. *Social Legal Studies, 16*(3), 383–403. https://doi.org/10.1177/0964663907079765

Mullin, J. (2017, February 16). Dad who live-streamed his son's birth on Facebook loses in court. *Ars Technica*. Retrieved from https://arstechnica.com/tech-policy/2017/02/dad-who-live-streamed-his-sons-birth-on-facebook-loses-in-court/

National Railroad Passenger Corp. v. Cimarron Crossing Feeders, LLC, No. 16-cv-1094-JTM. (2017, September 26). *United States District Court, D. Kansas*. Retrieved from https://scholar.google.com/scholar_case?case=11226481787724908277

New Castle County, Delaware, Code of Ordinances. (2019). Chapter 2—Administration. *Municipal Code Corporation*. Retrieved from https://library.municode.com/de/new_castle_county/codes/code_of_ordinances?nodeId=PTIICO_CH2AD

New Jersey General and Permanent Statutes (updated through P.L. 2019, ch. 513 and J.R. 33 of P.L. 2019). (2019). *New Jersey Legislature*. Retrieved from https://lis.njleg.state.nj.us/nxt/gateway.dll?f=templates&fn=default.htm&vid=Publish:10.1048/Enu

New York v. Ferber, 458 U.S. 747. (1982). *Supreme Court of the United States*. Retrieved from https://scholar.google.com/scholar_case?case=1226851723986989726

Palmetto Bay, Florida, Code of Ordinances. (2019). Chapter 2—Administration. *Municipal Code Corporation*. Retrieved from https://library.municode.com/fl/palmetto_bay/codes/code_of_ordinances?nodeId=COOR_CH2AD

Police Dept. of Chicago v. Mosley, 408 U.S. 92 (1972). Supreme Court of United States. Retrieved from https://scholar.google.com/scholar_case?case=7757495192285749706

Protection of Human Subjects, 45 CFR, Part 46. (2009, January 15). *U.S. Department of Health and Human Services*. Retrieved from https://www.hhs.gov/ohrp/sites/default/files/ohrp/humansubjects/regbook2013.pdf.pdf

Public Law No. 115–164, H.R. 1865. (2017). Allow States and Victims to Fight Online Sex Trafficking Act of 2017. *CONGRESS.GOV*. Retrieved from https://www.congress.gov/bill/115th-congress/house-bill/1865

Ravitz, J. (2014, March 7). "Upskirt" ban in Massachusetts signed into law. *CNN*. Retrieved from https://www.cnn.com/2014/03/07/justice/massachusetts-upskirt-bill/

Stampler, L. (2014, April 11). Facebook reveals which countries censor citizens' news feeds. *Time*. Retrieved from https://time.com/59567/facebook-countries-censor-report-india/

Stillwater, Oklahoma, Code of Ordinances, No. 3439, (Supp. No. 7). (2019). *Municipal Code Corporation*. Retrieved from https://library.municode.com/ok/stillwater/codes/code_of_ordinances

Strachan, J. C., & Kendall, K. E. (2004). Political candidates' convention films: Finding the perfect image—an overview of political image making. In C. A. Hill & M. Helmers (Eds.), *Defining visual rhetorics* (pp. 135–54). Lawrence Erlbaum.

Terms of Service. (2020). *Facebook*. Retrieved from https://www.facebook.com/legal/terms

Texas Statutes. Sec. 22.01[Assault]. (2019). Penal Code: Title 5. Offenses against the Person, Chapter 22. Assaultive Offenses. *Texas Constitution and Statutes*. Retrieved from https://statutes.capitol.texas.gov/Docs/PE/pdf/PE.22.pdf

U.S. Customs & Border Protection. (2007). *Welcome to the United States: A guide for international visitors* (CBP Publication 0000-0146). Retrieved from https://www.cbp.gov/sites/default/files/documents/WelcomeToTheUS.pdf

United States Code. (2020, April 10). Public Law 116-138 (04/10/2020): Title 18, Chapter 110 - Sexual exploitation and other abuse of children, § 2251. Sexual exploitation of children. *Office of the Law Revision Counsel of the United States House of Representatives*. Retrieved from https://uscode.house.gov/download/download.shtml

Vigliarolo, B. (2020, April 9). Who has banned Zoom? Google, NASA, and more. *TechRepublic*. Retrieved from https://www.techrepublic.com/article/who-has-banned-zoom-google-nasa-and-more/

Walsh v. Latham, No. A136016. (2014). *Court of Appeals of California, First District, Division One*. Retrieved from https://scholar.google.com/scholar_case?case=15371767228421757566

White, M. (*1999*). Television liveness: History, banality, attractions. *Spectator. 20*(1), 39–56. Retrieved from https://cinema.usc.edu/assets/099/15896.pdf

Wisconsin v. Mitchell, 508 U.S. 476. (1993). *United States Supreme Court*. Retrieved from https://scholar.google.com/scholar_case?case=6356850277412073701

Woodhull Freedom Foundation v. United States. (2018, June 28). The United States District Court for the District of Columbia: Declaration of Ricci Levy in support of motion for preliminary injunction. *Woodhull Freedom Foundation*. Retrieved from https://www.woodhullfoundation.org/wp-content/uploads/2018/06/Woodhull-FOSTA-Levy-Declaration.pdf

Woodhull Freedom Foundation v. United States, 948 F.3d 363 (D.C. Cir. 2020). (2020, January 24). *United States Court of Appeals for the District of Columbia Circuit*. Retrieved from https://www.cadc.uscourts.gov/internet/opinions.nsf/CD2E207B01AAFA4F852584F90053EE7D/$file/18-5298-1825427.pdf

Wright v. Warner Books, Inc., 953 F.2d 731. (1991). *United States Court of Appeals, Second Circuit*. Retrieved from https://scholar.google.com/scholar_case?case=4969177147306679183

Zambelli, A. (2013, March 1). A history of media streaming and the future of connected TV. *The Guardian*. Retrieved from https://www.theguardian.com/media-network/media-network-blog/2013/mar/01/history-streaming-future-connected-tv

Zeran v. America Online, Inc., 129 F.3d 327. (1997). *United States Court of Appeals, Second Circuit*. Retrieved from https://scholar.google.com/scholar_case?case=3112726467460676187

Chapter Seven

You Can Doesn't Mean You Should

The Rationale and Ethics of Live Streaming Crimes

Melissa L. Beall, Shing-Ling S. Chen,
and Laura Terlip

Live broadcasting used to be an activity restricted to organizations that control the use of radio and television stations, out of the reach of rank and files. Thanks to live streaming, live broadcasting is now at the fingertips of millions of social media users. Live streaming, an online technology that simultaneously records and broadcasts in real time, much like live broadcasts of radio and television signals over the airwaves, is available on social media. Hence, much like radio and television broadcasters, ordinary social media users are now able to broadcast events live. However, unlike radio and television broadcasting, which are regulated by Federal Communications Commission (FCC), a federal government agency that regulates communications by radio, television, wire, satellite, and cable, live streaming is not. Without any legal binding, live streaming is open to free-wheeling uses and misuses by social media users.

Other than the easy accessibility, live streaming has a few advantages over radio and television broadcasting. An advantage that a user of live streaming has, absent in radio and television broadcasting, is the reciprocal connection with viewers in a synchronized fashion. Live streaming brings a streamer and his/her audience together in real time, across space, to experience an event together. While live streaming, the streamer knows how many audiences he/she has and who log on, a knowledge that radio or television broadcasters do not have when broadcasting live.

In addition, live streaming permits the synchronized two-way communication, where live streamers receive immediate reactions from viewers, a feature not available to radio and television broadcasters. Reactions from radio listeners and TV viewers may come in telephone calls or fan mails, but they are asynchronized. Most of the radio listeners and TV viewers do not respond to radio or TV stations, and hence, they are passive consumers. Live stream viewers, unlike the passive audience of radio and television broadcasting, could easily respond to the streamer in real time with comments and emojis. Therefore, viewers not only view the live streamed event unfolds, but also contribute to the construction of a live stream community with their reactions by clicking emotive icons on the bottom of the screen—like love, haha, wow, sad, and angry—in addition to leaving a comment. Live stream viewers not only watch an event live but also witness the reactions of other viewers as floating emotive icons continuously move through the screen, and comments continuously appear. Hence, the experience of live streams is more comprehensive than the experience of live broadcasts on radio or television, where viewers are unable to immediately respond to the broadcasters, nor are they aware of the reactions of other audience members who are not in their immediate presence. Therefore, live streaming by allowing an instant response to the streamers, and immediate knowledge of other viewers' reactions closely resembles communications in face-to-face mode.

With these unique features, live streaming is a popular form of communication that allows streamers and viewers to experience significant events together, across space. Live streaming a birthday or wedding celebration, a sporting or concert event, or a backstage celebration of a victory, allow hundreds if not thousands of viewers to experience a significant event together live. A live streaming celebration is a community celebrating live, across space. However, uses of live streaming, not accountable to legal regulations, are open to misuses as well. Live-streaming antisocial activities were common occurrences. This chapter examines the legal context, the occurrences, and the rationale of live streaming crimes, as live streaming crimes represent the most controversial activities among all antisocial activities live streamed. The ethics of live streaming crimes are also considered.

BROADCASTING VIOLENCE AND GORE

In the United States, Federal law prohibits obscene, indecent, and profane content from being broadcast on the radio or TV. Obscene content refers to depicting or describing sexual content in an offensive way, while indecent content is the portrayals of sexual or excretory organs or activities, and profane content, grossly offensive language uses (FCC, 2017). Violating any of these rules, a radio or television station would have its station license revoked by FCC, or a fine or a warning issued by FCC.

Violence, due to its dramatic nature, is a common theme on television. Violent TV content includes the portrayals of the intentional use of physical force or power to injure, damage, or destroy, resulting in injury or death. In the United States, although federal law prohibits obscene, indecent, and profane content from being broadcast on the radio or TV, FCC does not regulate violent television programs (FCC, 2017). Instead, FCC oversees the television content rating system, known as the TV Parental Guidelines. The system is a voluntary participation system, with ratings determined by the participating networks. Among the six rating categories—TV-Y, TV-Y7, TV-G, TV-PG, TV-14, TV-MA—the rating category that addresses graphic violence is TV-MA. TV programs rated TV-MA, contain intense violent content such as blood and gore, among other matters such as dark humor, frequent profanity, and strong sexual themes (Labaton, 2007). However, the system has no legal implications for viewer/parental reference only.

Live streaming exists in this double legal vacuum of regulating violence in broadcast media. First, live streaming is not regulated by the FCC. Secondly, with FCC regulations (2017), there is no forceful legal control over violent media content such as broadcasting trauma. On the scale of free speech versus protection against trauma, the scale is found to be tilting toward free speech. It is understandable that, with this double legal vacuum, streamers are operating as digital Lone Rangers in a no man's land. Although prosocial live streams enhance the quality of lives of many, allowing many dispersed audiences to partake in significant events as they unfold, antisocial live streams which have been reported in the middle 2010s, may not enhance the quality of lives of their viewers.

LIVE STREAMING CRIMES

Twitter launched Periscope, a live stream app, in spring 2015. It was reported that Periscope had 10 million users in 2015, with 1.9 million daily active users in 2017, and it has been used for 200 million broadcasts in 2017 (Aslam, 2020). Although Periscope's guidelines ban explicit, graphic content, many used the platform to showcase crimes. Reports of live streaming crimes were found beginning the mid-2010s (Sacramento [CBS13], 2015; WTSP-TV 10 pm News Staff & Flowers, 2015). Notable cases are reported below.

Live-Streamed Battery and Suicide

In April 2016, a live streamed battery was reported. In the video, two teenagers assaulted a drunken man in Bordeaux, France, with one of the teenagers who live streamed the assault on Periscope. The two teens could be seen on the streamed video, bragging and laughing about the attack (Blaise & Morenne, 2016).

A live streamed suicide was also reported in April 2016, when a French woman, Océane, while live streaming herself on Periscope and interacting with her followers, threw herself under a train at Égly station, south of Paris. The video was widely circulated on YouTube, with the suicide blackout (Blaise & Morenne, 2016). It was reported that the woman had suffered abuse from her ex-boyfriend. In the video before the suicide, the woman said, "The video I am doing right now is not made to create buzz, but rather to make people react, to open minds, and that's it" (Blaise & Morenne, 2016, para 7).

Live-Streamed Rape

On April 26, 2016, an incident of live-streamed rape was reported. An Ohio teenager, Marina Lonina, witnessed a 17-year-old friend being raped. However, instead of helping her friend out, Lonina live streamed the sexual assault (McPhate, 2016). The day before the assault, Lonina and the victim met the perpetrator, Raymond Gates, a 29-year-old man, for the first time at a mall. The two girls agreed to meet Gates the next day at a residence. The next day, when the three gathered at the residence, Gates pinned the victim down and raped her. Lonina did not "call 911 and hit the guy over the head with a chair" (Kazdin, 2016, para 4); instead, she filmed the sexual attack. Lonina "not only failed to help the victim, she pointed her phone and streamed a live video of it on the Periscope app" (McPhate, 2016, para 1). A friend of Lonina's in another state saw the video and contacted the authorities. As a result, Lonina faced a series of charges as severe as those facing Gates. Both Lonina and Gates were charged with kidnapping, rape, sexual battery, and pandering sexual matter involving a minor (McPhate, 2016).

The prosecutor said that in the ten-minute video, the victim could be heard saying "no" and "help me," while Lonina could be heard laughing. While live streaming the assault, Lonina became enthralled by positive feedback collected. According to the prosecutor, "She [Lonina] got caught up in the likes" (McPhate, 2016, papa 9) that her live streamed video received. The prosecutor reported that "For the most part she [Lonina] is just streaming it on the Periscope app and giggling and laughing" (McPhate, 2016, papa 15). In 2017, Lonina was sentenced to nine months in jail. Gates received a nine-year jail term (BlueLivesMatterArchi, 2017).

Live-Streamed Torture

An incident of live-streamed torture occurred in January 2017, in Chicago, when a mentally disabled man, an 18-year-old white youth, visited a group of individuals, four African-Americans. What started as a play flight led to a prolonged assault where the four individuals abused the disabled man, by binding his hands with orange cords, covering his mouth with tape, kicking and hitting him, as well as slashing his scalp (Smith & Chokshi, 2017). The victim was also forced to kiss the floor and drink from a toilet bowl (Zurcher, 2017). The four individuals carried out these physical assaults while taunting anti-white messages, cursing and laughing. One of the four individuals live streamed the abuse using a cellphone camera. The abuse, a 28-minute video, was shown live on Facebook. It was evident that the four individuals carried out the torture with an intent to gain public attention, as they constantly monitored the amount of attention they received while live streaming. Phippen (2017) reports,

> At one point, dissatisfied with how few people have tuned in to watch the group assault the man, the woman with the cell phone says to her internet following, "You all ain't even commenting on my shit. Ain't nobody watching my shit." (para 4)

Although the video did not garner much attention when it was live streamed, the recording and sharing capacities of social media did allow the video to reach a wide audience. The video caused widespread outrage. President Barack Obama characterized the live streamed torture as "despicable" (Yan, Jones, & Almasy, 2017, para 25), while Chicago Mayor Rahm Emanuel described the video, sickening, and Illinois Governor Bruce Rauner called the video, horrific (Main, Charles, & Grimm, 2017). The four individuals were later arrested and charged with aggravated kidnapping, hate crimes, aggravated unlawful restraint, and aggravated battery with a deadly weapon (Smith & Davey, 2017). In 2017 and 2018, the four suspects pleaded guilty to committing a hate crime, intimidation, and aggravated battery, and were sentenced from four years of probation to eight years in prison (Crepeau, 2017, 2018; Pathieu & Hope, 2018; AP, 2018).

Live-Streamed Massacre

On March 15, 2019, in Christchurch, New Zealand, two consecutive mass shootings occurred at two mosques where fifty-nine people were killed and forty-nine injured. Australian Prime Minister Jacinda Arden described this apparent terrorist attack, as "an extraordinary and unprecedented act of violence" (*New York Times*, 2019, para 1). One of the reasons why this act of violence was extraordinary and unprecedented was because the killings were partially live streamed on Facebook. The lone gunman who carried out the shootings is an Australian white nationalist. On the day of the attack, before the shootings, the gunman posted links to a white-nationalist manifesto on

Twitter. He also posted on 8chan, an online forum, a link to his Facebook page where he indicated that he would broadcast live video of the shootings.

The gunman live streamed the first 17 minutes of his attack on Facebook Live, which began with driving to the Al Noor mosque, the first mosque where mass shootings took place and ended with driving away from the mosque. The live video was shot using a helmet camera, worn by the gunman. The video began with the gunman driving a vehicle, where the gunman's face could occasionally be seen in the rearview mirror. The video then showed the gunman pulled up in front of the Al Noor mosque. The video continued to show the gunman approached the mosque on foot with his weapon visible and began shooting at people at the entrance. In the video that followed was his firing on the worshipers. It was reported,

> On Friday, a gunman strapped on a helmet camera, loaded his car with weapons, drove to a mosque in Christchurch, New Zealand, and began shooting at anyone who came into his line of vision. The act of mass terror was broadcast live for the world to watch on social media. (Warzel, 2019, para 1)

What was live streamed was "a 17-minute video showing a man dressed in black shooting at fleeing worshipers and into piles of bodies with a semi-automatic rifle" (Graham-McLay, Ramzy, & Victor, 2019, para 4). It was also reported that in the video, it showed the gunman "methodically moving from room to room and shooting into piles of bodies slumped on the green carpets. Several victims can be seen in the footage, many lying on top of one another motionless in a corner of the room" (Graham-McLay, Ramzy, & Victor, 2019, para 20). At one point, the gunman exited the mosque and returned to his car for another gun. When he reentered the mosque, he shot several bodies at close range. After a few minutes, he returned to his vehicle and drove away. "There wasn't even time to aim, there were so many targets," the gunman was heard saying in the video (Graham-McLay, Ramzy, & Victor, 2019, para 22).

People around the world were stunned by what they witnessed on the Internet, "one of the most disturbing, high-definition records of a mass-casualty attack of the digital age—a grotesque first-person-shooter documentation of man's capacity for inhumanity" (Warzel, 2019, para 3). Prime minister Arden characterized the horrific day by saying, "This is and will be one of New Zealand's darkest days" (Graham-McLay, Ramzy, & Victor, 2019, para 6). The gunman was arrested shortly afterward. He was charged with 51 murders, 40 attempted murders, and engaging in a terrorist act. Although he had initially pleaded not guilty, on March 26, 2020, he pleaded guilty to all charges. He was convicted to be sentenced on a later date (Hollingsworth & Whiteman, 2020).

SEEKING MAXIMUM VIRALITY

Crimes, due to their illegal status, are attention getters. Violence is drama. Live streamed crimes, especially, illegal acts that cause others or self-physical harm, are the considerations of live streamers who seek attention to their acts, and virality of their videos. The intention to seek attention and virality is evident as one compares live streamed crimes with conventional crimes. Live streamed crimes are significantly different from conventional crimes such as murders, robberies, and thefts. Offenders of conventional crimes sought secrecy, while offenders of live streamed crimes sought publicity. When the offenders of conventional crimes were successful in hiding their identities, their offenses would turn into cold cases, where suspects of the offenses could not be identified. In live streamed crimes, however, all the offenders could easily be identified, as hiding their identities was an antithesis of their offenses. Live streamed offenders could either be seen or heard on the live streamed videos, or their account names on the social media, used to live streamed the videos, gave out their identities.

The felons of conventional crimes constructed criminal acts by having their victims as well as law enforcement in mind. The felons of live streamed crimes committed criminal acts, however, by taking into the consideration of their victims, as well as their live audience. Felons of conventional crimes would carefully plan and carry out their offenses to avoid having witnesses or leaving material evidence behind, in order to escape being identified and charged by law enforcement. For felons in live streamed crimes, witnesses or audience are welcomed. In the live streamed massacre described above, for example, the consideration for the viewers could be detected when the gunman announced his attack ahead of the shootings on Facebook, which could be considered as asking his audience to "stay tuned." The gunman's consideration of his viewers was further illustrated by him talking to his audience during the shootings, "There wasn't even time to aim, there were so many targets" (Graham-McLay, Ramzy, & Victor, 2019, para 22).

It is noted that conventional crimes are purposefully constructed as low visibility events where the aggressors strive to hide their identities, whereas live streamed crimes are intended as high visibility events where the aggressors seek maximum visibility (Surette, 2015). Needless to say, the maximum visibility of live streamed crimes is achieved with the use of live broadcasting, recording, and sharing capacities of social media. One can argue that social media are responsible for the emergence of live streamed crimes, as in live streamed crimes, criminal acts are purposefully created and distributed to achieve maximum virality.

It is argued that the emergence and growth of live streamed crimes are tied not only to the pervasive use of social media but also to the emergence of celebrity culture. The prevalent use of social media informs the users that what is presented on the social media commands attention and validation, and hence, generates the desire among the users to not only be the consumers of attention but also become the sources of attention. It is noted that becoming a celebrity has become a focus of public interest and a career goal for many (Cashmore, 2014). If social media did not create this public interest and career goal, they certainly help to sustain them by allowing seeking virality and fame, as easy as pushing a button on one's digital device.

The desire to achieve virality and fame on social media is prevalent, and successful examples are many. Ryan Kaji, an eight-year-old child, is the highest-earning YouTube personality in the world. Kaji makes millions reviewing toys online. Kaji's inspiration for entering the field was the question, "How come I'm not on YouTube when all the other kids are?" (Dinges, 2019, para 10). Kaji's desire to seek attention on social media turned into a major financial success, thanks to the easy accessibility of social media. Other celebrities who achieved fame due to their viral social media appearances include Justin Bieber, Shawn Mendes, Charlie Puth, and Ed Sheeran.

When commenting on the live streamed rape described above, critics quickly pointed out that Lonina became an accomplice due to "her psychological need for approval and the thrill of the event were greater than her concern or empathy for her friend during a serious sexual assault" (Kazdin, 2016, para 7). It was noted that Lonina was lost in the likes she was receiving, indicating that she was enjoying the attention that she was getting by presenting a criminal act for public consumption (Kazdin, 2016). It was argued that Lonina derived a sense of satisfaction by live streaming rape, because, according to Pamela Rutledge, director of the Media Psychology Research Center,

> Most people feel totally unfulfilled in their lives, unaccomplished, especially adolescents, young adults. "By posting it, it elevates everyone's mundane like to something—I don't know—special? Even if it's pervertedly special. But I guess they don't care because the reinforcement value is very powerful" (the explanation of N.G. Berrill, a forensic psychologist and the executive director of the New York Center for Neuropsychology and Forensic Behavioral Science, as quoted in Kazdin, 2016, para 23).

The live streamed rape illustrates that social media have fostered an increased need for validation (Kazdin, 2016); after all, social media are where the attention is. While Lonina was lost in the attention she received by live-streaming rape, the four individuals who live streamed torture in Chicago in 2017, certainly were frustrated by failing to gain the anticipated attention as one of them stated, "You all ain't even commenting on my shit. Ain't nobody watching my shit" (Phippen, 2017, para 4). Based on the argument of seeking attention on social media, one can argue that the two teenagers who assaulted a drunken man, with one of them live streamed the battery, in Bordeaux,

France, in 2016, did so to gain attention, evidenced by how they bragged and laughed during the attack. Bragging was due to battery being an attention-getter while laughing was due to battering a drunken man had an added comical element, so did the two teenagers thought.

The live streamed suicide in Paris, France, could be considered as another incident to seek attention on social media, although the woman who committed suicide stated that she did so not to create buzz. The highest sacrifice one could give for attention would be one's life, as the death of a human life commands the highest shocking value. Live streaming one's suicide on social media, served to call attention to oneself and the issue one's suicide represented.

The need for attention and validation of one's conduct was certainly the notion behind the live streamed massacre. It was argued that social media, with the capacities of broadcasting, recording, and sharing, are engineered for maximum virality. "The killer wanted the world's attention, and by committing an act of mass terror, he was able to get it" (Warzel, 2019, para 8). Knowing very well the gunman's need for attention and validation, Prime Minister Arden vowed to never say the gunman's name, in order to deny him the attention he craved. About the gunman, Prime Minister Arden said in an address to Parliament, "He is a terrorist. He is a criminal. He is an extremist. . . . But he will, when I speak, be nameless" (Cave & Steel, 2019, para 2).

The offenders of the live streamed crimes reported above, if not already being sentenced to various jail terms, will receive such legal punishments in due time. However, beyond legal issues, these cases of live streamed crimes also call for an examination of the ethics of live streaming. As noted earlier, live streaming is operating in a legal vacuum, without the regulation of FCC (2017). In addition, there are no federal guidelines controlling the broadcasts of violence or gores (Feldman, 2013). Given the easy accessibility and prevalent use of social media, never had a crime or trauma so easily to be broadcasted. The ethical question to address is, should one live stream a crime or trauma, even if the technology permits one to do so? To address ethical issues of media practices, communitarian ethics, extrapolated by Clifford Christians, John Ferre, and P. Mark Fackler (1993), offers useful guidance, as it is an ethical framework that provides a comprehensive consideration of stakeholders involved, individual users and the community as a whole.

COMMUNITARIAN ETHICS

Christians and associates (Christians, Ferre, & Fackler, 1993) advocate communitarian ethics as a moral philosophy for journalists who have mass communication capacities. Given that live streamers have the broadcasting capacity, one of the mass communication capacities, communitarian ethics certainly is applicable to live streamers. Communitarian ethics is an alternative moral philosophy to individualism, advocated by liberal theorists. Under individualism, individual autonomy is the sole consideration, which led individual media users to act as "lone rangers" (Christians, Ferre, & Fackler, 1993, p. 70) with free-wheeling uses of media. As discussed earlier, the lack of legal control, live streamers are free to use the technology in any way to express their personal interest. Hence, under libertarian individualism, Christians and associates (1993) note that anarchy is likely to occur. With libertarian individualism, misuses of live streaming occurred, evident by incidents of live streamed crimes—battery, suicide, rape, torture, and massacre. Live streaming crimes demonstrate how individual users pursued their autonomy and exercised individual rights for their personal interest, seeking attention and validation for themselves.

Christians and associates believe that media users should not act as "Lone Rangers" (Christians, Ferre, & Fackler, 1993, p. 70), but persons-in-community. That is, they believe that media users should act as vested stakeholders in a community, and operate with a consideration of the community. After all, "Social systems precede their occupants and continue after them" (Christians, Ferre, & Fackler, 1993, p. 62). Media users "are not alone in the world and should not behave as if they were" (Christians, Freer, & Fackler, 1993, p. 112). Therefore, instead of live streaming crimes to gain attention or achieve validation, media users should be responsible to society when live streaming. That is, live streamers need to be socially responsible.

However, to be socially responsible does not call for complete conformity to social dictations, as illustrated in an autocratic social system. Individual autonomy is an important element in the formulation of communitarian ethics, as important as the common good. Conformity would wipe out individual autonomy; hence, conformity is incongruent with the formulation of communitarian ethics. The formulation of communication ethics is constructed to avoid both anarchy, pure individualism, and conformity, pure autocracy. Communitarian ethics offers a comprehensive treatment of media ethics as it calls for a balanced relationship between the common good and individual autonomy. The creativity and autonomy of live streamers are valued; however, creative energy has to be used in a socially responsible fashion.

REFERENCES

AP. (2018, July 12). Final defendant in the videotaped beating case pleads guilty. *AP News.* Retrieved from https://apnews.com/e4d8d440900a426f88fa7c72e0cc9fb4

Aslam, S. (2020, January 13). Periscope by the numbers: Stats, demographics & fun facts. *Omnicore.* Retrieved from https://www.omnicoreagency.com/periscope-statistics/

Blaise, L., & Morenne, B. (2016, May 12). Suicide on Periscope promotes French officials to open inquiry. *The New York Times.* Retrieved from https://www.nytimes.com/2016/05/12/world/europe/periscope-suicide-france.html?_r=0

BlueLivesMatterArchi. (2017, April 15). Marina Lonina, who live-streamed rape of juvenile, gets sentenced. *BlueLivesMatter*. Retrieved from https://defensemaven.io/bluelivesmatter/news/mari na-lonina-who-live-streamed-rape-of-juvenile-gets-sentenced-0grRSS2CqE669ZH78QGduQ

Cashmore, E. (2014). *Celebrity culture*. New York: Routledge.

Cave, D., & Steel, E. (2019, March 19). New Zealand is loath to use the suspect's name to avoid amplifying his cause. *The New York Times*. Retrieved from https://www.nytimes.com/2019/03/19/world/asia/new-zealand-shooting-suspect-name.htm

Christians, C., Ferre, J., & Fackler, P. (1993). *Good news: Social ethics and the press*. New York: Oxford University Press.

Crepeau, M. (2017, December 8). Woman pleads guilty to hate crime in beating of disabled teen live on Facebook. *Chicago Tribune*. Retrieved from https://www.chicagotribune.com/news/breaking/ct-met-facebook-live-beating-disabled-teen-20171208-story.html

Crepeau, M. (2018, April 20). Women given prison for role in streaming live on Facebook a beating of teen with disabilities. *Chicago Tribune*. Retrieved from https://www.chicagotribune.com/news/breaking/ct-met-facebook-live-hate-crime-guilty-20180420-story.html

Dinges, G. (2019, October 17). 7-year-old makes $22 million per year on YouTube, more than anyone else. *The Fayetteville Observer*. Retrieved from https://www.fayobserver.com/news/20191017/7-year-old-makes-22-million-per-year-on-youtube-more-than-anyone-else

Federal Communications Commission (FCC). (2017). Obscene, indecent and profane broadcasts. Retrieved from https://www.fcc.gov/consumers/guides/obscene-indecent-and-profane-broad casts

Feldman, A. (2013). Can the FCC ban gore and violence from TV?, *Constitution Daily*. Retrieved from https://constitutioncenter.org/blog/can-the-fcc-ban-gore-and-violence-from-tv

Graham-McLay, C., Ramzy, A., & Victor, D. (2019, March 14). Christchurch mosque shootings were partly streamed on Facebook. *The New York Times*. Retrieved from https://www.nytimes.com/2019/03/14/world/asia/christchurch-shooting-new-zealand.html

Hollingsworth, J., & Whiteman, H. (2020, March 26). Accused Christchurch mosque shooter pleads guilty to killing 51 people. *CNN.com*. Retrieved from https://www.cnn.com/2020/03/25/asia/christchurch-shooting-tarrant-plea-intl-hnk/index.html

Kazdin, C. (2016, April 25). Psychologists weigh In on the teen who live-streamed her friend's rape. *Vice*. Retrieved from https://www.vice.com/en_us/article/jpyw5k/psychologists-weigh-in-on-the-teen-who-live-streamed-her-friends-rape

Labaton, S. (2007, April 26). F.C.C. moves to restrict TV violence. *The New York Times*. Retrieved from https://www.nytimes.com/2007/04/26/business/media/26fcc.html

Main, F., Charles, S., & Grimm, A. (2017, January 15). 4 face hate crime charges in videotaped attacks. *Chicago Sun-Times*. Retrieved from https://chicago.suntimes.com/2017/1/15/18364523/4-face-hate-crime-charges-in-videotaped-attack

McPhate, M. (2016, April 19). Teenager is accused of live-streaming a friend's rape on Periscope. *The New York Times*. Retrieved from https://www.nytimes.com/2016/04/19/us/periscope-rape-case-columbus-ohio-video-livestreaming.html

New York Times. (2019, March 14). Christchurch shooting live updates: 49 are dead after 2 Mosques are hit. *The New York Times*. Retrieved from https://www.nytimes.com/2019/03/14/world/asia/new-zealand-shooting-updates-christchurch.html

Pathieu, D., & Hope, L. (2018, July 5). Man gets 8 years after guilty plea in Chicago Facebook live torture, beating. *ABC Chicago Channel 7 News*. Retrieved from https://abc7chicago.com/man-gets-8-years-after-guilty-plea-in-chicago-facebook-live-torture-beating/3713952/

Phippen, J. (2017, January 6). The desire to live-stream violence. *The Atlantic*. Retrieved from https://www.theatlantic.com/news/archive/2017/01/chicago-beating-facebook-live/512288/

Sacramento[CBS13]. (2015, August 28). Police: Men hunted victim in midtown Sacramento on Periscope. Retrieved from https://sacramento.cbslocal.com/2015/08/28/police-men-hunted-vict im-in-midtown-sacramento-on-periscope/

Smith, M., & Chokshi, N. (2017, January 4) 4 questioned after video shows racially charged beating in Chicago. *The New York Times*. Retrieved from https://www.nytimes.com/2017/01/04/us/chicago-racially-charged-attack-video.html?action=click&module=RelatedCoverage&pgtype=Article&region=Footer

Smith, M., & Davey, M. (2017, January 5). 4 black suspects charged in videotaped beating of white teenager in Chicago. *The New York Times*. Retrieved from https://www.nytimes.com/2017/01/05/us/chicago-racially-charged-attack-video.html?action=click&module=RelatedCoverage&pgtype=Article&region=Footer

Surette, R. (2015). Performance crime and justice. *Current Issues in Criminal Justice*, Vol. 27, Issue 2, p. 195–216.

Warzel, C. (2019, March 15). The New Zealand massacre was made to go viral. *The New York Times*. Retrieved from https://www.nytimes.com/2019/03/15/opinion/new-zealand-shooting.html

WTSP-TV 10 pm News Staff, & Flowers, G. (2015, October 13). Woman live-streams herself while 'drunk' driving. *USA Today*. Retrieved from https://www.usatoday.com/story/news/nation-now/2015/10/13/woman-live-streams-herself-while-drunk-driving/73858228/

Yan, H., Jones, S., & Almasy, S. (2017, January 5). Chicago torture video: 4 charged with hate crimes, kidnapping. *CNN.com*. Retrieved from https://www.cnn.com/2017/01/05/us/chicago-facebook-live-beating/index.html

Zurcher, A. (2017, January 5). Four charged with hate crime for Chicago Facebook Live attack. *BBC News*. Retrieved from https://www.bbc.com/news/world-us-canada-38525549

Chapter Eight

Watch at Your Own Risk

Trauma and Live Stream Viewing

Melissa L. Beall, Shing-Ling S. Chen, and Laura Terlip

A live stream is live broadcast. The effects of live stream viewing could best be ascertained by examining the experiences of viewing live broadcasts. When differentiating the formats of live broadcasting media and print media, sociologist Carl Couch (2017) noted that one of the major differences is the amount of control users have over the content. Couch indicated that readers of print media can exercise control over the materials read, while live broadcast audiences have no control over the content. Readers can flip through pages to get a sneak preview of what is coming up and decide whether to read or not, however, broadcast audiences do not know what is going to happen next. The fact that audiences of live broadcasts do not know what is coming up, gives the audiences no control over their experiences. The live broadcast audiences have no control simply because the events are happening now as they view them.

Not knowing what is going to happen next is a condition, not solely residing in live broadcasting. The condition also happens often in face-to-face communication. When one converses with the other, one does not and could not fully anticipate the response coming from the other, and hence, one is often surprised pleasantly or unpleasantly by the other person's reply.

On March 31, 1994, Madonna, an American singer who has been known for pushing the boundaries of social norms, appeared on *Late Show with David Letterman*, an American late-night talk show hosted by David Letterman on CBS. The interview was extremely controversial as Madonna extensively used obscenity and profanity in her statements, including many expletives. Madonna's extensive uses of antics, including saying "f——" 14 times, during the interview made the episode the most censored talk-show in the history of American network television (Tucker, 1994). Madonna appeared to be rather spontaneous in the interview, as Letterman reacted to her spontaneity with an uneasy caution that the TV audience probably would not like her bad language late at night.

During the interview in the studio, as Madonna continued to swear, the director showed an elderly couple in the audience who was visibly shocked by Madonna's language use. Hence, although the TV audience was protected from Madonna's obscene and profane language, due to the censorship performed for later broadcast, the live audience in the studio was unable to escape the trauma of Madonna's continuous verbal assault.

TRAUMA AND LIVE BROADCAST VIEWING

The live audience is vulnerable, in the studio, or at home. The trauma associated with viewing live broadcasts could be best illustrated by the experiences of viewing the launching of Space Shuttle *Challenger* in January 1986. On January 28, 1986, Space Shuttle *Challenger* was scheduled to launch. The mission was the tenth flight for the *Challenger* orbiter. The crew members consisted of five NASA astronauts, one payload specialist, and a civilian schoolteacher, Christa McAuliffe. The launch was broadcast live on television, in the United States as well as globally. It was reported that about 17 percent of the American population watched the live broadcast (History.com Editor, 2020).

The intense interest in viewing the launch was mainly due to the presence of McAuliffe, who would have been the first teacher in space. Broadcasting the launch was believed to be not only an effective public relations event for NASA, but also a positive stimulant to increase the interest in space science among children. With the live broadcast, "millions of children in schools across the nation took a break from learning their ABCs to watch the space shuttle takeoff. It was supposed to be a moment of joy, but it quickly turned into one of the defining tragedies of the decade" (Bell, 2013, para. 1).

Seventy-three seconds into its flight, space shuttle *Challenger* exploded and broke apart, killing all seven crew members abroad. Seven astronauts, including a schoolteacher, lost their lives in front of a global TV audience, including millions of school children (Mack, 2016). Cheers turned to tears in classrooms across the country. Witnessing the explosion, children watched their real heroes die in an awful explosion, and the experience represented "a premature loss of a certain kind of innocence" (Mack, 2016, para. 3). Some believed that the death of a teacher, shown on live television, left children scared and confused. The incident has since been described as "the first ever national trauma on children" (Bell, 2013, para. 2).

Understanding the horror that the children had witnessed, and the trauma that children had experienced, President Ronald Reagan gave a memorable speech following the tragedy in which he spoke directly to those children. In the speech, Reagan stated, "I know it's hard to understand, but sometimes painful things like this happen" (NASA History Office, 2004, para. 6). Reagan continued to state that the tragedy was part of the process of exploration and discovery, and encouraged the children to be brave to continue the journey into the future.

Post-Traumatic Stress Disorder (PTSD)

Experiencing or witnessing a terrifying event can trigger a mental health condition, post-traumatic stress disorder (PTSD). Symptoms include flashbacks, nightmares, severe anxiety, and uncontrollable thoughts about the event (Mayo Clinic Staff, 2020). It is noted that most people who go through traumatic events would temporarily have difficulties adjusting or coping with the aftermath. Symptoms of PTSD may start within one month of a traumatic event. Over time, symptoms may fade. However, if the difficulties persist or become worse, months after the events, then, it is believed that people would have PTSD.

After the *Challenger* space shuttle explosion, researchers (Terr et al., 1999) examined if latency-age children and adolescents developed symptoms of PTSD after viewing such a horrifying event. It was reported that more than 60 percent of the children and adolescents studied, feared at least one stimulus related to *Challenger* within the first 5–7 weeks of the explosion. The East Coast and latency-age children appeared significantly more symptomatic than did the West Coast and adolescent groups (Terr et al., 1999). Over the 14-month study period, most symptoms found among children in the study faded (Terr et al., 1999). The children who showed symptoms of PTSD in 1986 did not exhibit these symptoms in 1987. It is also reported that adolescents expressed diminished expectations for the future. In addition, many children in the study reported a changed approach to space careers. Concurring with the study by Terr and Associates (1999), many researchers pointed out how children exhibited symptoms of trauma due to viewing the explosion of space shuttle *Challenger*. It was reported that some youngsters suffered lingering nightmares of the explosion of the shuttle, and hence, were afraid to sleep alone (Bell, 2013). Some children were reported to associate the *Challenger* tragedy with their own dangerous wishes and fears, while other children were reported to exhibit a heightened concern for the well-being of their parents, and hence, became clingy and reluctant to have their parents leave (Bell, 2013).

TRAUMA AND LIVE STREAM VIEWING

As indicated earlier in the discussion, a live stream is a live broadcast. When a live broadcast could trigger a traumatic experience, so does a live stream. On March 15, 2019, two shootings occurred at mosques in Christchurch, New Zealand. The shootings, which resulted in 51 deaths and 49 injured, were partially live streamed on Facebook by the gunman. A 17-minute video live streaming the first shooting was posted on the gunman's Facebook page. The video was captured by a head camera, worn by the gunman. The video showed the gunman, who drove to Al Noor Mosque in central Christchurch where the first of the two shootings took place, parked his car, picked up a number of rifles, walked toward the mosque, and began shooting as he approached the mosque. The video showed the gunman continue shooting as he entered the mosque and killed 41 worshipers (Roose, 2019).

Facebook received complaints of the live streamed video approximately 12 minutes after the live stream ended (BBC, 2019). Within minutes of being notified, Facebook removed the video. It is reported that the original video had been viewed no more than 200 times, and the video was viewed around 4,000 times before Facebook removed it (BBC, 2019). However, "Autoplay video and trending hashtags can make anyone an unwilling witness to violent material. Free, simple tools allow anyone to upload it" (Bogle, 2019, para. 2). "Indeed, millions of copies of the Christchurch shooting were uploaded to Facebook within the first 24 hours, and despite automated efforts that instantly removed most of them, hundreds of thousands still got through" (Akpan, 2019, para. 37). Facebook reported having removed 1.5 million videos of the attack in the first 24 hours of the incident (Euronews, 2019).

Since the video had been widely circulated, it was believed that an untold number of people had seen the video. It is reported that the risk of developing PTSD is greater when the trauma is interpersonal, when an individual or a group harmed others. "A hate crime such as the Christchurch attack is likely to have a particularly toxic psychological effect on the victims" (Bryant, 2019, para. 11).

There was much concern about children who accidentally stumbled on such a horrifying video, as some educators noted that once one had seen a traumatic event, one could not unseen it (Sargent, 2019). Child development experts advised parents of children who had seen the video to help their children process what they had seen, by consulting them that it was normal to be traumatized by seeing the video. The importance of discussing the video with the children was emphasized as it was believed to be the only way to eventually remove the images out of the children's heads. For adults who need help processing the horrifying images seen, it was advised that they seek help from counselors, or talk to friends about their experiences (Sargent, 2019).

CURBING THE MORBID CURIOSITY:
THE ETHICS OF SHARING TRAUMA

New Zealand police worked fiercely to have the footage of Christchurch shooting removed from the Internet, as copies of the live streamed video were reposted on many platforms and websites. New Zealand Internet service providers also stepped up efforts to stop the video circulating by blocking sites that were actively sharing it. However, "The footage was then replayed endlessly on YouTube, Twitter, and Reddit, as the platforms scrambled to take down the clips nearly as fast as new copies popped up to replace them" (Roose, 2019, para. 11). The video was continued to be shared and broadcast, despite calls from police, journalists, and researchers not to do so due to the graphic nature of the video and the trauma associated with viewing the video (Bryant, 2019). Internet users continued "to seek out footage, to download it, to share it in ways intended to circumvent Facebook and YouTube's censors" (Bogle, 2019, para. 5).

In order to effectively curb the sharing and broadcasting of the video, the New Zealand Office of Film and Literature Classification quickly classified the video as "objectionable" in order to make it illegal for anyone in New Zealand to view, possess, or distribute the video in any form (News Team of Inform the Public, 2019). Offenders would face up to 14 years' imprisonment. It was reported that at least eight people had been arrested for such an offense, sharing the video or related materials (Clarkson, 2019).

The ardent interest in sharing the video of the Christchurch shooting raised an ethical question, given the known trauma resulting from viewing the video, should one share the video? Concerning the experience of the viewers, should one share a video, horrifically graphical? The ethical perspective that centers the experience of the viewers is feminist communitarian ethics, extrapolated by Norman Denzin (1997).

Based on Communitarian Ethics, constructed by Clifford Christians and associates (Christians, Ferre, & Fackler, 1993), Denzin worked to advance the framework, lacing with the concern about the experience of the recipients in a communication act. Clifford and associates emphasized the importance of the consideration of the community, when a communication professional, such as a journalist, makes an ethical decision about his/her conduct. Denzin, building on the importance of the notion of community, further advanced the consideration of the recipients in the communication act.

The approach of feminist communitarian ethics, in agreement with the discussion of communitarian ethics, presumes that the community is prior to individuals and that human identity and experience are constructed through social interaction (Denzin, 1997). Feminist communitarian ethics calls for a communication act to be rooted in community, and neighborliness, the concerns for others. To do so, a communicator should take into account the interest of the community as well as the well-being of the recipients of one's conduct. The concerns for the community and the recipients of one's communication act are the cornerstones of the formulation of feminist communitarian ethics (Denzin, 1997).

Hence, before broadcasting or sharing a video, a user should consider the impact of such a conduct on the community instead of just his/her own interest such as seeking the attention of others. With social media being the dominant form of communication these days, many users seek fame and attention by broadcasting and sharing viral videos. When an unusual event occurred, an instinct of social media users would often prompt the users to raise their cell phones to capture the incident, sometimes regardless of the safety of others involved. On July 4, 2019, when a police officer confronted a passenger on a train in Taiwan, the passenger went berserk and viciously stabbed the officer (Everinton, 2019). Instead of helping out the police officer in danger, many passengers on the train stood back and held up their phones to video the confrontation. As the videos and photos of the stabbing went viral, the police officer later died of stabbing wounds. The failure of the bystanders to assist the police officer, and the obsession with videoing the stabbing, generated a social uproar. Hence, before one broadcasts or shares, one should set aside the desire to seek the limelight of being the source of a viral video, and consider the safety of the community—everyone involved in the situation.

In addition, by taking into account the well-being of the recipients of one's communication act, a social media user should be prompted to consider the impact of one's conduct before sharing a horrific video such as the Christchurch shooting video. The concern of the known trauma, temporary or long term, resulting from viewing a horrific video, should serve to halt any social media user from spreading the video further on the Internet. Even though one may be a digital rubbernecker, that does not mean everyone else on the Internet would be one as well. Feminist communitarian ethics calls for thoughtful considerations of the experience of the recipients of one's communication act. Watching a live stream, one runs the risk of seeing a trauma; when seeing a trauma, it is advised that one helps curb the morbid curiosity and stop sharing.

ACKNOWLEDGMENT

Authors wish to thank Sy-Duan Lee, President of MOMO TV, Taiwan, for the assistance in obtaining information about the stabbing incident on the train in Taiwan, to be incorporated in the chapter.

REFERENCES

Akpan, N. (2019, April 17). Coverage of mass killings is bad for mental health—yet makes people seek more. *PBS News Hour.* Retrieved from https://www.pbs.org/newshour/science/coverage-of-mass-killings-is-bad-for-mental-health-yet-makes-people-seek-more

BBC. (2019, March 21). Christchurch shootings: "Bad actors" helped attack videos spread online. *BBC.com.* Retrieved from https://www.bbc.com/news/technology-47652308

Bell, D. (2013, January 28). Challenger explosion was country's first endeavor in comforting grieving children. *USnews.com.* Retrieved from https://www.usnews.com/news/blogs/press-past/2013/01/28/challenger-explosion-was-countrys-first-endeavor-in-comforting-grieving-children

Bogle, A. (2019, March 18). Social media deserves blame for spreading the Christchurch video, but so do we. *ABC.net.* Retrieved from https://www.abc.net.au/news/science/2019-03-19/facebook-to-blame-for-christchurch-live-video-but-so-are-we/10911238

Bryant, R. (2019, March 19). How to take care of your mental health after the Christchurch attacks. *The Conversation.* Retrieved from https://theconversation.com/how-to-take-care-of-your-mental-health-after-the-christchurch-attacks-113733

Christians, C. G., Ferre, J. P., & Fackler, P. M. (1993). *Good news: Social ethics and the press.* New York: Oxford University Press.

Clarkson, D. (2019, April 15). Warning over threats in Christchurch terror attack video prosecutions. *Stuff.* Retrieved from https://www.stuff.co.nz/national/christchurch-shooting/112051430/warning-over-threats-in-christchurch-terror-attack-video-prosecutions

Couch, C. (2017). *Information technologies and social orders,* 2nd edition, edited by Mark D. Johns. New York: Routledge.

Denzin, N. K. (1997). *Interpretive Ethnography: Ethnographic practices for the 21st century.* Thousand Oaks, CA: Sage.

Euronews. (2019, March 17). New Zealand gunman streamed mosque shooting live on Facebook. *Euronews.com.* Retrieved from https://www.euronews.com/2019/03/15/new-zealand-gunman-streamed-mosque-shooting-live-on-facebook

Everinton, K. (2019, July 4). Video shows crazed passenger stab police officer to death on train in SW Taiwan. *Taiwan News.* Retrieved from https://www.taiwannews.com.tw/en/news/3738080

History.com Editors. (2020, January 28). The space shuttle Challenger explodes after liftoff. (Original published, November 24, 2009). *History.com.* Retrieved from https://www.history.com/this-day-in-history/challenger-explodes

Mack, E. (2016, January 27). I watched live from my first-grade class as Challenger exploded. *Cnet.com.* Retrieved from https://www.cnet.com/news/i-watched-live-from-my-first-grade-class-as-challenger-exploded/

Mayo Clinic Staff. (2020). Post-traumatic stress disorder (PTSD). *Mayoclinic.org.* Retrieved from https://www.mayoclinic.org/diseases-conditions/post-traumatic-stress-disorder/symptoms-causes/syc-20355967

NASA History Office. (2004, June 7). Explosion of the Space Shuttle *Challenger*: Address to the nation, January 28, 1986, by President Ronald W. Reagan. *NASA History.* Retrieved from https://history.nasa.gov/reagan12886.html

News Team of Inform the Public. (2019, July 31). Brenton Tarrant—Christchurch mosque shootings. *InformthePublic.org.* Retrieved from https://informthepublic.org/brenton-tarrant-christchurch-mosque-shootings/

Roose, K. (2019, March 15). A mass murder of, and for, the Internet. *The New York Times.* Retrieved from https://www.nytimes.com/2019/03/15/technology/facebook-youtube-christchurch-shooting.html?action=click&module=Spotlight&pgtype=Homepage

Sargent, E. (2019, March 21). Christchurch shootings: You watched the shocking video but how do you forget it? *Stuff.* Retrieved from https://www.stuff.co.nz/national/christchurch-shooting/111427399/christchurch-shootings-you-watched-the-shocking-video-but-how-do-you-forget-it

Terr, L. C., Bloch, D. A., Michel, B. A., Shi, H., Reinhardt, J. A., & Metayer, S. (1999, October 1). Children's symptoms in the wake of *Challenger*: A field study of distant-traumatic effects and an outline of related conditions. *The American Journal of Psychiatry*. https://doi.org/10.1176/ajp.156.10.1536

Tucker, K. (1994, April 15). Madonna's shocking David Letterman interview. *Entertainment* (ew.com). Retrieved from https://ew.com/article/1994/04/15/madonnas-shocking-david-letterman-interview/

Index

About the Editors and Contributors

EDITORS

Shing-Ling S. Chen is professor of mass communication in the Department of Communication and Media at the University of Northern Iowa.

Zhuojun Joyce Chen is professor emeritus in the Department of Communication and Media at the University of Northern Iowa.

Nicole Allaire is associate teaching professor in the Department of English at Iowa State University.

ABOUT THE CONTRIBUTORS

Melissa L. Beall is professor of communication studies at the University of Northern Iowa. Her teaching and research interests include intercultural communication, communication theory, listening, and communication education.

Genelle I. Belmas is an associate professor at the William Allen White School of Journalism and Mass Communications at the University of Kansas. She specializes in media law and is the coauthor of *Major Principles of Media Law*.

Clifford G. Christians is research professor of communications, professor of journalism and professor of media studies emeritus at the University of Illinois Urbana-Champaign. He is the author, coauthor, or editor of *Responsibility in Mass Communication*, *Teaching Ethics in Journalism Education*, *Communication Ethics and Universal Values*, *Jacques Ellul: Interpretive*

Essays, Ethics in Intercultural Communication, Communication Theories in a Multicultural World, Media Ethics and Global Justice in the Digital Age, and several others.

Matt Corr is professor of media and communication at Shenandoah University in Winchester, Virginia. His current areas of interest include health communication, rhetoric, and immersive learning. He coaches the Shenandoah University Debate Team as well as the Ethics Bowl team.

Chelsea Daggett is assistant professor of communication at Frostburg State University. She has been published in *Participations* and several anthologies. Her current research represents a continuation of her dissertation work on the news-making legacy of the Columbine Massacre and mass shooting coverage. Her research focuses on media ethics, mass shootings in public memory, and drag queen subcultures.

Brian N. Larson is associate professor of law at Texas A&M University's School of Law. He researches rhetoric and argumentation, especially in legal and professional communication. He focuses on rhetorical and argumentation theory in context and practice, using text-analytic, computational, and cognitive methods. Other research interests include the law of online contracts and empirical research methods. Before coming to Texas A&M, he had a 20-year career as an attorney and business executive.

Nicolas M. Legewie is a postdoctoral researcher at the German Institute of Economic Research (DIW Berlin). He teaches and writes about social mobility, migration, social networks, research methodology, and research ethics. He is currently exploring perceptions of privacy in relation to online videos.

Tim Michaels is an instructor in the Communication Department at Slippery Rock University of Pennsylvania where he teaches courses on civil discourse and serves as the head coach of the Slippery Rock Debate Society. His research interests include argumentation, political rhetoric, and communication ethics.

Anne Nassauer is an assistant professor in the Department of Sociology at the John F. Kennedy Institute, Freie Universität Berlin. Her research and teaching focus on microsociology, video data analysis, violence, emotions, and criminal behavior. She has used twenty-first-century video data in her analyses of protest violence, uprisings, armed store robberies, and rampage school shootings.

Laura Terlip is a faculty member in the Department of Communication and Media at the University of Northern Iowa. Her scholarship and teaching focus on organizational communication practices and communication ethics.

Wendy M. Weinhold is assistant professor of journalism at Coastal Carolina University. Her work focuses on the changing definition of U.S. journalists in the digital age. Her interests include critical theory and feminist criticism. Her articles have been published in *Feminist Media Students* and *Journalism Studies*. She has more than a decade of experience as a journalist, serving as a reporter for newspapers and public radio stations in Nebraska, Illinois, and South Carolina.